ALSO BY MARK JONES LORENZO

Affront to Meritocracy: Stories of Overlooked Talents,
Ignored Abilities, and Hidden Truths

● Not Ok ●

●Not Ok●

A REQUIEM FOR GW-BASIC*

Mark Jones Lorenzo

SE BOOKS

Philadelphia | Pittsburgh

* *GW-BASIC is a registered trademark of the Microsoft Corporation, which did not in any way endorse or assist in the production of this product.*

Ψ

SE BOOKS
5307 West Tyson Street
Philadelphia, Pennsylvania 19107
www.sebooks.com

Published in full-throated defiance of Yog's Law.

Cover design and art, as well as all illustrations in the text, by Mark Jones Lorenzo.

Manufactured in the United States of America.

10   9   8   7   6   5   4   3   2   1

Library cataloging information is as follows:

Lorenzo, Mark Jones
 Not ok : a requiem for GW-BASIC / Mark Jones Lorenzo.
p. ; cm.
 Includes bibliographical references.
 I. Title
1. Basic (Computer programming language) 2. Programming (Computers)
 QA76.73.B3 F53 2015
 001.6422'53097—js22
20144985140
ISBN: 978-1-508-59067-5

Dedicated to the many generations of computer-literate children

who sadly will never know the simple pleasures

of GW-BASIC programming

● ● ●

"[T]he medium is the message. This is merely to say that the personal and social consequences of any medium—that is, of any extension of ourselves—result from the new scale that is introduced into our affairs by any new technology…. Many people would be disposed to say that it was not the machine, but what one did with the machine, that was its meaning or message."

—Marshall McLuhan, *Understanding Media*

"BASIC lets you write programs the way Mozart wrote music, by improvising as you go along."

—Eugene Galanter, co-founder of cognitive psychology

• Contents •

• PART 2: GRAPHICS-AND-TEXT PROGRAMS •

Ok

Introduction

Ok. Two letters, two syllables. A very simple word with a nearly two-hundred-year-old history.

The word *Ok* is likely an American original, gaining popularity right around the presidential election of 1840, which pitted incumbent Martin Van Buren against challenger William Henry Harrison. Van Buren's nickname was Old Kinderhook—abbreviated to the snappy *Ok.*

Ok has evolved with the times and is now perhaps the Swiss Army knife of words: its usage can vary tremendously depending on the context. *Ok* can mean anything from acquiescence to approval, and oftentimes hints at mediocrity. But in the GW-BASIC programming language, *Ok* is more than just some equivocal, half-hearted pleasantry or tacit acknowledgement—it is an invitation to a world of possibility.

• • •

Beginner's All-purpose Symbolic Instruction Code, or BASIC, was developed in 1964 at Dartmouth College in New Hampshire by mathematicians John G. Kemeny and Thomas E. Kurtz. They wanted to make a programming language that was user-friendly even to the non-mathematician.

By the time personal computers arrived in the late 1970s, variants of BASIC were more than just packaged as software—these computers literally *booted* directly to ROM BASIC. Popular microcomputers such as Tandy's TRS-80 and Apple's Apple II made use of so-called direct (or immediate) mode BASIC interpreters. BASIC ruled the machine.

Eventually, when IBM ventured into the personal computer market with the IBM PC, they outsourced the creation of IBM BASIC to a small company called Microsoft, which had already produced versions of BASIC for the primitive Altair 8800. Microsoft quickly got to work on a line of BASIC software, including, eventually, GW-BASIC.

GW-BASIC* (and its clone, BASICA) has something in common with Latin: it's a long-dead language which has nonetheless exerted considerable influence on the lexicon, grammar, and syntax we still use today. Unlike Latin, though, GW-BASIC is no longer taught in schools—despite BASIC being one of the easiest languages with which to learn programming—though old standby IBM PC-compatible computers are still overwhelmingly likely to be used there. GW-BASIC has mostly fallen into disuse, its decline greatly hastened once graphical user interfaces like Windows began to proliferate, leaving pure text-based MS-DOS (Microsoft Disk Operating System) programs to wither away.

As the decades have worn on GW-BASIC's glaring deficiencies have piled up, like massive heaps of sand of which silicon chips are made. Someone learning GW-BASIC now might ask questions (all in an incredulous manner) such as: *You've got to use line numbers?* Yes, since the interpreter needs to distinguish between the program code and the direct mode commands. *All variables are global?* There's no way to set variables to be local. *No code encapsulation?* Code cannot be hidden, and don't even ask about object-orientated programming. *Debugging is all ad hoc?*

---

* Although Bill Gates likely came up with the name GW-BASIC, the etymology of the "GW" prefix is very murky; the initials are probably an acronym for *Gee-Whiz*.

There's no dedicated debugger, if that's what you're asking! (Microsoft did offer a standalone GW-BASIC compiler, called BASCOM, but we won't touch on that here.)*

Even the whole notion of a direct mode interpreter seems rather quaint, especially when we compare GW-BASIC to its (sort of) descendants, like Small Basic and Visual Basic. (Of course, there's a much closer relationship between QBasic and GW-BASIC, since QBasic is GW's sequel.) And yet—and *yet*—there's something to be said for GW-BASIC's simplicity, for not having to worry about writing programs with great sophistication, for finding clever workarounds while simultaneously buttressing what GW-BASIC can do so well (there are at least *several* things!). The *Ok* prompt greets you with a blank canvas in tow; *Ok* is paradoxically both an intimidating invitation—true, if you don't know any BASIC, you are most definitely *not ok*—and a warm, fuzzy embrace of user friendliness, enveloping you in a protective cocoon, whispering provocatively: go ahead, experiment with me a bit, try some things; nothing bad can happen in this digital sandbox beyond a benign syntax error or two. Time to fashion your

---

* The most trenchant criticisms are relayed in the article "Programming Language Choice: A Positive Albeit Ambiguous Case for BASIC Programming in Secondary Science Teaching" (1986), by William W. Cobern. BASIC doesn't require a structured programming style, so "most students approach BASIC programming solutions to a problem with little forethought or planning. They program on a 'stream of conscious' basis. As the programs lengthen, the lack of planning usually results in...spaghetti code...." Cobern then counters with a vote of confidence in favor of unstructured programming (which he quotes from the experimental psychologist Eugene Galanter): "BASIC lets you write programs the way Mozart wrote music, by improvising as you go along." Touché.

creations, *ex nihilo*. So tell me: How can you resist the *Ok* prompt?

I wasn't yet born when Altair BASIC, the first incarnation of Microsoft's BASIC programming platform, came out. Instead, I first encountered GW-BASIC right around my eighth birthday, and I couldn't resist. By my tenth I was cranking out silly (and mostly useless) programs during the long, boring stretches of winter and summer breaks that are the bane of elementary school students everywhere. Feeding instructions to computers at such an early age shaped the way I thought about things, elements in my life not related to computers, later on—how I wished that there were algorithms, recipes, sets of instructions I could cue up and follow for those tasks that others performed so easily, so fluidly: like greasing the wheels of social machinery or playing sports.

Marshall McLuhan supposedly said that "we shape our tools and then our tools shape us." My tool of GW-BASIC programming unwittingly shaped me, maybe even socialized me, despite that surfeit of algorithms I so desperately and fruitlessly sought not being readily available for the non-computerized situations in my life. Though, admittedly, a heavy dose of nostalgia fuels my continued interest in the language, my sustained love for GW-BASIC permits me to be willfully blind to its limitations.

• • •

NOT OK is not meant to be an exhaustive tour through GW-BASIC history or commands or statements or functions or programming techniques, nor is it intended as some kind of learn-GW-BASIC-in-ten-easy-steps tutorial, nor is it designed as some sort of teleological work, although it contains bits of all of those things. Instead, the book brushes up against the absolute limits of the GW-BASIC interpreter toolbox, gravitating toward take-no-prisoners mathematics only when absolutely necessary, whilst shying away from PEEKs, POKEs, and other assembly language-type subroutines. Appropriately, **NOT OK**'s scope is especially vast; the approach is meant to be as accessible as possible while also not sparing many details, serving as both a GW-BASIC appetizer and a main course.* And unlike most other computer programming books, in which the keywords or the concepts are the focus, here the programs are the centerpiece from which everything else follows.

NOT OK is written more in the style of books like *Game Playing with BASIC* (1977) by Donald D. Spencer, *PC Graphics: Charts, Graphs, Games and Art on the IBM PC* (1983) by Dick Conklin, *Computer Monsters* (1984) by Stephen Manes and Paul Somerson, *Thrilling Games for the Tandy Color Computer* (1983) by Hal Renko and Sam Edwards, and *The Color Computer Playground* (1983) by Fred D'Ignazio—books that revolve around BASIC programs that perform carefully circumscribed tasks or permit the

---

* If you want a look at more complicated GW-BASIC games and utilities than **NOT OK** has to offer—sacrificing accessibility for complexity, with assembly routines not off-limits—check out these two websites: *Back to BASICs* at http://peyre.x10.mx/GWBASIC/index.htm and *KindlyRat* at http://www.oocities.org/KindlyRat/GWBASIC.html. But, if you're a GW-BASIC neophyte, don't look at these sites just yet; work through at least some of the programs in this book first to whet your appetite.

user to play simple games; books from a simpler time in which the joy comes from the journey to the code, rather than just from running the programs themselves. My inspiration comes from these books, and others like them, old-timey books that are no-nonsense utilitarian code-centric tomes about BASIC, yet also glow with the obvious care and passion their authors took crafting the code. Books that cleverly detail how to exploit the limitations of the language, with a cogent simplicity and a sharp focus, yet are rife with the spirit of self-discovery. Books that have delicious algorithmic recipes to stew up, in type-in form. Books—let's call them mashup *BASIC Cookbooks*—that almost transform BASIC coding into a delectable romantic pursuit, but which are—alas—no longer being written.

I hope that **NOT OK** is a worthwhile entry into this buried and perhaps mostly forgotten niche genre. I hope that the programs on the following pages will delight with their simplicity and focus. I also hope to rekindle in folks around my age (or older) that same GW-BASIC itch, reminding erstwhile programmers of the supreme satisfaction to be had while coding BASIC, and maybe, just maybe, introduce the language, with all of its simple pleasures and lovable foibles, to a younger set.

● ● ●

There are two sections in **NOT OK**: the text-only programs (PART 1) and the graphics-and-text programs (PART 2). Although most chapters examine only a single program in detail, some other chapters group together programs with a common theme. Read the book in order and you'll notice that, in both sections, programs in successive chapters get progressively more and more complex—well, more or less.

Each chapter is split into four parts: (1) An introduction to the program (or associated programs), which relays some context and the *raison d'etre*, along with a description of a sample run; (2) A look at some of the nuts and bolts of the algorithm; (3) The code itself; and (4) Suggestions for improving the program (or, if it is more agreeable, *challenges for the reader*, depending on your perspective).

None of the programs is "complete," whatever that means; certainly there are no masterpieces of originality or design or logic within these pages, though perhaps several programs, such as **ADD.BAS** and **POSITION.BAS** and **STAMP.BAS**, come within a hair's breadth. Instead, I am counting on the reader to be inspired to modify and improve or finish the programs herein with his (or her) own flourishes, even if the inspiration is driven by a *frustration* with the way I code (which may be too sparsely commented or too loose or too unstructured or too casual for some to take).* It'll be your job to forge the diamonds from the coal.

To that end, I am not posting the programs' code online. If you wish to run any of the type-ins, you have two options: type the programs into GW-BASIC, line by line,† or work through the logic in your head and run them in your mind's eye. Certainly this approach is a significant departure from other contemporary computer books on modern programming languages. Yes, perhaps nostalgia plays some part in driving my approach—after all, when I learned GW-BASIC many years ago, there was no Inter-

---

* My coding style is far from poetic. Side note: If you're interested in GW-BASIC but are less mathematics- and more humanities-orientated, you might want to conjure up some *code poetry*, computer code written to resemble poetry that can be read by humans and executable by computers.

† For readability's sake, all program listings in this book utilize a "hanging indent" despite this particular formatting neither being canonical (with respect to other BASIC cookbooks) nor commensurate with GW-BASIC's on-screen display of code.

net, and rarely did computer texts even come packaged with floppy disks (or *diskettes*? Is one term male, the other, female?) full of the programs' code (*The Rainbow* magazine, centered on Tandy Color Computer BASIC, which was a close cousin of GW-BASIC, offered a service by mail: readers could send away for diskettes of the code)—but I've found that by expending the time and effort typing in code (in any language, not just GW-BASIC) a line at a time, rather than just copying and pasting someone else's code haphazardly, I get a much better sense of the logic behind the code. Typing each character slows me down just enough to open up the mental space necessary to realize how the code might be improved, or how the program could be made more functional or user-friendly.

• • •

When Michelangelo was asked how he made his statue of David, he supposedly explained, "You just chip away the stone that doesn't look like David." I encourage you to be Michelangelo and carve out your own digital algorithmic Davids, not only by improving the programs here, but by fashioning your own, original GW-BASIC programs. Your programming chops will be sharpened with the effort, you'll help to keep GW-BASIC fresh and vital, and you'll have some fun to boot.

So let's not permit the subtitle of this book to become a reality—let's not cue up the funeral dirge for GW-BASIC just yet, because that is most certainly *not ok*. Long live GW-BASIC, and turn the page to get started. *Ok?*

Getting Started with GW-BASIC

Ok

RUN_

To load and run GW-BASIC, your most authentic option is to procure an old IBM compatible PC with MS-DOS as its operating system, running on an Intel x86 (e.g., 80386 or 80486) processor. GW-BASIC was included with most versions of DOS, until about the mid-1990s.

You should have an executable GW-BASIC file either on the hard drive or on a floppy disk; the file is likely named **BASIC.EXE, GWBASIC.EXE,** or **BASICA.EXE**. At the **C:\\>** DOS prompt, type **DIR** to see the files in the directory (if you think GW-BASIC is inside a subdirectory of the drive—let's say in a directory called **BAS**—then, at the DOS prompt, type **CD BAS** first and press ENTER, then **DIR** to see a list of the files). When you find a BASIC executable file, simply type the file's name, without the file extension, and press ENTER.

If, however, BASIC resides on a floppy drive—usually represented by a letter like A (or B)—then, at the DOS prompt, type **A:** (or **B:**) and then press ENTER. Use the **DIR** command to see the contents of the floppy drive. And, again, when you find a BASIC executable file, simply type the file's name, without the file extension, and press ENTER.

Note that all BASIC programs will be automatically saved in the directory (and drive) in which the BASIC executable file resides, unless you specify otherwise.

● ● ●

Suppose you have a GW-BASIC executable file, but no older computer to run it on. You still have several options.

First up, option one: up until Windows 7 (i.e., native 64-bit operating systems on PCs), Windows was able to run most older DOS programs. If you have Windows 7 or Windows 8 (or beyond), these files won't run without a Windows XP emulator. The best is courtesy of Microsoft, called Windows *Virtual PC*. *Virtual PC* has a Windows XP Mode option that will run most DOS executable files.

Or, option two: download, install, and run *DOSBox*, an x86 DOS emulator, which is freely available at http://www.dosbox.com. Once you run *DOSBox*, you are presented with a **Z:\>** prompt. You'll first need to "mount" a disk drive onto the emulator. For example, if your BASIC executable file is in a directory called **BAS** on the **C:** drive, then you'd type this in (and hit ENTER):

MOUNT C C:\BAS

Then, when you go into your newly created **C:** drive (by typing **C:** and ENTER), any and all files in the **BAS** directory are listed—and BASIC will run like a charm.

Even better, *DOSBox* is available for Mac OSX as well. Most of the programming and debugging in this book was completed on an iMac only a couple of years old. Specifically, here's how: I created a folder called **BAS** in my **Applications** directory; the folder housed a BASIC executable file along with a number of BASIC programs. After double-clicking *DOSBox*, at the **Z:\>** prompt I typed the following:

MOUNT C /applications/

From there, the **C:** drive linked up directly with my **Applications**, as well as with the folder containing my BASIC files, called **BAS**—which was now accessible by simply typing **CD BAS** and pressing RETURN.

If you do run GW-BASIC on the Mac, though, you need to be aware of the differences in the keyboard layout—namely, there's no labeled PAUSE and BREAK keys, which are critical to debugging. If you wish to pause a program, hit the F16 button. And, any time you want to break, press CONTROL along with F15. (By the way, the PAUSE and BREAK keys work just fine using *DOSBox* on a PC.)

• • •

If none of the options above are appealing, here's another: download a program that emulates GW-BASIC directly. The best such program out there is called PC-BASIC, and it is freely available for download at **http://pcbasic.sourceforge.net**. PC-BASIC works quite well, and runs on multiple operating systems, but it is not a perfect emulator of GW-BASIC. Caution: some programs in this book—especially those that are more graphics-intensive—don't quite run as advertised on PC-BASIC. (The same goes for QBasic, a GW-BASIC successor; although QBasic might run most GW-BASIC programs with little complaint, there will be subtle differences in execution. By the way, if you can't manage to obtain an original QBasic executable file, QBasic has its own downloadable emulator as well, at **http://www.qb64.net**.)

• • •

After reading **NOT OK**, you may wish to check out some Internet resources as well. The most comprehensive GW-BASIC website, run by Neil C. Obremski, is located at **http://www.gw-basic.com**. There you'll find discussion boards, links to other BASIC-themed websites, and original BASIC programs ready to download.

• PART 1: TEXT-ONLY PROGRAMS •

Writing Backwards
LOAD "BACKWRIT.BAS"
Ok
RUN_

Type a letter. Any letter. Try *q*, for instance. And then *q* appears on the blank screen—but not where you expect it to be. The letter shows up on the top right of the screen. Pick another letter: maybe *p* this time. It appears on the right side of the screen, too—but to the immediate *left* of *q*.

Pick more letters to type. A *d*. An *r*. A *w* (the only letter with more than one syllable), an *s*, and a *t*. And what is the result? *tswrdpq*. Type in *fred* and out comes *derf*.

• • •

When run,* the program waits patiently for a keyboard prompt—any prompt—to be assigned to the **INKEY$** variable. Once a letter or number or other character is typed, the **LOCATE** statement is used to place the cursor on the

---

* To run a program: (1) Type the code in, pressing ENTER after each line; (2) Check to make sure you entered the code in correctly by typing **LIST** and hitting ENTER; and (3) Type RUN and press ENTER. To stop the execution of a program at any time, hold down the Ctrl key and tap the Pause/Break key. And to save a program, type out **SAVE"** along with the program's name. So, to save **BACKWRIT**, you'd type **SAVE"BACKWRIT"** and press ENTER.

far right of the screen. With each additional character, **LOCATE** moves leftward by one unit (that's where the **X=X-1** counter comes into play)—until hitting the left side of the screen, at which point it resets to the right (the **X=75**) and moves down a line (the **Y=Y+1**).

By the way, there's one keyboard button when pressed that will not print on the screen: the ESCAPE key, better known as **CHR$(27)** to the GW-BASIC-initiated.

• • •

```
BACKWRIT.BAS
5 X=75:Y=1
10 CLS
20 I$=INKEY$
30 IF I$="" THEN 20
31 IF I$=CHR$(27) THEN END
35 IF X=1 THEN X=75:Y=Y+1
40 LOCATE Y,X:PRINT I$;:X=X-1
45 GOTO 20
```

• • •

Although short and simple, the program could stand some improvements. First, replacing the **GOTO** with a **WHILE-WEND** loop wouldn't be the worst idea in the world; there'd be no whiff of spaghetti code.

Second, it's tough to keep track of what's being typed while it's being typed backwards. Imagine being able to type some letters, words, phrases in at the start—forwards, left-to-right—and then hitting a button (let's say, the ESCAPE key) to find that same text instantly transposing itself in a backwards manner. An array (or set of arrays) might be needed to capture that initial forwards-input.

Doubling Your Money
LOAD "MONEY.BAS"

Ok
RUN_

There is an ancient legend of a chessboard and a grain of rice. Although there are many versions, more or less it goes like this: A king, losing a battle of wits to a clever opponent, decides to give the victorious man whatever he wishes.

"Put a grain of rice on the first square of a chessboard," he says to the king. "Then two grains on the second square, four on the third, and so forth, doubling the number of grains with each successive square."

The king, almost insulted at the seemingly paltry demand, readily agrees to the clever man's choice of a prize. Quickly it becomes apparent, however, that—because of exponential growth—more rice grains than there exist on the Earth would be needed to fulfill the clever man's request. The king nonetheless solves the problem, however: he beheads the man.

Instead of grains of rice, the MONEY.BAS program listed below starts your salary at a new, short-term job at the measly amount of one penny—but the salary doubles each day. Pressing the spacebar moves time forward: one cent total, three cents total, seven cents total, and so on. Although the job lasts only twenty-one days, by its end you've earned a pretty penny.

• • •

After (informally) declaring two variables by seeding them with initial values, the program clears the screen, gives a little context, and waits for the user to tap the spacebar to accelerate the money totals courtesy of the power of exponential growth (if only it were that easy in real life!). Note that INKEY$ waits for " ", which signifies a spacebar tap (we'll see an alternative to the scare quotes when we examine ASCII codes later on). Also note the PRINT USING statement, which allows the output to be specially formatted—in this case, as money.

In line 60 the DAY variable is incremented by one and the MONEY variable is doubled (and money previously earned is appended to the total).

● ● ●

MONEY.BAS
```
1 REM MONEY
2 DAY=1:MONEY=.01
10 CLS
20 PRINT"If you start out with one cent and obtain
   double that each day, the amount of money you
   earn will be astronomical! Press spacebar to in
   crease the day, and keep in mind that the total
   money is money earned since the beginning of the
   job (total = 21 work days)."
30 LOCATE 15,1:PRINT"DAY:";DAY
35 LOCATE 16,1:PRINT"TOTAL $:";MONEY
40 I$=INKEY$
50 IF I$=" " THEN GOTO 56
55 GOTO 40
56 IF DAY=21 THEN GOTO 40
60 DAY=DAY+1:MONEY=(MONEY*2)+MONEY
70 LOCATE 15,1:PRINT"DAY:";DAY
75 LOCATE 16,1:PRINT USING"$#########.##";MONEY
80 GOTO 40
```

● ● ●

The most glaring limitation of the program is the short-term nature of the job. Twenty-one days doesn't come close to matching the chessboard's sixty-four squares described in the ancient story. The problem is that GW-BASIC resorts to scientific notation (using the ugly E notation rather than the elegant ten-to-a-power) as numbers grow very large, ultimately quitting with an "Overflow" error when the total gets too out of hand. There are work-arounds, however; for instance, refer to the program **ADD.BAS**, presented later in this book, which can add two numbers scores of digits in length.

Calculating Tax

```
LOAD "TAXES.BAS"
Ok
RUN_
```

Ben Franklin famously quipped that the only certainties in life are death and taxes (although he's not the first to make this trenchant observation).

After asking the cost of the item and its sales tax percentage, the amount of sales tax, along with the total price of the item, is displayed on the screen.

Finally, the option to either calculate tax on another item or exit the program is presented. Use the cursor to highlight your choice, and then tap ENTER.

• • •

Although it's a simple, the program reveals how many such basic calculations requiring user input could be written in GW-BASIC—the language can double as a super-programmable calculator. (Texas Instruments, makers of the most popular lines of graphing calculators, utilize a version of BASIC.) Note line **110**, which turns the percent (*per* one hundred) tax back into a proportion. Tax calculations are completed within the **PRINT** statements themselves.

More interesting is the short "YES" or "NO" menu prompting the user to either exit or try another: such a menu could be expanded, in other programs, to many different commands—although only one command is permitted per line when using a **LINE INPUT** statement. (The standard GW-BASIC keystroke menu, displayed at the screen's gutter, is shut off with the **KEY OFF** statement in the first line.)

● ● ●

TAXES.BAS

```
45 SCREEN 9:KEY OFF
50 COLOR 1,1:CLS:COLOR 15
60 PRINT:PRINT:PRINT"FINDING SALES TAX"
80 INPUT"COST OF ITEM";COST
85 INPUT"SALES TAX (IN %)";TAX
90 CLS
100 PRINT"WITH TAX AT ";TAX;"%,"
110 TAX=TAX/100
120 PRINT"THE TAX IS $";COST*TAX
130 PRINT"THE TOTAL COST WITH TAX IS $";COST*
    TAX+COST
150 PRINT:PRINT"ANOTHER?":PRINT"YES":PRINT"NO"
160 LINE INPUT U$
170 IF U$="YES" THEN GOTO 50
180 IF U$="NO" THEN CLS:END
190 GOTO 160
```

● ● ●

There are other types of tax besides sales tax. More complex programs might be able to handle a myriad of tax calculations.

Diagnostic Tests
LOAD "DISEASE.BAS"
Ok
RUN_

Taking a diagnostic test for a suspected medical ailment is scary. What's even scarier is that doctors frequently don't know how to interpret the results of the tests properly to their patients (e.g., see the comprehensive research by Gerd Gigerenzer, among others).

Suppose you take a blood test for diabetes, which is 98 percent accurate for those who have the disease. If you don't have the diabetes, however, the test will show a (false) positive result in about five percent of cases.

According to the American Diabetes Association, roughly 5.9 percent of all Americans have the disease (this is called the *prevalence*). You take the test, and it shows a positive result. How worried should you be?

The *positive predictive value* gives the probability of the disease, given that you obtained a positive result on a diagnostic test. At first you might believe it to be 98 percent, since, as stated above, the test is "98 percent accurate for those who have the disease." But this doesn't tell the whole story.

Recall that only about six percent of the population has diabetes—and you don't know whether you have it or not (that's why you're taking a diagnostic test to find out!). Thus you need to also consider the false positive rate.

The formula to find the positive predictive value is

$$P(disease \mid +) = \frac{P(disease \cap +)}{P(+)}$$

The | symbol means "given," and the ∩ means "intersection" (in other words, what's in common between the two sets). Finding the intersection of having the disease along with obtaining a positive result on the test simply means multiplying the two percentages; finding the denominator—the probability of obtaining a positive result—requires you to add up the probabilities of the two possible positive results: positive if you have the disease (a *true positive*) and positive if you don't have the disease (a *false positive*). Stated more precisely using a formula,

$$P(disease \mid +) = \frac{incidence \times truepos}{preval \times truepos + nonpreval \times falsepos}$$

The *preval* above refers to the prevalence.

With all this in mind, we return to the central question of this chapter: If you test positive for diabetes, how worried should you be? Run **DISEASE.BAS** to find out. The answer may surprise you.

• • •

Beyond the positive predictive value calculation on line **150**, the code is very straightforward. Observe that a table of disease versus test results is displayed on-screen. Also, the **TAB(*n*)** function (see line **60**) moves the cursor over *n* spaces to a new position on the line.

• • •

DISEASE.BAS
```
10 KEY OFF:SCREEN 9:COLOR 15,1:CLS
20 PRINT"PROBABILITY OF YOU HAVING A DISEASE"
```

```
30 INPUT"What percent of people in the population
   have the disease (prevalence)";PRE
40 INPUT"What percent of people who have the dis
   ease test positive for it";TPOS
50 INPUT"What percent of people who do not have
   the disease test positive for it";FPOS
55 PRINT
60 PRINT TAB(25) "DISEASE"
70 PRINT "TEST RESULT           YES       NO"
80 PRINT "+             True positive False posi
   tive"
90 PRINT "                    ";TPOS;"
   ";FPOS
95 PRINT
100 PRINT "-        False negative    True nega
    tive"
110 PRINT "                   ";(100-TPOS);"
    ";(100-FPOS)
120 PRINT
130 PRINT"The positive predictive value is the
    probability of having the disease,"
140 PRINT"given that a positive result on the di
    agnostic test was obtained."
150 PRINT:PRINT"The positive predictive value of
    this test is ";(((PRE/100)*(TPOS/100))/
    ((PRE/100)*(TPOS/100)+((100-PRE)/100)*
    (FPOS/100)))*100;"%."
155 PRINT:PRINT"ANOTHER?":PRINT"YES":PRINT"NO"
160 LINE INPUT U$
170 IF U$="YES" THEN GOTO 10
180 IF U$="NO" THEN CLS:END
190 GOTO 160
```

● ● ●

It might be more effective to show the calculations step-by-step, perhaps even using *natural frequencies* (counts of people) instead of percentages. Graphically displaying tree diagrams and pictographs might be helpful as well.

Oh, and one more thing: e-mail this program to your doctor—he or she just might need it.

Counting Up
LOAD "AGEBMI.BAS"

Ok

RUN_

How old are you, really? Some people are strangely too sensitive to give their *real* age.

After inputting your age—let's say *36*—out comes how long you've been alive in days, hours, minutes, and seconds. Not quite a *How many piano tuners are there in Chicago* Fermi problem-like feat, but more accurate than your average back-of-the-envelope calculation.

But **AGEBMI.BAS** does more. After querying you on your height (in inches) and weight (in pounds)—more personal information that people are also sometimes reluctant to part with—the program quickly calculates your BMI, or body mass index, which is an important (albeit overly simplified) measurement of your body fat. And, finally (and usefully), **AGEBMI.BAS** interprets your BMI.

• • •

Several variables are required for the program: **AGE**, **WEIGHT**, and **HEIGHT**, which are user-inputted, and **BMI**, which is calculated on-the-fly.

Notice that the number of days in a year is assumed to be 365.25—the extra fourth is because of the extra day in leap years, although even 0.25 isn't quite right because of the weirdness necessitated by leap-year divisibility calculations. Though an "infallible" pope introduced it, the Gregorian calendar doesn't solve all the issues of the Julian calendar it replaced.

Also notice the conditional statements that interpret the BMI measurement (in lines **90** to **120**). Once a BMI criterion is met—such as BMI greater than 30, for instance—the program relays the appropriate information and then terminates.

● ● ●

AGEBMI.BAS
```
5 REM AGE-BMI CALCULATOR
8 CLS
10 INPUT"WHAT IS YOUR AGE";AGE
12 INPUT"WHAT IS YOUR WEIGHT (IN POUNDS)";WEIGHT
14 INPUT"WHAT IS YOUR HEIGHT (IN INCHES)";HEIGHT
20 PRINT"YOU HAVE BEEN ALIVE:"
30 PRINT AGE*365.25" DAYS"
40 PRINT (AGE*365.25)*24" HOURS"
50 PRINT (AGE*365.25*24)*60" MINUTES"
60 PRINT (AGE*365.25*24*60)*60" SECONDS"
70 REM DETERMINE BMI, AND WHAT IT MEANS
80 BMI=(WEIGHT/(HEIGHT*HEIGHT))*703     '703 IS A
   CONVERSION FACTOR
85 PRINT"YOUR BMI IS ";BMI
90 IF BMI<18.5 THEN PRINT"YOU ARE
   UNDERWEIGHT.":END
100 IF BMI>30 THEN PRINT"YOU ARE OBESE.":END
110 IF BMI>24.999 AND BMI<=30 THEN PRINT"YOU ARE
    OVERWEIGHT, BUT NOT OBESE.":END
120 PRINT"YOU ARE AT A NORMAL WEIGHT.":END
```

● ● ●

Because even the youngest user will enter in a big enough year to cause the number of seconds (at least) to turn into scientific notation—in the form of an ungainly E rather than the number ten—only approximate values to truly large numbers can be given directly.

Indirectly, however, perhaps more precise numbers can be shown—by counting differently. See the later chapter on the **ADD.BAS** program for the details.

Time's Up

LOAD "ALARM.BAS"

Ok

RUN_

Perhaps it's not a surprise to you that your computer has an internal clock in it, always ticking. So why not set it on a timer?

Run the program: you'll be immediately asked when you want the alarm to ring. Type in the time, press ENTER, and wait till your time's up.

• • •

In GW-BASIC, **TIME$** is reserved for the current time; likewise, **DATE$** is set to the current day's date. Once the alarm time and true time converge, the program plays a sound and jumps to a flashing-the-screen subroutine.

• • •

```
ALARM.BAS
10 SCREEN 9:SCREEN 0:KEY OFF:COLOR 15:CLS
11 CLS
12 LOCATE 2,20:PRINT"ALARM TIME (CURRENT TIME IS
   ";TIME$;")";
13 INPUT Y$
14 IF Y$="" THEN CLS:GOTO 20
20 LOCATE 10,25:PRINT TIME$
25 LOCATE 11,25:PRINT DATE$
26 IF TIME$=Y$ THEN SOUND 3000,20:GOTO 60
27 I$=INKEY$
28 IF I$="E" OR I$="e" THEN CLS:END
30 IF I$="A" OR I$="a" THEN GOTO 11
```

```
40 LOCATE 14,25:PRINT "Press 'E' to end, and 'A'
   to reset the alarm."
50 GOTO 20
60 CLS
70 FOR OUTER=1 TO 10
75 FOR LOOP=1 TO 15
80 COLOR ,LOOP:CLS
90 FOR PAUSE=1 TO 100:NEXT PAUSE
100 NEXT LOOP
105 NEXT OUTER
110 GOTO 10
```

● ● ●

The program is not flashy, in the nonliteral sense of the term; much more could be done with the user interface. For instance, perhaps digital clock faces could be presented—that, though, would require some sophisticated graphical manipulations.

Harder still, consider writing a program with an analog clock on-screen displaying the time. You'd have to use some trigonometry to get the rotations of the second, minute, and hour hands right. Not too hard a task for the more mathematically adventurous GW-BASIC programmer.

Fibonacci's Sequence
LOAD "FIBO.BAS"
Ok
RUN_

The famed Fibonacci sequence did not begin with Fibonacci but, like many Western-appropriated ideas, originated in the East.

Nonetheless, in the book *Liber Abaci* (1202), Fibonacci (also known as Leonardo of Pisa) lays down the sequence, as a model of the growth of a simplified population of rabbits. Suppose the gestation period for rabbits is a month. At first, there is one pair; at the end of a month, there is still one pair—but they have mated. The offspring are born at the end of the second month, making two pairs: the original set and a new set of rabbits. Another month, another pair, for a total of three pairs. This continues, ad infinitum.

Also, rather famously, the ratio of successive terms of the Fibonacci sequence converges to the *golden ratio* (although it is not the only such recursive sequence to do so):

$$\Phi = \frac{1+\sqrt{5}}{2} = 1.618034\ldots$$

The golden ratio pops up in nature and ancient (and modern) architecture and design, among other places.

When running the **FIBO.BAS** program, you are prompted to press the ESCAPE key to begin the sequence (and you can terminate it, once it begins, by hitting ESCAPE).

• • •

Line **20** sets initial values for the first generation of rabbits, while line **50** begins the calculation from there. After two ones, the next term is simply the sum of the previous two terms: in this case, two. And so forth.

• • •

FIBO.BAS
```
10 KEY OFF:SCREEN 9:COLOR 15,0:CLS
15 PRINT:PRINT TAB(16);"Fibonacci Sequence:"
16 PRINT"PRESS <ESC> TO BEGIN"
17 IF INKEY$<>CHR$(27) THEN 17
20 TEMP2=1:TEMP=1:P=1
30 PRINT TEMP,P,
40 FOR T=1 TO 33
50 TEMP=P:P=TEMP+TEMP2:TEMP2=TEMP
60 PRINT P,
65 IF INKEY$=CHR$(27) THEN END
70 NEXT T:PRINT:PRINT
```

• • •

The biggest problem with the program lies with a key GW-BASIC limitation. After thirty-three iterations the sums get too large for the interpreter to handle. A coding solution to this dilemma can (at least partially) be found in the program **ADD.BAS**, presented later on in this book.

Copernicus Method
LOAD "COPER.BAS"
Ok
RUN_

In his book *Time Travel in Einstein's Universe* (2002), the astrophysicist J. Richard Gott describes a revelation he had while standing at the Berlin Wall in 1969, eight years after it was built, wondering how long it would stand. Using the idea of the Copernican principle—which was named after the scientist Copernicus and states that there is nothing inherently special about the location of the Earth—Gott realized that there was nothing special about the time of his visit to the Berlin Wall. Thus, he predicted that there was a seventy-five percent chance that he was observing the wall after the first quarter of its life—since there are four quarters to the life of the wall, no matter how long it would last. (Note that it wouldn't have made sense for Gott to claim that he was seeing the wall after the first quarter of its life if he arrived in Berlin just when construction of the wall was completed; this would have been a *special* observation point in time.)

Gott took his observation one step further. Given that there was a seventy-five percent chance that he, in 1969, was observing the wall after the first quarter of its life, he predicted that he was either at the beginning of the wall's second quarter (exactly at the lower quartile, Q1), or at the beginning of the wall's fourth quarter (exactly at the upper quartile, Q3). Gott used some simple calculations to determine that the wall would last no more than twenty-four more years; he termed the calculations the "Copernicus method" of determining lifespan. The method permits different confidence percentages as well, but the larger the confidence, the bigger the prediction interval.

Gott noted that these sorts of predictions could be made with anything: how long your current relationship is going to last, how long you will live, how long before the extinction of the human race, how long shows on Broadway will run. The only information required is a non-special observation point. (For example, as Gott explains, you wouldn't use this method to calculate how long a friend's wedding is going to last precisely *one minute* after vows were exchanged—this is a special observation point, the point of the marriage's beginning.)

In fact, in 1993 he famously applied his Copernican method to calculating a 95% confidence interval for the survival of the human race. First of all, suppose right this moment is a non-special observation point—there is no reason to assume otherwise. Humans have been around for approximately 200,000 years. With 95% confidence, there is 2.5% on the low end, and 2.5% on the high end, so there are forty 2.5% intervals. In order to calculate the upper and lower limits of the 95% confidence interval, then, you'd have to multiply your observation point (in this case, 200,000 years) by 1/39—which assumes that we are 97.5% through the entire human race's lifespan—and by 39—which assumes that we have 97.5% of the human race's lifespan to go.

So how long will human beings be around? No need to stay in suspense: simply run the program below to find out. But remember, as Yogi Berra once said, it's difficult to make predictions, especially about the future.

● ● ●

Observe that line **50** simplifies the calculations of the upper and lower bounds of the confidence interval quite a bit by calculating an intermediate step and assigning the result to a variable called **PIECE**.

• • •

```
COPER.BAS
10 KEY OFF:SCREEN 9:COLOR 15,1:CLS
15 YEARS=0:CONF=50:PIECE=0
20 PRINT "COPERNICUS METHOD OF LIFETIME ESTIMATION
   by GOTT"
30 PRINT:PRINT "The reference point in time must
   not be special."
40 PRINT:INPUT "At this point in time, how many
   years old is the person/item/situation";YEARS
45 INPUT "Estimate remaining life with what confi
   dence percentage";CONF
47 IF CONF<0.5 OR CONF>99.5 THEN 45
50 PIECE=100/((100-CONF)/2)-1
60 PRINT:PRINT "Lower bound of remaining life (in
   years) is ";YEARS*(1/PIECE)
70 PRINT "Upper bound of remaining life (in years)
   is ";YEARS*PIECE
80 PRINT:PRINT"ANOTHER?":PRINT"YES":PRINT"NO"
90 LINE INPUT U$
100 IF U$="YES" THEN GOTO 10
110 IF U$="NO" THEN CLS:END
120 GOTO 90
```

• • •

This program could be made more interesting visually—perhaps a timeline display is in order, showing the upper and lower bounds as well as the observation points.

Football Scores
LOAD "FBSCORES.BAS"

Philosopher Thomas Hobbes, in *Leviathan* (1651), famously described life as "nasty, brutish, and short." If he had lived some four centuries later, he might have described life on the gridiron as much nastier, more brutish, and even shorter—American football is nothing if not a brutal, take-no-prisoners game, and the players, current and former, have paid the price for it (along with, in fewer instances than you'd think, some being paid handsomely for the privilege of being brutalized).

There have been so many football games already played that you might suspect that every score's been permuted. Not quite: for example, when the Philadelphia Eagles upset the then-defending world champion New York Giants in a playoff game on January 11, 2009, the final score was twenty-three to eleven; a final whistle had never before been blown with that combination of touchdowns and field goals.

With only a handful of ways to put points on the scoreboard—touchdown with no extra point (six points), touchdown with an extra point (seven points), field goal (three points), and safety (two points)—there aren't many ways to arrive at a team's final score in any particular game. (Note that the program ignores two-point conversions.)

FBSCORES.BAS helps you find a potential path, circuitous or not, to a football team's final point total.

• • •

By using the **INT** function, GW-BASIC checks to see if **2,
3, 6,** and/or **7** divide evenly into the entered points total
variable **SCORE**. See lines **32** to **55** for the details.

• • •

FBSCORES.BAS
```
10 KEY OFF:SCREEN 9:COLOR 15,1:CLS
15 PRINT "THERE ARE FOUR POSSIBILITIES OF A SINGLE
   SCORE BY A TEAM:"
16 PRINT"A 2 (safety); a 3 (field goal); a 6
   (touchdown); and a 7 (touchdown and extra
   point)."
20 PRINT:INPUT "INPUT THE TEAM'S TOTAL SCORE";
   SCORE
30 IF SCORE<2 THEN PRINT"SCORE IS IMPOSSIBLE":GOTO
   150
32 IF SCORE=2 THEN GOTO 100
35 IF SCORE/3=INT(SCORE/3) THEN GOTO 110
40 IF SCORE/6=INT(SCORE/6) THEN GOTO 120
45 IF SCORE/7=INT(SCORE/7) THEN GOTO 130
50 IF (SCORE-3)/2=INT((SCORE-3)/2) THEN GOTO 140
55 IF SCORE/2=INT(SCORE/2) THEN GOTO 100
100 PRINT"All you need is ";SCORE/2; "safety(ies)
    to get a score of ";SCORE;"."
105 GOTO 150
110 PRINT"All you need is ";SCORE/3; "field
    goal(s) to get a score of ";SCORE;"."
115 GOTO 150
120 PRINT"All you need is ";SCORE/6; "touchdown(s)
    to get a score of ";SCORE;"."
125 GOTO 150
130 PRINT"All you need is ";SCORE/7; "touchdown(s)
    + extra point(s) to get a score of ";SCORE;"."
135 GOTO 150
140 PRINT" You need one field goal. And then ";
    (SCORE-3)/2; "safeties to get a score of ";
    SCORE;"."
150 PRINT:INPUT"ANOTHER (TYPE 'YES' or 'NO')";
    PROMPT$
```

```
160 IF PROMPT$="YES" THEN 10
170 IF PROMPT$="NO" THEN CLS:END
180 GOTO 150
```

● ● ●

Some of the scoring paths that the program relays, though possible, aren't particularly realistic. For instance, here's **FBSCORES.BAS**'s solution to a final score of forty-three: one field goal and twenty safeties. Twenty safeties? In one game? Sheer nonsense. Coming up with more sensible scoring paths awaits the programmer needing a challenge. (And as a related, but much more difficult, challenge: Have **FBSCORES.BAS** relay *all possible paths* to any score under, say, seventy points.)

Working on Matrices
LOAD "MATRIX.BAS"

Ok

RUN_

Matrices are rectangular arrangements of numbers (or variables) in rows and columns, and in mathematics are very useful for organizing data as well as for solving equations.

For instance, suppose you wished to solve this system of equations:

$$\begin{cases} x - y = 2 \\ 4x - 6y = 4 \end{cases}$$

Setting up a matrix equation, as shown below,

$$\begin{bmatrix} 1 & -1 \\ 4 & -6 \end{bmatrix}\begin{bmatrix} x \\ y \end{bmatrix} = \begin{bmatrix} 2 \\ 4 \end{bmatrix}$$

puts you in position to isolate the *x-y* matrix on one side, which ultimately solves for both variables:

$$\begin{bmatrix} x \\ y \end{bmatrix} = \begin{bmatrix} 1 & -1 \\ 4 & -6 \end{bmatrix}^{-1}\begin{bmatrix} 2 \\ 4 \end{bmatrix} = \begin{bmatrix} 4 \\ 2 \end{bmatrix}$$

Although using matrices isn't particularly difficult, many of the calculations involving them are quite tedious. For example, to find an inverse matrix (denoted by the −1 exponent in the equation above) that is two rows by two columns, you'll need to find what's called the *determinant* first—calculated only from a square matrix, the determinant is a value that reveals certain properties of the matrix, such as if it's singular or not—and then transpose and flip the signs of other matrix elements. (Finding the determinant of a three-row-by-three-column matrix is really tedious.)

Computer algorithms usually work well when the steps of a procedure (especially a mathematical one) are unambiguous and exhaustive. Such is the case with matrix operations tackled by the **MATRIX.BAS** program below. Along with finding inverses and simple determinants, the program also allows for transposition (turning rows into columns and columns into rows).

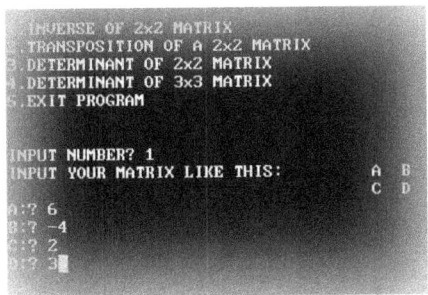

● ● ●

There are no complicated lines of code here; once the elements of the matrix are inputted, it's all just grunt work, just plug-and-chug, and GW-BASIC acquits itself well yet again as a programmable calculator.

● ● ●

MATRIX.BAS
```
10 KEY OFF:SCREEN 9:COLOR 15,1:CLS
15 PRINT"MATRIX CALCULATING PROGRAM"
17 PRINT
```

```
20 PRINT"1.INVERSE OF 2x2 MATRIX"
21 PRINT"2.TRANSPOSITION OF A 2x2 MATRIX"
22 PRINT"3.DETERMINANT OF 2x2 MATRIX"
23 PRINT"4.DETERMINANT OF 3x3 MATRIX"
25 PRINT"5.EXIT PROGRAM"
29 PRINT:PRINT
30 INPUT"INPUT NUMBER";NUM
31 A=0:B=0:C=0:D=0:E=0:F=0:G=0:H=0:I=0
40 IF NUM=1 THEN GOTO 60
41 IF NUM=2 THEN GOTO 125
42 IF NUM=3 THEN GOTO 170
43 IF NUM=4 THEN GOTO 220
45 IF NUM=5 THEN CLS:END
55 GOTO 30
60 PRINT"INPUT YOUR MATRIX LIKE THIS:          A
   B"
70 PRINT"                                      C
   D"
80 INPUT"A:";A
85 INPUT"B:";B
90 INPUT"C:";C
95 INPUT"D:";D
100 E=((A*D)-(C*B))
105 IF E=0 THEN GOTO 120
110 PRINT ((1/E)*D);" ";((1/E)*-B)
115 PRINT ((1/E)*-C);" ";((1/E)*A)
116 GOTO 15
120 PRINT"YOU CANNOT FIND THE INVERSE OF THIS
    MATRIX!":GOTO 15
125 PRINT"INPUT MATRIX AS               A  B"
126 PRINT"                              C  D"
130 INPUT"A:";A
135 INPUT"B:";B
140 INPUT"C:";C
145 INPUT"D:";D
150 PRINT"                       ";A;" ";C
155 PRINT"                       ";B;" ";D
160 GOTO 15
170 PRINT"INPUT MATRIX AS               A  B"
180 PRINT"                              C  D"
190 INPUT"A:";A
191 INPUT"B:";B
192 INPUT"C:";C
193 INPUT"D:";D
```

```
200 PRINT ((A*D)-(B*C))
210 GOTO 15
220 PRINT"INPUT MATRIX AS                    A    B
    C"
230 PRINT"                                   D    E
    F"
240 PRINT"                                   G    H
    I"
250 PRINT"NOTE: THE DIAGONAL METHOD WILL BE USED
    TO FIND THE DETERMINANT"
251 INPUT"A:";A
252 INPUT"B:";B
253 INPUT"C:";C
254 INPUT"D:";D
255 INPUT"E:";E
256 INPUT"F:";F
257 INPUT"G:";G
258 INPUT"H:";H
259 INPUT"I:";I
260 PRINT (A*E*I)+(B*F*G)+(C*D*H)-(G*E*C)-(H*F*A)-
    (I*D*B)
270 GOTO 15
```

● ● ●

The program could be streamlined quite a bit without losing any of its functionality. For instance, only a single subroutine should be devoted to entering in a matrix, and the elements of the matrix should be assigned values as part of an array, rather than having their own separate variables (like **A**, **B**, **C**, and so forth, as the program is clumsily written now). That way, more flexibility would be permitted—and more difficult matrix operations could be performed.

Defining Functions
LOAD "FUNC.BAS"

Ok

RUN_

Simple mathematical functions map ordinates (the y values) to abscissas (the x values) in a very specific way: each x value, when plugged into a function, yields one—and only one—y value.

For instance, consider the following function:

$$f(x) = 3x + 1$$

If we plug 4 in for x, we get out a unique value for y, 13, as shown below.

$$f(4) = 3 \cdot 4 + 1 = 12 + 1 = 13$$

GW-BASIC allows for user-defined functions, with varying numbers of inputs. Examine the code of **FUNC.BAS**, and then run the program: you supply the inputs, and the outputs are printed to the screen.

$\bullet\ \bullet\ \bullet$

The magic lies with the **DEF FN** statement: lines **25** and **60** define two different functions, while lines **35** and **90** evaluate them at user-inputted values.

$\bullet\ \bullet\ \bullet$

FUNC.BAS

```
10 KEY OFF:SCREEN 9:COLOR 15,0:CLS
20 PRINT"WE WILL DEFINE A FUNCTION F(X) = 3X+1
25 DEF FNFUN(X)=3*X+1
30 INPUT"EVALUATE F(X) FOR X=";X
35 P=FNFUN(X)
40 PRINT "F(";X;")=";P
50 PRINT:PRINT"WE WILL NOW DEFINE A FUNCTION
   G(X,Y) = 2X+3Y"
60 DEF FNFC(X,Y)=2*X+3*Y
70 INPUT "X=";X
80 INPUT "Y=";Y
90 Q=FNFC(X,Y)
100 PRINT"G(";X;",";Y;")=";Q
110 PRINT:END
```

● ● ●

The **DEF FN** statement, when used appropriately, can be a powerful ally in helping to simplify a program's code. The catch? Every function's name must begin with the letters FN.

Finding Derivatives
LOAD "DERIVE.BAS"
Ok

RUN_

Taking derivatives is a fundamental operation in calculus. A derivative of a function is its rate of change, or *slope*, with respect to some variable.

It's straightforward to find the slope of a linear function, which graphs as a straight line, since the slope—the *rise/run*, or the *y* units traveled divided by the *x* units traveled when constructing the line—is constant everywhere on a line. If we have two unique points on a line, (x_1, y_1) and (x_2, y_2), the slope can be found by using the formula

$$m = \frac{rise}{run} = \frac{y_2 - y_1}{x_2 - x_1}$$

But what happens if our function isn't linear? Can we still find its slope?*

With some qualifications,† the answer is yes. The key is to examine smaller and smaller segments of the function,

---

* If you're not feeling comfortable with the notion of slope, you might want to read the later chapter on the SLOPE.BAS program before continuing.

† Namely: discontinuities, sharp edges, and certain kinds of inflection points, because a tangent line cannot be properly drawn at any of these spots. Without a tangent line—a line

calculating the slope of those tightly bounded segments. Using Δ (pronounced "delta") to represent a small quantity, and rewriting the slope formula, we obtain

$$m = \frac{f(x + \Delta) - f(x)}{\Delta}$$

which will find the slope of a function over an interval of size Δ. The smaller the Δ, the better.

But how small does Δ need to be? Certainly it can't be zero, since Δ is in the denominator of the slope equation. Instead, mathematicians use the concept of the *limit* to "approach" a value—in this case zero—as closely as possible. Rewriting the slope formula with limit notation gives

$$\lim_{\Delta \to 0} \frac{f(x + \Delta) - f(x)}{\Delta}$$

This particular limit is formally referred to as the *definition of the derivative*.

Let's look at an example. The derivative of

$$f(x) = 4x^2$$

can be obtained by plugging the function *f(x)* into the definition of the limit:

$$\lim_{\Delta \to 0} \frac{4(x + \Delta)^2 - 4(x)^2}{\Delta}$$

---

that just barely "touches" the function at precisely one point— you cannot determine the steepness or sign of the slope at a point of interest.

$$\lim_{\Delta \to 0} \frac{4\left(x^2 + 2x\Delta + \Delta^2\right) - 4(x)^2}{\Delta}$$

$$\lim_{\Delta \to 0} \frac{4x^2 + 8x\Delta + 4\Delta^2 - 4x^2}{\Delta}$$

$$\lim_{\Delta \to 0} \frac{8x\Delta + 4\Delta^2}{\Delta}$$

$$\lim_{\Delta \to 0} \frac{\Delta(8x + 4\Delta)}{\Delta}$$

$$\lim_{\Delta \to 0} 8x + 4\Delta$$

This simplified limit is easy to find: simply plug zero in for Δ.* Thus,

$$f'(x) = \frac{df}{dx} = 8x^1 = 8x$$

Both the f-prime and df/dx notation signify a first derivative of the function $f(x)$. The slope of $f(x)$ is not a fixed number, but changes, depending on the x value. Take $x = 6$, for instance. The slope of $f(x)$ at $x = 6$ is $f'(6) = 8 \cdot 6 = 48$. Hence, a tangent line drawn at $(6, f(6))$ on a graph of $f(x)$ has a slope of 48.

---

* Note that we were unable to plug in zero until the final simplification because delta was lodged in the limit's denominator—so we still would have been attempting to divide by zero, always a mathematical no-no.

Using the definition of the derivative can result in a lot of simplification work, though. The same derivative of $f(x)$ could have also been found by simply multiplying the exponent by the coefficient (here, multiplying two by four) and then subtracting one from the exponent.

Note that $f(x)$ is a monomial; because garden variety monomials' derivatives are relatively straightforward to obtain, a computer program, like DERIVE.BAS, can easily model the mathematical process. (Although, technically, negative integer exponents disqualify the function from being a monomial, the program can find derivatives of these functions too.)

When run, the DERIVE.BAS program prompts you for a monomial in $k*x\char`\^n$ form, where k is the coefficient and n is the power (both values must be integers), and then outputs its derivative.

● ● ●

Several conditional statements handle the special cases (see lines 36 to 38) but, otherwise, the calculations are very straightforward here.

● ● ●

DERIVE.BAS

```
5 KEY OFF:SCREEN 9:COLOR 15,0:CLS
7 PRINT"Find Simple Derivatives!"
10 LOCATE 4,5:PRINT"ENTER IN FUNTION USING THIS
   FORMAT: K*x^n":PRINT
15 PRINT"Please use only integers for the values
   of K and n":PRINT
20 INPUT"What is K";K
30 INPUT"What is power n";N
35 NW=N-1
36 IF NW=0 THEN 60
37 IF NW=1 THEN 45
38 IF NW=-1 THEN 65
39 IF NW<-1 THEN 55
```

```
40 PRINT "d/dx(";K;"x^";N;") = ";K*N;"x^";NW
43 END
45 PRINT "d/dx(";K;"x^";N;") = ";K*N;"x"
50 END
55 PRINT "d/dx(";K;"x^";N;") = ";K*N;"/ x^";-(NW)
57 END
60 PRINT "d/dx(";K;"x) = ";K*N
63 END
65 PRINT "d/dx(";K;") = ";0
70 END
```

• • •

While the challenge might be apparent, it is incredibly difficult to grapple with: write a program to find the derivative of *any* function (if such a derivative can be obtained). Different classes of functions would necessitate their own derivative-calculating algorithms: besides monomials, polynomial, exponential, trigonometric, and hyperbolic are just some of many possible classes of functions to consider. In addition, step-by-step procedures for handling the product, quotient, and chain rules would have to be written. The task, though daunting because of the large number of permutations of functions, is not impossible for the intrepid GW-BASIC programmer.

Adding Up

LOAD "SIGMA.BAS"

Ok

RUN

In mathematics, the Greek letter uppercase sigma, or Σ, represents summation: given some function and an index of summation (often represented by i or n), add the terms from a lower to an upper bound. For example, the summation

$$\sum_{i=1}^{10} i = 1 + 2 + 3 + \cdots + 9 + 10$$

is equal to fifty.

Once the function is entered into the code, **SIGMA.BAS** will ask for the limits of the summation and proceed to print out the terms as well as the sum of all of the terms.

• • •

Line **60** contains the summation function. In this case, it is

$$\sum \frac{i^2}{2}$$

The function can be changed to anything you wish, but the function input must occur *outside* of a program run.

• • •

SIGMA.BAS

```
10 KEY OFF:SCREEN 9:COLOR 15,0:CLS
15 X=0:SUM=0
30 INPUT"You should have already inputted the
   function in the program's code. Start at:";ST
40 INPUT"Finish at:";FI
45 PRINT"{ ";
50 FOR X=ST TO FI
60 SUM=SUM+((X^2)/2):PRINT ;((X^2)/2);
70 NEXT X
80 PRINT;" }"
90 PRINT:PRINT"Finite sum of terms: ";SUM
```

• • •

The challenge here is obvious: permit the user to input a summation function within the program itself—i.e., via an **INPUT** prompt.

An even more difficult challenge: add code that correctly calculates sums of infinite series, thus permitting the upper bounds of summations to be infinity. Hint: you might want to restrict your attention, at least at first, to infinite geometric series; your program would have to recognize this class of summations.

Solve It
LOAD "EQUATION.BAS"

Ok

RUN

▪▪

Suppose we want to solve a one-variable equation like this:

$$x - 10 = -x + 10$$

We would simply group the variables on one side, and the constants on the other, and isolate x. In the equation above, x equals ten.

Once an equation is entered into a line of code, the **EQUATION.BAS** program will ask for a lower and an upper bound and cycle through numbers—beginning with integers, then progressing to tenths, hundredths, and thousandths places—until a match to both sides of the inputted equation is found.

● ● ●

Before running, an equation first needs to be entered in line **50**. The **FOR/NEXT** loop starts incrementing by one unit through the bounds, and then increments by ever-smaller one-over-factor-of-ten amounts if necessary—examine the **STEP** statement for the details.

● ● ●

EQUATION.BAS
```
10 KEY OFF:SCREEN 9:COLOR 15,1:CLS:ST=1
```

```
15 PRINT"Make sure the equation has been entered
   in line 50 first!"
20 INPUT"Lower bound of x:";IX
30 INPUT"Upper bound of x:";XI
40 FOR X=IX TO XI STEP (1/ST)
50 IF (X-10)=(-X+10) THEN PRINT"x= ";X:END
60 NEXT X
70 ST=ST*10:GOTO 40
```

● ● ●

Similar to the programs SIGMA.BAS and DERIVE.BAS, the user is only allowed to input the equation directly into the code, rather than dynamically during a program run. This is cumbersome and certainly not user-friendly.

A more subtle limitation? You are only permitted only one variable in the inputted equations. With, say, two variables, you would also need two equations in order to solve for both variables. Expanding this program so it can handle two or more variables (and two or more equations, linear or otherwise) is no easy feat—but certainly within the realm of possibility.

Assignments

LOAD "AVGCALC.BAS"

Ok

RUN_

You're a student—or a teacher. There are a number of assignments, all out of a different number of points, that you wish to average. And this won't be the last time this term that you'll want to calculate such an average.

How about writing a program? After asking for the number of assignments to average, the score of each assignment, as well as its "perfect score," must be inputted. And then—presto!—the average of all your assignments is displayed.

• • •

A **FOR/NEXT** loop takes care of most of the program's business (see lines **30** to **60** for the details). The variable **S** compiles a running total of the numerator of the final average, while the variable **R** does the same for the denominator.

• • •

AVGCALC.BAS
```
10 KEY OFF:CLS:SCREEN 7:COLOR 15,1
20 INPUT" NUMBER OF ASSIGNMENTS:";V
30 FOR H=1 TO V
40 PRINT:INPUT"SCORE OF STUDENT:";G
45 INPUT"PERFECT SCORE:";P
50 S=S+G:R=R+P
60 NEXT H
```

```
70 A=S/R*100
80 PRINT"  THE STUDENT SCORED A:";INT(A)
```

• • •

The only option, as it stands now, is in varying the number of assignments entered. But this isn't true to life—or school.

Perhaps certain assignments carry more weight than others, beyond just their point totals. For example, a midterm might count for thirty percent of the grade, while a number of other assignments would fall into a "homework" category worth, let's say, ten percent of the semester's grade. Improving the program to be dynamic enough to handle the vagaries of school assignments would improve its usefulness greatly.

Rolling Dice
LOAD "DICE.BAS"

Ok

RUN

Roll a single, fair die: there are six possible outcomes, one for each face. Roll two fair dice, and the number of outcomes swells to thirty-six: you could roll a one and a two, a two and a three, a three and a four…

Now consider the sum of the rolls of the two dice. (The casino game craps is structured around these sums.) Seven is the most likely sum, whereas the sums of two and twelve are the least likely.

Although we could demonstrate the probabilities empirically by picking up two physical dice and rolling them many times while recording our results, GW-BASIC can easily perform the same process and show the sums on-screen. You can set the speed of each roll (asked for at the beginning of the program via the prompt *Delay?*), and stop the dice rolls at any time by hitting the ESCAPE key.

• • •

Notice the randomization function:

```
INT(1+6*RND(1))
```

It will not work to merely code, let's say, `RND(6)`, since the `RND` function will simply output a random[*] number in

---

[*] Well, not really; it's actually *pseudorandom*, as we'll explore

a bounded interval from zero to one. The **INT** part of the randomization expression makes sure that the output value is an integer, and the **1+6** part ensures the random number is between one and six: one of the six faces of a rolled die.

• • •

DICE.BAS
```
1 KEY OFF
5 RANDOMIZE TIMER
6 DIM ROLL(12)
10 COLOR 15,1:CLS
11 LOCATE 10,30
13 PRINT"ROLLING TWO DICE!"
15 INPUT"DELAY AFTER EACH ROLL";DELAY:CLS
20 I=INT(1+6*RND(1)):Q=INT(1+6*RND(1))
25 LOCATE 3,7
30 PRINT "ROLL OF DIE 1:";I;"   ";"ROLL OF DIE
   2:";Q;"   ";"SUM OF ROLLS:"I+Q
35 FOR PAUSE=1 TO DELAY:NEXT PAUSE
40 IF I+Q=2 THEN ROLL(2)=ROLL(2)+1
41 IF I+Q=3 THEN ROLL(3)=ROLL(3)+1
42 IF I+Q=4 THEN ROLL(4)=ROLL(4)+1
43 IF I+Q=5 THEN ROLL(5)=ROLL(5)+1
44 IF I+Q=6 THEN ROLL(6)=ROLL(6)+1
45 IF I+Q=7 THEN ROLL(7)=ROLL(7)+1
46 IF I+Q=8 THEN ROLL(8)=ROLL(8)+1
47 IF I+Q=9 THEN ROLL(9)=ROLL(9)+1
48 IF I+Q=10 THEN ROLL(10)=ROLL(10)+1
49 IF I+Q=11 THEN ROLL(11)=ROLL(11)+1
50 IF I+Q=12 THEN ROLL(12)=ROLL(12)+1
60 LOCATE 10,1:PRINT"ROLL SUM OF 2:";ROLL(2)
61 LOCATE 11,1:PRINT"ROLL SUM OF 3:";ROLL(3)
64 LOCATE 12,1:PRINT"ROLL SUM OF 4:";ROLL(4)
```

in a later chapter, the number being based off of an initial seed produced by the computer's internal clock—hence the RANDOMIZE TIMER function. Although, for our purposes, pseudorandom is sufficiently indistinguishable from truly random.

```
65 LOCATE 13,1:PRINT"ROLL SUM OF 5:";ROLL(5)
66 LOCATE 14,1:PRINT"ROLL SUM OF 6:";ROLL(6)
67 LOCATE 15,1:PRINT"ROLL SUM OF 7:";ROLL(7)
68 LOCATE 16,1:PRINT"ROLL SUM OF 8:";ROLL(8)
69 LOCATE 17,1:PRINT"ROLL SUM OF 9:";ROLL(9)
70 LOCATE 18,1:PRINT"ROLL SUM OF 10:";ROLL(10)
71 LOCATE 19,1:PRINT"ROLL SUM OF 11:";ROLL(11)
72 LOCATE 20,1:PRINT"ROLL SUM OF 12:";ROLL(12)
74 ALL=ROLL(2)+ROLL(3)+ROLL(4)+ROLL(5)+ ROLL(6)+
   ROLL(7)+ROLL(8)+ROLL(9)+ROLL(10)+ROLL(11)+ROLL(1
   2)
75 LOCATE 22,1:PRINT"SUM OF ALL ROLLS:";ALL
77 IF INKEY$=CHR$(27) THEN END
80 GOTO 20
```

● ● ●

These rolls of two dice are only of *fair* dice. What if instead you wish to roll two dice that are unfair (i.e., weighted)? The probabilities of landing on each face would change. Furthermore, what if you wished to roll dice that don't have six faces? Perhaps a program with more die-rolling options is in order.

Rolling Dice Again

LOAD "DICE2.BAS"

Ok

RUN_

Instead of rolling two fair dice in three dimensions, imagine rolling two dice of *n* number of sides on a number line of a finite width (equal lengths from zero, however). If the sum of the rolls satisfies two conditions with respect to the number line, you win; otherwise, you lose. DICE2.BAS will run any number of such trials that you wish, all the while calculating the empirical probability of winning the game.

• • •

Note that the program selects *negative* random numbers in lines 100, 105, and 110 by subtracting from the randomization expressions; GW-BASIC cannot otherwise "directly" obtain negative random numbers.

• • •

```
DICE2.BAS
10 KEY OFF:SCREEN 9:CLS:COLOR 15,0:RANGE=0:A=0:
   B=0:ROLL=0:WIN=0:TRIAL=0:RANDOMIZE TIMER
20 INPUT"WHAT IS THE RANGE, +/- 0, OF YOUR NUMBER
   LINE";RANGE
30 INPUT"HOW MANY SIDES DOES THE 'DIE' HAVE";SIDES
40 INPUT"HOW MANY TRIALS";TRIALS
90 FOR LOOP=1 TO TRIALS
100 A=INT(1+RANGE*2*RND(1))-RANGE
105 B=INT(1+RANGE*2*RND(1))-RANGE
```

```
110 ROLL=(INT(1+SIDES*2*RND(1))-SIDES)+(INT(1+
    SIDES*2*RND(1))-SIDES)
120 IF ROLL<A AND B<A THEN WIN=WIN+1
130 IF ROLL>A AND B>A THEN WIN=WIN+1
135 LOCATE 12,5:PRINT"A=";A;" B=";B;" ROLL=";ROLL
140 LOCATE 13, 15:PRINT"TRIAL #:";LOOP
150 LOCATE 15,15:PRINT WIN/LOOP
160 NEXT LOOP
```

● ● ●

Displaying a number line on the screen, along with plot-
ting a dot at each dice roll sum, would add visual flourishes
to an otherwise very rudimentary program.

The Decision Maker
LOAD "DM.BAS"

Ok

RUN_

The Magic 8-Ball was invented by Albert Carter in the 1940s, although it didn't take the plastic crystal ball form—after all, it's supposed to be a fortune teller, right?—we're now familiar with until Abe Bookman encased the toy in a clear sphere, and eventually in a black-and-white plastic sphere. Today, the Magic 8-Ball is made by (and a registered trademark of) Mattel, Inc.

The DM.BAS program, short for "Decision Maker," is effectively an electronic version of the 8-Ball (sans flashy graphics simulating the real thing). Many, but not all, of the answers printed on the 8-Ball's floating die are programmed in DM.BAS.

Once you ask the computer a question, it "computes" the answer and displays it on-screen. Positive answers are shown in green, negative answers in red, and the sole equivocal answer is in yellow.

• • •

There are nine possible "decisions," enumerated in lines 110 to 126, all corresponding to a random number chosen in line 100. The flashing *Computing…* text is simply for show. Probably.

• • •

DM.BAS

```
10 KEY OFF:SCREEN 9:RANDOMIZE TIMER
20 COLOR 15,1:CLS
30 PRINT:PRINT:PRINT:PRINT TAB(10) "The Decision
   Maker"
50 FOR F=1 TO 10000:NEXT F
60 CLS
70 LINE INPUT"ASK YOUR QUESTION:";D$
80 COLOR 4,1:CLS
81 FOR M=1 TO 2
90 PRINT:PRINT:PRINT:PRINT:PRINT:PRINT:PRINT:
   PRINT:PRINT TAB(10) "COMPUTING..."
95 FOR MN=1 TO 3000:NEXT MN
96 COLOR 4,1:CLS
97 FOR MCV=1 TO 2000:NEXT MCV
98 NEXT M
100 I=INT(1+9*RND(1))
105 PRINT:PRINT:PRINT TAB(15);
110 IF I=1 THEN COLOR 2:PRINT"It's certain!"
112 IF I=2 THEN COLOR 2:PRINT"Without any doubt!"
114 IF I=3 THEN COLOR 2:PRINT"You can rely on it!"
116 IF I=4 THEN COLOR 2:PRINT"Your outlook's
    good!"
118 IF I=5 THEN COLOR 14:PRINT"Please ask me again
    later..."
120 IF I=6 THEN COLOR 4:PRINT"Well, don't count on
    it."
122 IF I=7 THEN COLOR 4:PRINT"My reply is no."
124 IF I=8 THEN COLOR 4:PRINT"Your outlook is not
    so good."
126 IF I=9 THEN COLOR 4:PRINT"It's very, very
    doubtful."
128 COLOR 15
130 PRINT:PRINT"Another? (Type 'Y' or 'N').";
140 INPUT T$
150 IF T$="Y" OR T$="y" THEN GOTO 10
160 CLS:END
```

• • •

Besides increasing the number of decisions, adding 8-Ball-like graphics is far and away the most significant improvement you could make to **DM.BAS**.

Pseudorandom Numbers
LOAD "PSEUDO.BAS"
Ok
RUN_

GW-BASIC's **RND** function does not manufacture *true* random numbers from thin air; rather, the function generates what are called *pseudorandom* numbers, and require an initial (and varying) random number "seed" so the patterns of numbers produced for every program's run are different. This seed usually takes two forms: if the **RANDOMIZE** statement is used, the user is prompted to enter a number; if, instead, the **RANDOMIZE TIMER** statement is coded, the computer quietly pulls a number from the computer's internal clock. **RND** works, behinds the scenes, using an recursive function.

Trying to find the *specific* mathematical algorithm that GW-BASIC uses to generate pseudorandom numbers, though, has proven difficult. In the article "A Theoretical and Empirical Comparison of Mainframe, Microcomputer, and Pocket Calculator Pseudorandom Number Generators" (in the academic journal *Behavior Research Methods, Instruments, & Computers*), author Patrick Onghena writes that

> [t]he Advanced BASIC (IBM, 1986), GW-BASIC (Microsoft, 1987), and QBASIC (Microsoft, 1991) programming languages provide the function **RND**, which is initialized by the **RANDOMIZE** command together with a number between -2^{15} and $2^{15}-1$, and which returns a pseudorandom single-precision number between **0** and **1**…. [T]he generating algorithm is un-

documented in the manual. Our letters to Microsoft Inc. about the algorithm remain unanswered.

Onghena wrote that in 1993. Needless to say, I'm pretty confident that Microsoft isn't going to reveal their GW-BASIC pseudorandom-number generator algorithm any time soon.

Nonetheless, Microsoft's website states that "Microsoft Basic uses the linear-congruential method [a common class of pseudorandom number generator algorithms] for random-number generation in the **RND** function," but the "Basic" in question isn't GW-BASIC, but likely Quick-Basic and/or Visual Basic. The program that follows is an attempt to pare down the website's algorithm to something more manageable by GW-BASIC.

When **PSEUDO.BAS** is run, you'll be asked for an initial seed, and then "random" numbers will be generated on-screen, all without the use of the **RND** function.

• • •

The flashpoint in the code is on line **50**: this is the recursive function that generates the pseudorandom numbers. The **MOD** operator permits modulus arithmetic, giving the remainder of a quotient. Line **80** continues the succession of pseudorandom integers.

• • •

PSEUDO.BAS

```
10 KEY OFF:SCREEN 9:SCREEN 0:COLOR 15,1:CLS
15 PRINT"LINEAR-CONGRUENTIAL METHOD FOR RANDOM-
   NUMBER GENERATION"
20 A=213
30 C=2531
40 INPUT"RANDOM NUMBER SEED (FROM 1 TO 100)";INI
45 IF INI>100 THEN 40
46 IF INI<1 THEN 40
50 X=(INI*A+C) MOD 2^6
```

```
60 PRINT X
70 'TAKE RESULT AND PLUG BACK INTO THE FORMULA
80 X2=(X*A+C) MOD 2^6
90 PRINT X2
95 PRINT:PRINT"PRESS <ENTER> FOR NEXT RANDOM
   NUMBER... (OR TYPE Q TO QUIT)..."
96 LINE INPUT N$
97 IF N$="Q" THEN CLS:END
100 X=X2
120 GOTO 70
```

• • •

There are a number of ways **PSEUDO.BAS** might be fruit-fully tweaked. For instance, the initial values of **A** and **C** could be altered, and the recursive function itself could be modified.

The American Standard Code for Information Interchange, or ASCII, is an digital map of characters to numbers.[*] For instance, the uppercase *J* is corresponds to ASCII code 74.

The codes represent more than just letters and numbers. ASCII code 236 represents the infinity symbol, for example, while 227 is assigned to π.

There are two programs presented in this chapter: CHRGC.BAS and RNDCHR$.BAS.

CHRGC.BAS permits you to scroll through all the ASCII character codes displayable by GW-BASIC, simply by pressing the + and − keys. RNDCHR$.BAS is an ASCII codes' screensaver (although such programs are no longer needed with modern computer displays).

● ● ●

Both programs make use of the CHR$ function. CHR$ converts the ASCII code to the character it represents. Since the ASCII codes run from 1 to 255, the programs need to ensure that CHR$ remains within those bounds.

● ● ●

_____

[*] The industry standard is now Unicode.

CHRGC.BAS

```
10 KEY OFF:N=1:SCREEN 9
20 COLOR 1,1:CLS:COLOR 15
40 LOCATE 12,37:PRINT CHR$(N)
41 LOCATE 3,30:PRINT"CHR$:";N:G$=INKEY$
42 IF G$="" THEN GOTO 41
43 IF G$="+" THEN N=N+1
44 IF G$="-" THEN N=N-1
46 IF G$=CHR$(27) THEN CLS:END
50 IF N=>255 THEN N=1:CLS
55 IF N<1 THEN N=254:CLS
60 GOTO 40
```

RNDCHR$.BAS

```
10 KEY OFF:SCREEN 9:COLOR 14,0:CLS
20 F=INT(1+255*RND(1))
21 C=INT(1+15*RND(1)):IF C=8 THEN GOTO 21
22 X=INT(1+24*RND(1)):Y=INT(1+80*RND(1))
30 IF F=7 THEN GOTO 20
35 IF F=12 THEN GOTO 20
40 COLOR C:LOCATE X,Y:PRINT CHR$(F);;
45 IF INKEY$=CHR$(27) THEN CLS:END
50 GOTO 20
```

● ● ●

Combining both programs into one (with a menu giving
you an option of which subprogram to jump to) might be
a marginal improvement but is certainly not necessary;
after all, RNDCHR$.BAS, a screensaver, is just for kicks,
contrary to CHRGC.BAS, which functions as a reference of
ASCII codes that you might want to use for other programs.

Music!
LOAD "MUSIC.BAS"

Ok

RUN_

The futurist Ray Kurzweil first drew national attention as a teenager, way back in the mid-1960s, when he appeared on the then-popular CBS show *I've Got a Secret*: his prodigious mathematical and musical talents came together as he played a piece on the piano for a studio audience that a computer—running off of a program that he wrote—had earlier (and off-camera) composed.

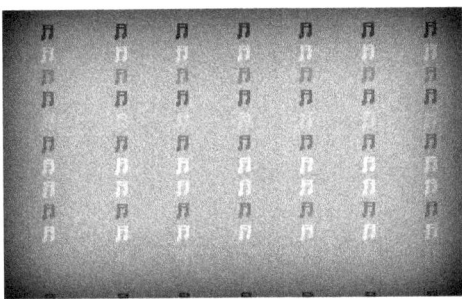

When you run **MUSIC.BAS**, you'll hear a composition from your computer, too—except, well, it won't sound like much, beyond some random notes strung together with no melody, rhyme, or reason. Kurzweil, hearing your computer's tone-deaf piece, might be horrified enough to recant his most preposterous belief: that of the imminent singularity.

• • •

The **SOUND** statement has two parameters: frequency and duration. Both have been randomized here, with the frequency not permitted to be below 500 hertz and the duration not allowed under five clock ticks (yes, that's a real unit of measurement; there are roughly five clock ticks per second). Colorful musical notes, which are printed on-screen using **CHR$**, won't help save your ears, sadly.

• • •

```
MUSIC.BAS
10 RANDOMIZE TIMER:SCREEN 9:COLOR 15,1:CLS
20 R=INT(1+15*RND(1))
21 IF R=1 THEN GOTO 20
25 COLOR R
30 FOR T=1 TO 5:PRINT ,CHR$(14);:NEXT T
35 SOUND INT(1+200*RND(1))+500,INT(1+10*RND(1))+5
40 GOTO 20
```

• • •

Though you'll never be able to code an electronic Mozart or Mahler, programming in some basic musical rules, and generating random notes within those bounds, would greatly improve **MUSIC.BAS**.

Morse Code
LOAD "MORSE.BAS"

Ok

RUN_

Perhaps relaying Morse code permits a better use of the **SOUND** statement than do digital musical compositions. Over a century before Claude Shannon revolutionized information theory, American Samuel Morse (along with several others) developed a communications system of electrically coded pulses, which came to be called Morse code. Telegraphs were used to transmit the signals.

Run **MORSE.BAS** to hear—and see—the old code in action.

• • •

Using **INKEY$, MORSE.BAS** waits patiently for you to type a letter (only the letters A through K are programmed in); then, the Morse code is transmitted—well, at least to your ears. Typing a lowercase *c* will clear the screen, while a lowercase *s* will insert a space.

• • •

MORSE.BAS
```
10 KEY OFF:SCREEN 7:COLOR 5,3:CLS
20 PRINT TAB(10) "MORSE CODE EQUALIZER"
30 COLOR 8
40 I$=INKEY$
41 IF I$="c" THEN GOTO 10
43 IF I$="s" THEN PRINT;" ";
50 IF I$="A" THEN PRINT"A ._ ";:PLAY"MB C8 C4"
```

```
60 IF I$="B" THEN PRINT"B _... ";:PLAY"MB C4 C8 C8
   C8"
70 IF I$="C" THEN PRINT"C _._. ";:PLAY"MB C4 C8 C4
   C8"
75 IF I$="D" THEN PRINT"D _.. ";:PLAY"MB C4 C8 C8"
80 IF I$="E" THEN PRINT"E . ";:PLAY"MB C8"
85 IF I$="F" THEN PRINT"F .._. ";:PLAY"MB C8 C8 C4
   C8"
90 IF I$="G" THEN PRINT"G _ _. ";:PLAY"MB C4 C4
   C8"
95 IF I$="H" THEN PRINT"H .... ";:PLAY"MB C8 C8 C8
   C8"
100 IF I$="I" THEN PRINT"I .. ";:PLAY"MB C8 C8"
105 IF I$="J" THEN PRINT"J ._ _ _  ";:PLAY"MB C8
    C4 C4 C4"
110 IF I$="K" THEN PRINT"K _._ ";:PLAY"MB C4 C8
    C4"
120 IF I$=CHR$(27) THEN CLS:END
500 GOTO 40
```

• • •

The challenge here is obvious: finish (Morse) coding the
alphabet!

Square Rooting
LOAD "SQRT.BAS"

GW-BASIC has a square root function; it's called **SQR**. If you want the square root of, say, the number eight, you'd type in **PRINT SQR(8)** and out would come **2.828427** (the output's decimal terminates, unlike the true decimal expansion of the square root of eight—which goes on forever without a pattern, since the number is irrational).

But the program **SQRT.BAS** does something more novel: it uses an recursive algorithm to find the square root of an inputted number. After entering a number at the prompt *Square Root of*, the program also queries the user for a starting number—in other words, a point at which to begin the iterations. Tapping the spacebar lets you see each step, as the square root is homed in on until, eventually, the numbers stop changing and—*voilà*—you have your square root approximated as a decimal.

• • •

No matter what number is chosen as the starting number (within reason), the recursive algorithm obtains the square root within only a handful of steps. Carefully examine lines **40** and **50**: first, the variable **M** is narrowed down with a quotient, and then its result is summed to variable **C**, the starting number (which may increase or decrease the number). The process then repeats recursively, summing less and less to **C** each time until no more changes are apparent—at which point the best approximation to the square root has been calculated.

• • •

SQRT.BAS

```
10 SCREEN 7:COLOR 15,1:KEY OFF:CLS
15 DIM S,C
20 INPUT"Square Root of:";S
30 INPUT"Number to start at: ";C
40 CLS:M=((S-C*C)/(2*C))
50 C=C+M
60 PRINT:PRINT TAB(3);CHR$(251);S;" is:
   ";C:PRINT:PRINT"Press <SPACE> for another itera-
   tion (or ESCAPE to quit)"
70 I$=INKEY$
75 IF I$=CHR$(32) THEN 40
80 IF I$=CHR$(27) THEN END
90 GOTO 70
```

• • •

The algorithm is not, unsurprisingly, the only avenue to finding square roots. Perhaps a program utilizing several different rooting algorithms (such as the long division method) is in order, with the steps clearly shown on the screen. In addition, it would be nice if more digits after the decimal point could be evaluated and displayed.

Denominators

LOAD "LCD.BAS"

When adding or subtracting fractions—unlike multiplying or dividing them—the fractions' denominators must be the same. In order to the find the lowest common denominator (or least common denominator) of two (or more) fractions, you need to find the *smallest* whole number that both denominators divide into evenly. Seems like a process tailor-made for a computer.

Run LCD.BAS and simply enter in your two denominators; out pops not only the LCD, but also how the LCD was calculated.

• • •

The trick in the program lies with variable Q. Examine the formula (in line 50): Q=(DB*M)/DA, where M is initialized to 1 and is incremented by one unit until the quotient is an integer; see line 60 for the integer test.

• • •

LCD.BAS
```
10 KEY OFF:SCREEN 9:COLOR 15,1:CLS
20 PRINT"* L C D   C A L C U L A T O R *"
30 INPUT"ENTER FIRST DENOMINATOR:";DA
35 INPUT"ENTER SECOND DENOMINATOR:";DB
40 M=1
50 Q=(DB*M)/DA
55 LOCATE 5,10:PRINT DB*M;"/";DA;"=";(DB*M)/DA
```

```
60 IF Q=INT(Q) THEN 90
70 M=M+1
80 GOTO 50
90 PRINT"LCD(";DA;";";DB;")=";
100 PRINT DB;"X";M;"=";DB*M
110 PRINT:INPUT"ANOTHER(Y/N)";F$
120 IF F$="Y" THEN GOTO 10
130 IF F$="N" THEN CLS:END
140 GOTO 110
```

• • •

The algorithm only finds the LCD of two denominators. It wouldn't be that much work to expand the code to allow for finding the LCD of n denominators at once.

Prime Numbers
LOAD "PRIMES.BAS"

Ok

RUN_

Although the ancient mathematician Euclid was probably not the first to prove the infinitude of primes—i.e., that there are an uncountable amount of prime numbers—his proof is surely the most famous, requiring little prior mathematical knowledge.

Recall that a prime number is any whole number with only itself and the number one as divisors (although the number one, by definition, is not prime).* Euclid began by supposing that the number of primes were finite, and we had a list of them all. He then said to multiply all those primes together, and to call this product P.

Now, add one to P; designate this new number Q. There are two possibilities: either Q is prime (meaning that the number of primes is not finite after all) or it is not. But if Q is not prime, then there is some prime number that divides into Q, but it can't be a number from the original

---

* The number one is not prime because, when making a factor tree of any whole number, the number one could be made to repeat any number of times you wish, unlike any other prime factor. Since every whole number decomposition must have a unique number of prime factors (think of the primes like the "atoms" that build whole numbers—their appearance or lack thereof is not merely arbitrary), the number one cannot be considered to be prime.

finite list of primes since the remainder when dividing Q by any of those primes would have to be 1.

So, either way, we have a contradiction: every prime cannot be on Euclid's original, "finite" list of primes. Thus, there must be infinitely many primes.

We can never list all the primes out, and no computer can print them all on-screen no matter how long we wait. But there are algorithms to determine if a number is prime, as well as to generate lots of primes quickly. One of the oldest of the latter algorithms is called the Sieve of Eratosthenes, and works iteratively. Starting from the smallest primes, multiples of every prime are declared composite, leaving the primes in their wake. Other algorithms test primes in sequential order.

PRIMES.BAS prompts you to either check if a single number is prime or simply see quick sequential primes. To see if a single number is prime, type it in: the computer will check rapidly if the number has any divisors besides one, report the results, and query for another number. If a negative number is entered, the programs throws you back to the main menu.

The sequential primes option displays primes in sequential order as quickly as possible on the screen. The loop can be stopped at any time by hitting the ESCAPE key.

● ● ●

When checking if a number is prime, notice that only divisors (excluding the number one) up to the square root of the given number need to be sequentially checked: see lines **40** and **140**. On those two lines, the **INT**, or convert-to-integer, function is used; if the quotient inside the **INT** is an integer, the number **P** is not prime, but composite.

● ● ●

PRIMES.BAS

```
5 KEY OFF:SCREEN 9:COLOR 15,1:CLS
6 GOTO 200
10 CLS
20 INPUT"IS IT A PRIME NUMBER? INPUT NUMBER TO SEE
   (or negative to stop):";P
23 IF P=1 THEN PRINT"NOT PRIME, BY
   DEFINITION":GOTO 20
24 IF P=0 THEN PRINT"NOT PRIME":GOTO 20
25 IF P<0 THEN 5
30 FOR L=2 TO INT(SQR(P))
40 IF (P/L)=INT(P/L) THEN PRINT P;" IS NOT PRIME!!
   (";L;"IS A DIVISOR.)":GOTO 20
50 NEXT L
60 PRINT P;" IS A PRIME NUMBER"
70 PRINT:GOTO 20
100 CLS:P=1
120 P=P+1
125 IF INKEY$=CHR$(27) THEN 200
130 FOR L=2 TO INT(SQR(P))
140 IF (P/L)=INT(P/L) THEN GOTO 120
150 NEXT L
160 PRINT P;
170 GOTO 120
200 CLS
205 PRINT"PRIME NUMBERS":PRINT
210 PRINT"HIGHLIGHT WHAT YOU'D LIKE TO DO:"
220 PRINT:PRINT"CHECK IF NUMBER IS PRIME"
230 PRINT"SEE A LIST OF PRIMES (PRESS ESC TO
    STOP)"
240 PRINT"EXIT"
250 LINE INPUT PROMPT$
260 IF PROMPT$="CHECK IF NUMBER IS PRIME" THEN 10
270 IF PROMPT$="SEE A LIST OF PRIMES (PRESS ESC TO
    STOP)" THEN 100
280 IF PROMPT$="EXIT" THEN CLS:END
290 GOTO 250
```

• • •

The list of primes is tested sequentially. That's ineffi-
cient—watch the loop for a while, and you'll notice how
the program progressively slows down with each higher

number to test. Perhaps modifying the program to use the Sieve of Eratosthenes, or some other algorithm (Mersenne primes, anyone?), would be more efficient.

Triangles
LOAD "PASCAL.BAS"

Ok

RUN_

French mathematician Blaise Pascal, though he lived four centuries ago, is known for a great many things. Philosophy, science, mathematics—little went untouched by the great thinker.

You probably remember his eponymous Triangle from grade school. Although he is credited with its discovery, Pascal's Triangle has turned up in writings centuries before (another example of a Western-appropriated idea); nonetheless, Pascal brought great mathematical rigor to the proceedings.

Pascal's Triangle is constructed by starting with 1s at its top and both outer diagonals downward, with the numbers inside the diagonals obtained by summing the left and right values immediately above. The resulting rows are the binomial coefficients (and the values of mathematical combinations).

The program presents you with two options: either view a significant portion of Pascal's Triangle constructed on the fly (by pressing *1*) or a single row (by pressing *2*).

• • •

For both options, two arrays are used: **P** and **TEMP**, which both have space for one thousand array elements. (Arrays are much more flexible than regular variables, which can only take one value, because arrays can house many indexed values.) Lines **75** and **275** calculate elements within the outer diagonals of Pascal's Triangle or an *n*th row of the Triangle, respectively, depending on the user's entry at the start of the program.

• • •

PASCAL.BAS

```
0 KEY OFF:SCREEN 9:COLOR 15,0:CLS
1 PRINT"PASCAL'S TRIANGLE"
5 INPUT"Type 1 to see many rows of Pascal's trian
  gle, or type 2 to see a specific row";PROMPT
6 IF PROMPT=1 THEN 10
7 IF PROMPT=2 THEN 215
8 GOTO 5
10 CLS
15 PRINT TAB(10);"Pascal's Triangle :"
20 X=2:G=0
30 DIM P(1000):DIM TEMP(1000)
40 TEMP(1)=1:TEMP(2)=1
45 FOR C=2 TO 12
50 X=X+1:F=F+1
60 FOR A=1 TO X
70 P(1)=1:P(X)=1
75 IF A<>X OR A<>1 THEN P(A)=TEMP(A-1)+TEMP(A)
80 NEXT A
90 R=((178/X-1)+4):LOCATE F,R
95 FOR G=1 TO X
100 PRINT P(G);
120 NEXT G
130 FOR Z=1 TO X
140 TEMP(Z)=P(Z)
150 NEXT Z
170 NEXT C
200 END
215 CLS
220 X=2:G=0
230 DIM P(1000):DIM TEMP(1000)
240 TEMP(1)=1:TEMP(2)=1
241 INPUT"Nth row of Pascal's Triangle--->";V
242 IF V>50 THEN GOTO 241
245 FOR C=2 TO V
250 X=X+1:F=F+1
260 FOR A=1 TO X
```

```
270 P(1)=1:P(X)=1
275 IF A<>X OR A<>1 THEN P(A)=TEMP(A-1)+TEMP(A)
280 NEXT A
330 FOR Z=1 TO X
340 TEMP(Z)=P(Z)
350 NEXT Z
370 NEXT C
380 FOR G=1 TO X:PRINT P(G);" ";:NEXT G
```

● ● ●

Pascal's Triangle goes on forever, bloating more and more at its bottom. Obviously, because the binomial coefficients grow so fast as the rows increase, only a handful of complete rows can be shown on the screen (and the user input for the nth row is limited as well). Perhaps this can be expanded, though certainly not indefinitely.

In addition, the handful of rows shown in the first portion of the program aren't perfectly centered. The fault lies in line **90** and the **LOCATE** statement, specifically with the variable **R**'s value from row to row. Some measure of tweaking is necessary for a symmetrical display.

Pi Approximation
LOAD "PIER.BAS"
Ok

RUN_

The ratio of a circle's circumference to its diameter is given by the Greek letter π, pronounced "pi." In decimal form,

$$\pi = 3.1415926535897932384\ldots$$

The decimal expansion of π goes on forever and does not repeat; the constant is thus an *irrational number*, or a number that cannot be written as a quotient of two integers. (More precisely, π is a transcendental number, meaning it is not algebraic.)

Before the advent of calculating machines, digits of π had to be arrived at the hard way: through laborious manual calculations by hand. Approximations of π can be found in the Old Testament of the Bible (the units were cubits, and the approximation was about three) and in texts in ancient Greek (twenty-two over seven).

Eventually, the theory of infinite series, developed about four centuries ago, made manual calculation of π easier. Gottfried Wilhelm Leibniz and Leonhard Euler are two notable mathematicians who arrived at infinite series approximations of π. For instance, one of Euler's formulas found that $\pi^2/6$ is equal to the sum of the inverses of the squares.

Another such approximation formula, which equals $\pi/2$, is utilized in the code below. Each press of the

ESCAPE key prints another iteration of the approximation.

● ● ●

PIER.BAS uses two arrays: P and Q. The numerators of
the approximations' product are successively stored in P;
likewise for the denominators in Q. Lines 90 and 100
store the products.

● ● ●

PIER.BAS
```
5 'Equation for finding (PI/2)=((2K/2K-1)*(2K/2K
  +1))........
7 'Max Number of times allowed in this program: 33
10 KEY OFF:SCREEN 9:COLOR 15,0:CLS
15 PRINT"APPROXIMATION FOR PI USING ROUGHLY THIRTY
   ITERATIONS...":PRINT
20 A1=0:A2=0:K=1:DIM P(100):DIM Q(100)
30 FOR Y=1 TO 33 STEP 2
40 P(Y)=(2*K):P(Y+1)=(2*K)
50 Q(Y)=((2*K)-1):Q(Y+1)=((2*K)+1)
60 K=K+1
70 NEXT Y
75 A1=P(1):A2=Q(1)
80 FOR F=2 TO 33
90 A1=A1*P(F)
100 A2=A2*Q(F)
105 PRINT A1;" / ";A2; "x 2 = ";(A1/A2)*2
107 PRINT"PRESS <ESC> FOR NEXT ITERATION..."
108 IF INKEY$<>CHR$(27) THEN 108
110 NEXT F
120 PRINT"THAT'S AS FAR AS WE CAN APPROXIMATE PI"
```

● ● ●

Look at line 120: it's a printed reminder that GW-BASIC
can only take you so far with a numerical result. Although
you could make additional programs which approximate

π using other methods, you will always run up against such limitations.

Cone Approximation
LOAD "CONE.BAS"

Archimedes, an ancient Greek mathematician, first found the area of a circle by inscribing regular polygons of increasing numbers of sides inside a circle—essentially, he arrived at the result by approximating with simpler shapes. This process is common in mathematics; for example, consider Simpson's rule and the trapezoidal rule, which approximate numerical integration.

Suppose we wish to approximate the volume of a cone, which has a circular base and converges to a single point at its top. Utilizing thinly sliced horizontally stacked cylinders—beginning with the base, and each one getting slightly smaller—would probably be the best approach. The volume of a cone, by the way, is given by

$$V = \pi r^2 \frac{h}{3}$$

and we'll use this formula to see how far off our approximations of cone volumes are in **CONE.BAS**.

When you run the program, you're first asked how thin you wish to slice each cone—the thinner you slice, the better the approximation. Then, after inputting the radius of the base of the cone, the results appear on-screen.

• • •

A **FOR/NEXT** loop named **X** handles the (perhaps) many iterations needed for the cone volume approximation. Smaller and smaller inputs for **H**, the cylinder height, unsurprisingly take more and more time for the computer to process.

• • •

CONE.BAS
```
10 KEY OFF
20 SCREEN 9:COLOR 15:CLS
25 R=0:H=0:S=0
29 COLOR 1:PRINT"CONE APPROXIMATION PROGRAM--BASED
   ON STACKED CYLINDERS":COLOR 15
30 INPUT"HEIGHT OF EACH CYLINDER USED TO
   APPROXIMATE CONE";H
40 INPUT"RADIUS OF BOTTOM CYLINDER (ALSO WILL
   EQUAL HEIGHT OF CONE)";R
50 FOR X=0 TO (R/H)
60 S=S+(R-(X*H))^2:PRINT "(";R;"-(";X;"*";H;"))^2
   = ";(R-(X*H))^2
70 NEXT X
80 PRINT "ACTUAL CONE WITH RADIUS OF ";R;"
   IS:";(R^3)*(1/3);"PI."
90 PRINT "APPROXIMATION OF SAME CONE
   IS:";S*H;"PI."
100 INPUT "RUN ANOTHER? (Y or N)";I$:PRINT:PRINT
110 IF I$="Y" OR I$="y" THEN 25
```

• • •

Since **CONE.BAS** is built on estimating the volume of a three-dimensional cone, actually *showing* the cone, along with the simpler cylinders used to approximate it, would be much more visually interesting. In addition, other sorts of more complex shapes—which don't have ready-made formulas like cones do—could have their volumes estimated by these approximation methods, which trace their origins to antiquity.

Spriolaterals
LOAD "SPIRAL.BAS"
Ok
RUN_

The British biochemist Frank Odds was the first to describe spirolaterals, way back in the early 1970s. Spirolaterals are geometric forms created by drawing a line, rotating a certain number of degrees, drawing another line, rotating that same number of degrees, drawing yet another line, rotating again, ad infinitum. Some spirolaterals close in on themselves—in other words, after n number of turns, the starting point of the shape is reached. Not all spirolaterals are of this "closed" variety, however.

When **SPIRAL.BAS** is run, you are asked *Which direction?*—effectively, the program is querying you about the length of each line segment of the spirolateral. Once a negative number is entered, the program determines if the spirolateral is closed, and reports the number of steps n to return to the starting point (here, the origin), or not closed, shown by a never ending loop of rotations of ninety degrees each.

• • •

An array called **SPIRAL** stores the form of the geometric figure; up to thirty line segments can be inputted. But once a negative number is entered, a **FOR/NEXT** loop called **LOP** begins, reporting the line length and coordinates of the shape. If the coordinates land back on the starting point—the origin, $(0,0)$—then the loop terminates, and the closed nature of the geometric figure is reported. Otherwise, the loop doesn't cease unless the user taps the ESCAPE key.

• • •

SPIRAL.BAS
```
10 KEY OFF:COLOR 15,1:CLS
15 TEMP=0:TEST=1
20 DIM SPIRAL(30)
25 PRINT"PUT IN A NEGATIVE NUMBER TO HALT."
30 WHILE (TEST<30)
35 INPUT"Which Direction";SPIRAL(TEST)
36 IF SPIRAL(TEST)<0 THEN TEMP=TEST-1:TEST=29
40 TEST=TEST+1
50 WEND
60 'Declare Coordinates: X and Y
70 X=0:Y=0:DIRECTION=1:T=0
80 FOR LOP=1 TO TEMP
90 IF DIRECTION=1 THEN Y=Y+SPIRAL(LOP)
100 IF DIRECTION=2 THEN X=X+SPIRAL(LOP)
110 IF DIRECTION=3 THEN Y=Y-SPIRAL(LOP)
120 IF DIRECTION=4 THEN X=X-SPIRAL(LOP)
130 DIRECTION=DIRECTION+1
140 IF DIRECTION>4 THEN DIRECTION=1
145 T=T+1
150 PRINT SPIRAL(LOP),,"X=";X;,,"Y=";Y
160 IF X=0 AND Y=0 THEN GOTO 200
170 NEXT LOP
175 IF INKEY$=CHR$(27) THEN END
180 GOTO 80
200 PRINT:PRINT"TRUE--IT IS A CLOSED
    SPIROLATERAL."
210 PRINT "IT TOOK ";T;" TIMES TO COME BACK TO
    (0,0), THE STARTING POINT."
```

• • •

Since spirolaterals are best visualized geometrically rather than merely with coordinate pairs, actually *showing the figures on-screen* is surely the biggest possible improvement to the program. It would not be too complicated; utilizing several well-placed **PSET** statement would do the trick.

In addition, the rotation angle for spirolaterals does not need to be ninety degrees; any degree measurement could be used, as long as each rotation is of a constant degree measure. That's a more complicated process than simply drawing the shapes on the screen, since it requires a pinch of trigonometry.

Bubble Sorting

There are a number of common algorithms for sorting items in a list. The shell sort, cubesort, heapsort, mergesort, binary tree sort, and bubble sort are only a handful of many.

The bubble sort, for instance, compares sets of two elements in a list which are adjacent. If the first element in the set is bigger than the second, the elements in the set are swapped; if not, nothing is done. Then, the algorithm moves on to the next set of two elements in the list, and the same comparison is made. When no more swaps are required between all sets of adjacent elements, the algorithm terminates because the list is completely sorted (in ascending order).

SORT.BAS implements a bubble sort with at most 100 elements. You are prompted to enter positive numbers, one at a time, from a list (in any order, obviously). Entering a negative number will signal the end of the list. Finally, your list in the order it was entered, alongside the list in ascending order, will be displayed on the screen.

• • •

Without using arrays, the program would be much more difficult to construct (and inelegant). Arrays allow the flexibility to compare the sets of adjacent elements—see lines 90, 95, and 96 for the conditional comparisons. Also ob-

serve the multiple FOR/NEXT loops: the loops keep running until the entire list is sorted completely.

• • •

SORT.BAS
```
10 KEY OFF:SCREEN 9:COLOR 15,1:CLS
20 DIM ARRAY(100):TEMP=0
25 PRINT"Maximum Number of Entries: 100."
30 FOR DUMMY=1 TO 100
40 PRINT"Input Value #(";DUMMY;") -->(-1 TO
   STOP)";: INPUT A
45 IF A=-1 THEN 65
50 ARRAY(DUMMY)=A
60 NEXT DUMMY
65 CLS:PRINT"Original List:  ":FOR LA=1 TO (DUMMY-
   1):PRINT ARRAY(LA);"  ";:NEXT LA
70 FOR D=1 TO (DUMMY-2)
80 FOR GA=1 TO (DUMMY-2)
90 IF ARRAY(GA)>ARRAY(GA+1) THEN 100
95 IF ARRAY(GA)<ARRAY(GA+1) THEN 200
96 IF ARRAY(GA)=ARRAY(GA+1) THEN 200
100 TEMP=ARRAY(GA):ARRAY(GA)=ARRAY(GA+1):
    ARRAY(GA+1)=TEMP
110 GOTO 200
200 NEXT GA
210 NEXT D
220 PRINT:PRINT
230 PRINT"Sorted List:  ":FOR LA=1 TO (DUMMY-
    1):PRINT ARRAY(LA);"  ";:NEXT LA
```

• • •

Because a negative number halts the entry of list elements,
no negative numbers are permitted as list elements. Perhaps, instead of a negative number signifying the end of
the list, a single number—positive or negative—might be
the assigned "stopping number." But then, of course, that
stopping number would not be permitted as a list element,
either.

An alternative approach might be the program prompting the number of list elements in advance of their entry. Although this would permit any number as a list element, the dynamic nature of the list entry is lost.

Is there an approach that permits dynamic entry along with no stopping number(s)?

Lottery Numbers
LOAD "LOTTERY.BAS"

Ok

RUN

The lottery has oftentimes been called a tax on people who are bad at math. Even worse, the lottery can be considered a regressive tax, because each ticket costs disproportionately more for a poor person than a rich person—and poor people play the lottery with a much greater frequency than rich people do.

Avid lottery players swear by so-called lottery systems; many of these systems pick this week's numbers by examining previous weeks' winning numbers, looking for patterns in masses of data. Sounds good—many patterns will surely be found. Human beings (and, by extension, computer algorithms that human beings have written) are pattern-seekers, frequently seeing signal where there is merely noise. This is properly termed *apophenia*.

Unless there is some deliberate non-random method to the selection of the lottery numbers, the patterns in winning numbers of the past are simply *un*-predictive, pure and simple, of a set of future numbers. Past is not prologue here: each trial (i.e., each draw of numbers) is independent of any other, despite your intuition perhaps believing otherwise. Lottery balls don't have brains, so how could they remember when they came up in the past? (To believe they do remember, by the way, is deemed the gambler's fallacy. Despite what others would have you believe, there is no such thing as a "law of averages," in which numbers that haven't come up recently pop up to correct some sort of "imbalance.")

With all that in mind, the program LOTTERY.BAS simply creates random sets of numbers depending on a few criteria: how many sets, how many numbers in each set, and the upper bound for the numbers. Of course, each set of numbers is drawn without replacement.

• • •

The complexity in the program lies almost entirely in the fact that each set must be drawn without replacement: there can be no repeat numbers in any given set. An array, along with a couple of FOR/NEXT loops, ensures that if there are any repeats, the set is discarded and redrawn (see lines 15 to 60).

• • •

LOTTERY.BAS
```
5 RANDOMIZE TIMER
6 SCREEN 9:COLOR 15,1:CLS:KEY OFF
7 PRINT "LOTTERY NUMBER GENERATOR":PRINT
8 INPUT"HOW MANY SETS TO GENERATE ON-
  SCREEN";SETS:IF SETS<1 THEN 8
9 INPUT"HOW MANY LOTTERY NUMBERS IN EACH
  SET";NUM:IF NUM<1 THEN 12
10 INPUT"EACH LOTTERY NUMBER IS FROM 1 TO
   WHAT";MAX:IF MAX<2 THEN 13
11 DIM I(NUM)
14 FOR X=1 TO SETS
15 FOR A=1 TO NUM
20 I(A)=INT(1+MAX*RND(1))
25 NEXT A
30 FOR U=1 TO NUM-1
40 FOR W=U+1 TO NUM
50 IF I(U)=I(W) THEN GOTO 15
60 NEXT W,U
65 PRINT"SET #";X;":";
70 FOR F=1 TO NUM:PRINT I(F);"  ";:NEXT F
80 PRINT
90 NEXT X
```

● ● ●

Suppose you wish to draw five sets of ten numbers, with balls numbering from one to ten each. No matter how fast your computer's processor, this may take a while. Since each set must include every number from one to ten, if that particular unique set is not chosen randomly, the loops kick the program back to redraw the set—and this may happen dozens of times. Perhaps a different algorithm is in order to ensure a much quicker, more effective sampling without replacement.

In addition, lotteries such as the Powerball have draws from two different sets of balls (such as five white balls along with a red Powerball); including this as an option in the program LOTTERY.BAS would increase its usefulness. Just so long as you don't have the program analyze past winning combinations for patterns.

The Flip Game
LOAD "FLIP.BAS"

A randomized board of zeros and ones appears in a rectangular matrix on the screen. Each "flip" of a row changes the zeros to ones, and the ones to zeros. Likewise for
each flip of a column. Your mission: in the fewest number
of flips, turn the entire matrix into all zeros—or all ones.

A completely text-based game, FLIP.BAS uses letters
on the keyboard as shortcuts to execute a row or column
flip.

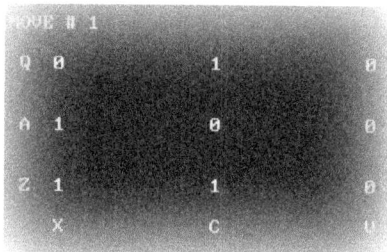

Also on the screen is a counter displaying the number of
flips performed so far. At any time the matrix can be reset
by pressing N, and you can exit the game by hitting the
ESCAPE key.

• • •

A RANDOMIZE TIMER statement makes sure that the
game board matrix is as randomized as possible at the

start, while the lines **12** to **20** set the initial random values
(of zero or one) for each cell in the matrix. After printing
the instructions and game board on the screen, **INKEY$**
(as usual) handles all the keyboard input without the need
for an **INPUT** statement. Finally, lines **800** to **810** take
care of the "flipping" as well as checking to see if you
won the game.

● ● ●

FLIP.BAS
```
10 KEY OFF:SCREEN 9:COLOR 15,0:COUNT=1
11 RANDOMIZE TIMER:'Randomize letters A-I
12 A=INT(RND(1)*2)
13 B=INT(RND(1)*2)
14 C=INT(RND(1)*2)
15 D=INT(RND(1)*2)
16 E=INT(RND(1)*2)
17 F=INT(RND(1)*2)
18 G=INT(RND(1)*2)
19 H=INT(RND(1)*2)
20 I=INT(RND(1)*2)
25 'Main Program
30 CLS
32 PRINT"--The Flip Game--"
33 PRINT:PRINT"Get all numbers to be zero or
   one!!"
34 PRINT"Type the letter next to the row or column
   to FLIP the zeros and ones"
35 PRINT"Press 'N' for a new game, or ESC to quit"
36 PRINT:PRINT:PRINT:PRINT:PRINT"You are on MOVE
   #";COUNT:PRINT
40 PRINT"          Q ";A;"          ";B;"
   ";C
45 PRINT:PRINT
50 PRINT"          A ";D;"          ";E;"
   ";F
55 PRINT:PRINT
60 PRINT"          Z ";G;"          ";H;"
   ";I
61 PRINT
```

```
65 PRINT"                X              C
   V"
70 I$=INKEY$
71 IF I$="N" THEN GOTO 10
72 IF I$=CHR$(27) THEN CLS:END
80 IF I$="Q" THEN GOTO 200
81 IF I$="A" THEN GOTO 210
82 IF I$="Z" THEN GOTO 220
83 IF I$="X" THEN GOTO 230
84 IF I$="C" THEN GOTO 240
85 IF I$="V" THEN GOTO 250
100 GOTO 70
200 A=A+1:B=B+1:C=C+1:COUNT=COUNT+1:GOTO 800
210 D=D+1:E=E+1:F=F+1:COUNT=COUNT+1:GOTO 800
220 G=G+1:H=H+1:I=I+1:COUNT=COUNT+1:GOTO 800
230 A=A+1:D=D+1:G=G+1:COUNT=COUNT+1:GOTO 800
240 B=B+1:E=E+1:H=H+1:COUNT=COUNT+1:GOTO 800
250 F=F+1:C=C+1:I=I+1:COUNT=COUNT+1:GOTO 800
800 IF A>1 THEN A=0
801 IF B>1 THEN B=0
802 IF C>1 THEN C=0
803 IF D>1 THEN D=0
804 IF E>1 THEN E=0
805 IF F>1 THEN F=0
806 IF G>1 THEN G=0
807 IF H>1 THEN H=0
808 IF I>1 THEN I=0
809 IF (A+B+C+D+E+F+G+H+I)=0 THEN GOTO 900
810 IF (A+B+C+D+E+F+G+H+I)=1 THEN GOTO 900
820 GOTO 25
900 'Win!!
901 CLS
902 PRINT:PRINT:PRINT:PRINT:PRINT
903 PRINT"You're a Winner!!!"
904 PRINT"And it only took you ";COUNT;" moves!"
905 END
```

• • •

Although the game is complete, it is not very visually interesting. Instead of restricting the game board to a text-based matrix, graphical flourishes could help enhance the experience.

Furthermore, the keyboard input is stilted; better instead to play the "Flip Game" with a joystick or a mouse, although you will have to venture into assembly language calls to do so. And to really ratchet up the pressure, why not insert a time limit or a flip-move limit (or both)?

Typing Practice
LOAD "TYPEPRAC.BAS"
Ok
RUN_

The "Flip Game" has no time limit; how about we con-struct a game with one?

Public schools used to have classes which taught stu-dents a single skill: typing. Yes, typing on a computer key-board—or, in the more distant past, a typewriter. Typing classes have fizzled out. So, instead, how about running a program to sharpen your typing skills?

Run **TYPEPRAC.BAS** and press the spacebar, and you have roughly five seconds to type the letters you see on-screen as quickly as you can. Needless to say, it's not easy—even for me, someone who was forced to take a public school typing class last century. A nice feature: as long as you don't exit out of **TYPEPRAC.BAS**, your high score is retained.

• • •

Instead of informally calling a portion of a program a "subroutine," as I've done in previous chapters, here we see a formal subroutine: look at lines **50** to **60**, which con-jure up a new random letter to quickly plaster on the screen using ASCII codes. The last line of the subroutine houses a **RETURN**—meaning *return* to the spot in the pro-gram whence the subroutine was called (which was, as you can see, in line **31**).

• • •

TYPEPRAC.BAS

```
5 HIGHSCORE=0
10 KEY OFF:SCREEN 7:COLOR 2,0:CLS:SCORE=0
11 RANDOMIZE TIMER
12 I$=CHR$(INT(1+25*RND(1))+65)
15 PRINT"TYPING PRACTICE!"
16 PRINT:PRINT"YOU HAVE 5 SECONDS, ONCE HITTING
   THE"
17 PRINT"ESCAPE KEY, TO TYPE THE LETTERS SHOWN"
18 PRINT"ON-SCREEN AS FAST AS YOU CAN...READY?
19 PRINT"TURN ON CAPS LOCK; HIT <SPACE> TO BEGIN!"
20 IF INKEY$<>" " THEN 20
21 CLS
22 FOR TIME=1 TO 4000
30 LOCATE 10,20:PRINT I$
31 IF INKEY$=I$ THEN GOSUB 50
40 NEXT TIME
45 GOTO 70
50 'SUBROUTINE: GET NEW RANDOM LETTER
55 I$=CHR$(INT(1+25*RND(1))+65)
56 SCORE=SCORE+1
60 RETURN
70 CLS
80 PRINT:PRINT "IN 5 SECONDS, YOU GOT ";SCORE;"
   RIGHT!":PRINT
82 IF SCORE>HIGHSCORE THEN HIGHSCORE=SCORE
90 PRINT"YOUR HIGHEST SCORE IS ";HIGHSCORE;"
   RIGHT."
95 PRINT:PRINT"PRESS <SPACE> FOR ANOTHER ROUND,"
96 PRINT"OR <ESCAPE> TO EXIT..."
100 Q$=INKEY$
110 IF Q$=" " THEN 10
120 IF Q$=CHR$(27) THEN CLS:END
130 GOTO 100
```

• • •

More options could be presented to the user to increase
(or decrease) the challenge, such as a restriction in the let-

ters shown (or perhaps only numbers) and adjustable time limits.

The Stroop Test

LOAD "STROOP.BAS"

Ok

RUN_

Reading is so automatic in adults that even if the word *RED* were shown in a different color (let's say green), a person's reading of the word *RED* would *interfere* with the recognition of the color of the word (green). This phenomenon is called the "Stroop effect," named after the psychologist John Stroop. Although he was not the first to notice this *theory of interference*, Stroop, back in 1935, was the first to conduct a formal experiment testing for it.

You don't need a team of psychologists to arrive at your doorstop to give you a Stroop test—GW-BASIC can implement one. Run **STROOP.BAS**, and you'll sit for two tests: in the first test, five words are printed on-screen whose colors match their color names; in the second test, another set of five words are shown, this time whose colors differ from their color names. Both tests are timed; you'll get your times (in seconds) after completing both. It is unlikely that you'll complete the second test in less time than the first one.

● ● ●

Lines **5** and **6** define a string array, which matches the colors' names to their numerical representations (for example, color **1** is assigned to blue). Next, lines **22** to **43** contain the code for the first test; note the subroutine calls, which check to see if you inputted the correct word color. Lines

122 to 142 contain the code for the second test. Finally, lines 275 and 280 display a rough approximation for the number of seconds each test took you to complete.

• • •

STROOP.BAS

```
4 'DEFINE COLORS INTO AN ARRAY (IGNORE COLOR 3)
5 DIM COL$(6)
6 COL$(1)="BLUE":COL$(2)="GREEN":COL$(6)="YELLOW":
  COL$(4)="RED":COL$(5)="PURPLE":COL$(3)="NOTHING"
10 KEY OFF:SCREEN 9:COLOR
   15,0:CLS:COUNT1=0:COUNT2=0
11 RANDOMIZE TIMER
15 PRINT"THE STROOP TEST"
16 PRINT:PRINT"THERE ARE TWO TESTS YOU WILL
   COMPLETE, AS FAST AS POSSIBLE."
17 PRINT"IN BOTH TESTS, YOU TYPE THE LETTER OF THE
   *COLOR* OF THE WORD, NOT WHAT"
18 PRINT"THE WORD ACTUALLY SAYS.
   Z=BLUE,X=GREEN,C=RED,V=PURPLE,B=YELLOW. THE
   CODES WILL"
19 PRINT"BE AT THE BOTTOM OF THE SCREEN. HIT
   <SPACE> TO BEGIN!"
20 IF INKEY$<>" " THEN 20
22 FOR LOOP=1 TO 5:CLS:COLOR 15:PRINT"TEST
   #1":LOCATE
   20,10:PRINT"Z=BLUE,X=GREEN,C=RED,V=PURPLE,B=YELL
   OW"
23 TEMPCOL=RWORD:RWORD=INT(1+6*RND(1)):IF RWORD=3
   THEN 23
24 IF RWORD=TEMPCOL THEN 23
30 COLOR RWORD:LOCATE 10,35:PRINT
   COL$(RWORD):CONTINUE=0
31 I$=INKEY$
32 COUNT1=COUNT1+1
35 IF I$="Z" THEN GUESS=1:GOSUB 45
36 IF I$="X" THEN GUESS=2:GOSUB 45
37 IF I$="C" THEN GUESS=4:GOSUB 45
38 IF I$="V" THEN GUESS=5:GOSUB 45
39 IF I$="B" THEN GUESS=6:GOSUB 45
40 IF CONTINUE=1 THEN 42 ELSE 31
42 NEXT LOOP
```

```
43 GOTO 120 'WHEN TEST #1 IS DONE, JUMPS TO TEST
   #2
45 'SUBROUTINE FOR TEST #1 TO SEE IF YOUR CHOICE =
   COLOR OF WORD
50 IF GUESS=RWORD THEN CONTINUE=1
60 RETURN
120 CLS:COLOR 15:PRINT:PRINT:PRINT:PRINT"PRESS THE
    <SPACE> TO BEGIN TEST #2"
121 IF INKEY$<>" " THEN 121
122 FOR LOOP=1 TO 5:CLS:COLOR 15:PRINT"TEST #2"
    :LOCATE 20,10:PRINT"Z=BLUE,X=GREEN,C=RED,
    V=PURPLE,B=YELLOW"
123 RWORD=INT(1+6*RND(1)):IF RWORD=3 THEN 123
124 RCOLOR=INT(1+6*RND(1)):IF RCOLOR=3 THEN 124
125 IF RCOLOR=RWORD THEN 124
130 COLOR RCOLOR:LOCATE 10,35:PRINT
    COL$(RWORD):CONTINUE=0
131 I$=INKEY$
132 COUNT2=COUNT2+1
135 IF I$="Z" THEN GUESS=1:GOSUB 145
136 IF I$="X" THEN GUESS=2:GOSUB 145
137 IF I$="C" THEN GUESS=4:GOSUB 145
138 IF I$="V" THEN GUESS=5:GOSUB 145
139 IF I$="B" THEN GUESS=6:GOSUB 145
140 IF CONTINUE=1 THEN 142 ELSE 131
142 NEXT LOOP
143 GOTO 270 'WHEN TEST #2 IS DONE, JUMPS TO
    RESULTS OF BOTH TESTS
145 'SUBROUTINE FOR TEST #2 TO SEE IF YOUR CHOICE
    = COLOR OF WORD
150 IF GUESS=RCOLOR THEN CONTINUE=1
160 RETURN
270 CLS:COLOR 15
275 PRINT"YOU TOOK APPROXIMATELY
    ";INT(COUNT1/800);" SECONDS TO COMPLETE TEST
    #1"
280 PRINT"YOU TOOK APPROXIMATELY ";INT(COUNT2/
    800);" SECONDS TO COMPLETE TEST #2"
295 PRINT:PRINT"PRESS <SPACE> TO TRY AGAIN,"
296 PRINT"OR <ESCAPE> TO EXIT..."
300 Q$=INKEY$
310 IF Q$=" " THEN 10
320 IF Q$=CHR$(27) THEN CLS:END
330 GOTO 300
```

• • •

The program needs more options. For starters, the user should be queried regarding how many words each test should display (right now, it's stuck on five words). The colors' input is also cumbersome, and thus wastes precious seconds; certainly there has to be a better way. Even the display of the words themselves isn't ideal—they are too small.

Factorial Numbers
LOAD "FACTY.BAS"

Ok

RUN

The mathematical expression 5! is not pronounced "FIVE!"—the exclamation point means *factorial*. 5! uncoils to five multiplied by four multiplied by three multiplied by two multiplied by one, which equals one hundred and twenty.

Factorials are useful with counting problems. For example, the number of ways to place five persons in a line is equal to 5!, since five possible people could be put first in the line, four people could be put second, and so on.

A computer program to evaluate factorials, such as 5!, is easy to create. But a little more complex, and more worthwhile? A program that works backwards, arriving at the *factorial number* (if such a number exists at all).

For example, at a prompt, enter the number 120, along with whole number lower and upper bounds to search through. At a flash, the computer arrives at the result: 5! Run the program again, this time inputting 130 (along with the bounds)—but there is no such factorial number.

• • •

Once the upper and lower bounds are entered in (see lines 60 and 70), the algorithm has the limits of its search: an outer FOR/NEXT loop cycles through the bounds, while an inner FOR/NEXT loop computes the factorials, methodically checking to see if there's a match.

• • •

```
FACTY.BAS
10 KEY OFF:SCREEN 9:COLOR 15,0:CLS
20 PRINT"Factorial Finder -- will find what number
   is result of a factorial."
30 PRINT"But most numbers are not a 'factorial
   number':"
40 PRINT"In form x! = your number."
50 PRINT:INPUT "Your number=";X:NUM=1
60 INPUT"Bounds:lower:";LO
70 INPUT"Bounds:high:";HI
80 IF X=1 THEN PRINT"= 1! or 0!":END
90 IF X=2 THEN PRINT"= 2!":END
100 FOR SEAR=LO TO HI STEP 1
110 FOR LOOK=SEAR TO 1 STEP -1
120 NUM=NUM*LOOK
130 NEXT LOOK
140 IF NUM=X THEN PRINT"= ";SEAR;"!":END
150 NUM=1:NEXT SEAR
160 PRINT"No factorial number!"
```

• • •

The biggest problem with the program has much more to do with the GW-BASIC interpreter than with the code itself: there's a limit to how large of a number you're permitted to input. Moreover, the higher the upper bound, the longer the algorithm will take to perform the search.

Permutations and Combinations
LOAD "PERCOMB.BAS"
Ok

RUN_

When arranging people (or objects) in a line, the order of the arrangements matter. This is referred to as a *permutation*. Consider a lineup of five people at the police station: how many ways can such a lineup be permuted? Well, any of the five alleged criminals can be put in the leftmost slot; then, there are four left for the slot next to him; then, three people; then, two; and, finally, one person remains for the final placement. That gives us 5!, or one hundred and twenty, ways to line up five malcontents at the station.

Contrariwise, the order of arrangements oftentimes doesn't matter. This is called a *combination*. Suppose, at work, you need a committee of five people out of the twenty-five people in your department. Here, it doesn't matter the order in which you choose the five people; it only matters that a unique subset of five folks is selected. We'll still use factorials to compute the answer, but the calculation is a bit different:

$$\binom{25}{5} = \frac{25!}{(25-5)!5!} = 53,130$$

So there are 53,130 unique subsets of five people from a set of twenty-five.

As a point of contrast, pretend instead that the order of the selection of five people (out of twenty-five) *did* in fact matter. We would find that there are

$$\frac{25!}{(25-5)!} = 6,375,600$$

ways to permute this arrangement—many more ways than a combination of five people taken from twenty-five.

PERCOMB.BAS can quickly calculate both permutations and combinations, only after asking the user some simple questions.

• • •

FOR/NEXT loops rule the day here; they're necessary for the intermediate factorial calculations. The variable TEMP is utilized repeatedly as a placeholder.

• • •

PERCOMB.BAS

```
5 TEMP=1    'Sets value of TEMP to one
10 KEY OFF:SCREEN 9:COLOR 15,1:CLS
20 PRINT"PERMUTATIONS VS COMBINATIONS"
30 PRINT:INPUT"Permutation (type 1) or Combination
   (type 2) or Exit (type 3)";T$
40 IF T$="1" THEN GOTO 70
50 IF T$="2" THEN GOTO 270
55 IF T$="3" THEN CLS:END
60 GOTO 30
70 PRINT:PRINT"Permutations: Order of arrangement
   matters."
80 INPUT"How many total items/people are
   there";TOTAL
85 TOTAL=INT(TOTAL)    'Make sure the TOTAL varia
   ble is an integer
90 INPUT "How many, of the total, do you wish to
   arrange in a line";SUBSET
95 SUBSET=INT(SUBSET)    'Make sure the SUBSET var
   iable is an integer
100 FOR LOOP1=1 TO TOTAL
110 TEMP=TEMP*LOOP1 'Calculates Factorial: LOOP!
120 NEXT LOOP1
```

```
130 NUMER=TEMP    'Sets the numerator to the fact
    orial LOOP!
135 TEMP=1   'Resets value of TEMP to one
140 FOR LOOP2=1 TO (TOTAL-SUBSET)
150 TEMP=TEMP*LOOP2  'Calculates Factorial:
    SUBSET!
160 NEXT LOOP2
170 DENOM=TEMP    'Sets the denominator to the
    factorial SUBSET!
175 TEMP=1   'Resets value of TEMP to one
180 PRINT:PRINT"The number of ways to arrange thes
    e items is: ";NUMER/DENOM
190 GOTO 30
270 PRINT:PRINT"Combinations: Order of arrangement
    doesn't matter."
280 INPUT"How many total items/people are there"
    ;TOTAL
285 TOTAL=INT(TOTAL)    'Make sure the TOTAL vari
    able is an integer
290 INPUT "What is the subset of the total you
    wish to find";SUBSET
295 SUBSET=INT(SUBSET)   'Make sure the SUBSET
    variable is an integer
300 FOR LOOP1=1 TO TOTAL
310 TEMP=TEMP*LOOP1  'Calculates Factorial: LOOP!
320 NEXT LOOP1
330 NUMER=TEMP    'Sets the numerator to the fac
    torial LOOP!
335 TEMP=1   'Resets value of TEMP to one
340 FOR LOOP2=1 TO SUBSET
350 TEMP=TEMP*LOOP2  'Calculates Factorial:
    SUBSET!
360 NEXT LOOP2
370 DENOM1=TEMP    'Sets the first part of denomi
    nator to the factorial SUBSET!
375 TEMP=1   'Resets value of TEMP to one
380 FOR LOOP3=1 TO (TOTAL-SUBSET)
390 TEMP=TEMP*LOOP3  'Calculates Factorial:
    (TOTAL-SUBSET)!
400 NEXT LOOP3
410 DENOM2=TEMP    'Sets the first part of denomi
    nator to the factorial SUBSET!
415 TEMP=1   'Resets value of TEMP to one
```

```
430 PRINT:PRINT"The number of ways to arrange the
    se items is: ";NUMER/(DENOM1*DENOM2)
440 GOTO 30
```

• • •

Despite the program working about as quickly as it possibly could, the code itself could be written more efficiently, more cleanly. Perhaps the factorial algorithm, instead of being repeatedly coded, could instead be inputted once as a subroutine and called multiple times. Other similar improvements are surely possible.

Measures of Dispersion
LOAD "SPREAD.BAS"
Ok

RUN_

If you're familiar with the mathematical discipline of statistics, then you know that when examining a data set, you'll want to measure certain things—such as its mean and median (the measures of central tendency, or measures of the center of the data), as well as its variance and standard deviation (the measures of dispersion, or measures of the spread of the data). Let's focus on the latter: quantifying how a data set's spread out.

To obtain a measurement of dispersion, it might seem most intuitive to procure the mean absolute deviation, or MAD: the mean of all of the data points' *distances* to the mean. Thus, MAD is calculated as

$$MAD = \frac{\sum |x_i - \bar{x}|}{n}$$

The absolute bars are present since distance can never be negative; thus, the smallest MAD can ever be is zero—only if every observation in the data set is identical.

Although intuitive, MAD is not a commonly used measure in statistics because taking an absolute value is not an algebraic operation—unlike, for instance, addition, taking roots, and raising to powers—and that leads to problems with more advanced statistical methods.

Instead of MAD, standard deviation is used (along with variance, which is standard deviation squared). The formula for standard deviation is similar to MAD, albeit without the absolute values.

$$s = \sqrt{\frac{\sum \left(x_i - \bar{x}\right)^2}{n-1}}$$

Roughly speaking, the standard deviation gives you the average distance of all the data points to the mean. So the standard deviation and the MAD will be commensurate, but usually not the same; hence the "Roughly speaking...."

The denominator of the standard deviation calculation is n–1, referred to in statistics as "n–1 degrees of freedom," because there are really n–1 (and not n) pieces of independent data since the deviations from the mean always sum to zero.

When you run **SPREAD.BAS**, you'll be asked how many pieces of data you wish to enter—the limit is twenty. Then you'll be presented not only with the values of the MAD, variance, and standard deviation of the entered data set, but the steps the program used to arrive at the calculations.

• • •

A number of arrays are defined in the first line of the program; each one has space for, at most, twenty entries. **SPREAD.BAS** leans on three loops: **LOOP1** to enter the data set, **LOOP2** to find the mean, and **LOOP3** to calculate MAD, variance, and standard deviation.

• • •

SPREAD.BAS
```
5 DIM NUMBERS(20):DIM DEVFM(20):DIM ABSDEV(20):DIM
  SQDEV(20)
10 KEY OFF:SCREEN 9:CLS
```

```
20 PRINT"CALCULATE THE MAD (MEAN ABSOLUTE
   DEVIATION), VARIANCE, AND STANDARD
   DEVIATION":PRINT
25 SUMNUM=0:SUMDEV=0:SUMABS=0:SUMSQ=0
40 INPUT"HOW MANY DATA POINTS (MAXIMUM IS
   20)";COUNT
45 IF (COUNT<1 OR COUNT>20) THEN GOTO 40
50 FOR LOOP1=1 TO COUNT
60 PRINT"ENTER IN POINT #";LOOP1;
70 INPUT NUMBERS(LOOP1)
80 NEXT LOOP1
90 FOR LOOP2=1 TO COUNT
100 SUMNUM=SUMNUM+NUMBERS(LOOP2)
110 NEXT LOOP2
120 MEAN=SUMNUM/COUNT
130 PRINT"THE MEAN IS:";MEAN
140 FOR LOOP3=1 TO COUNT
150 DEVFM(LOOP3)=NUMBERS(LOOP3)-MEAN
160 IF DEVFM(LOOP3)<0 THEN ABSDEV(LOOP3)=-1*
    DEVFM(LOOP3) ELSE ABSDEV(LOOP3)=DEVFM(LOOP3)
170 SQDEV(LOOP3)=(ABSDEV(LOOP3))^2
180 PRINT"#";LOOP3;":";NUMBERS(LOOP3);", DevFrom
    Mean=";DEVFM(LOOP3);", AbsDev=";
    ABSDEV(LOOP3);", SqDev=";SQDEV(LOOP3)
190 SUMDEV=SUMDEV+DEVFM(LOOP3)
200 SUMABS=SUMABS+ABSDEV(LOOP3)
210 SUMSQ=SUMSQ+SQDEV(LOOP3)
220 NEXT LOOP3
230 PRINT:PRINT"Sum of: DevFromMean=";SUMDEV;",
    AbsDev=";SUMABS;", SqDev=";SUMSQ
240 PRINT:PRINT "The MAD is:";SUMABS/COUNT
250 PRINT "The variance is:";(SUMSQ/(COUNT-1))
260 PRINT "The standard deviation
    is:";SQR(SUMSQ/(COUNT-1))
270 PRINT:INPUT"Another? Type 'YES' or 'NO'";I$
280 IF I$="YES" THEN GOTO 10
290 END
```

● ● ●

For what it does—and its scope is very narrow—it's tough to improve **SPREAD.BAS**, beyond permitting the entry of larger data sets. Perhaps **SPREAD.BAS** could form the basis of a statistical software program, which might permit more advanced calculations (and manipulations) of data sets, such as finding z-scores and *student* t-scores and p-values, as well as displaying dotplots or box-and-whisker and stem-and-leaf plots (two of statistician John Tukey's many contributions to the exciting, and still-burgeoning, field of statistics).

Flash Cards

LOAD "FLASH.BAS"

Ok

RUN

Using flashcards is one of the more effective ways to remember words and their definitions, among other things that can be mapped one-to-one, flashcard front-to-back. Unsurprisingly, GW-BASIC can simulate working with flashcards, albeit electronically on a glowing monitor.

Before running **FLASH.BAS**, you'll need to enter both the front and back of each "flashcard" straight into the **DATA** lines of the program. Furthermore, you will have to keep a count of how many unique flashcards you've entered into the code.

Once that's all set, **FLASH.BAS** deals a quick and random and endless procession of flashcards to help you memorize whatever you wish.

As **FLASH.BAS** is written below, though, German words and their English definitions serve as the example flashcards. There are thirty-eight unique flashcards, so **38** must be entered in at the opening prompt. And then, finally, you won't have to wonder any longer what the German term is for a Bavarian pretzel.

• • •

The **DATA** lines—of which you could add many more—do not need to be at the beginning of the program; you can insert them anywhere you wish. But any program with **DATA** must always have a **READ** statement: see line **80**,

which reads the English definition into the string variable
A$, and line 110, which reads the corresponding German
word into the string variable B$ (which always must be the
subsequent DATA element). And a conditional statement in
line 71 ensures that you're quizzed on a random *word*, rather than on a random definition.

● ● ●

FLASH.BAS

```
10 CLEAR:KEY OFF:SCREEN 9:COLOR 15,0:RANDOMIZE
   TIMER
20 DATA TO BE NON-NOTICABLE,AUFFALLEN,
   BALANCED,AUSGEWOGEN
21 DATA STATEMENT,DIE AUSSAGE,TO
   IMPRESS,BEEINDRUCKEN
22 DATA BAVARIAN PRETZEL,DIE BREZEL,TO
   CHARACTERIZE,CHARAKTERISIEREN
23 DATA CONTAINER,DER CONTAINER,GERMAN-
   SPEAKING,DEUTSCHSPRACHIG
24 DATA FAT,DICK,DIRNDL DRESS,DAS DIRNDLKLEID
25 DATA OUTSIDE,DRAUSSEN,INSIDE,DRINNEN
26 DATA THIRSTY,DURSTIG,AMBITIOUS,EHRGEIZIG
27 DATA TO RECOMMEND,EMPFEHLEN,TO
   EXPERIENCE,ERLEBEN
28 DATA TO FALL,FALLEN,PATIENT,GEDULDIG
29 DATA TO ENJOY,GENIESSEN,FACE,DAS GESICHT
30 DATA DIVIDED,GETEILT,POLITE,HOFLICH
31 DATA FOOD,DIE KOST,LEATHER SHORTS,DIE
   LEDERHOSEN
32 DATA EMPTY,LEER,WALL,DIE MAUER
33 DATA PAPER,DAS PAPIER,WALK,DER SPAZIERWEG
34 DATA STUBBORN,STUR,TO TRANSLATE,UBERSETZEN
35 DATA AWARE OF ENVIRONMENTAL
   PROBLEMS,UMWELTBEWUSST,TO SUSPECT,VERMUTEN
36 DATA SPOILED,VERWOHNT,CAUTIOUS,VORSICHTIG
37 DATA HIKING TRAIL,DER WANDERWEG,TO THROW,WERFEN
38 DATA THE WEST,DER WESTEN,TO BRING
   BACK,ZURUCKBRINGEN
39 DATA
40 DATA
65 PRINT"FLASHCARDS!"
```

```
66 PRINT
67 PRINT"YOU SHOULD HAVE ENTERED BOTH SIDES OF
   EACH FLASHCARD IN THE DATA LINES OF CODE."
68 INPUT"HOW MANY *TOTAL* FLASHCARDS DID YOU ENTER
   (count front and back as one card)";CARDS
69 CARDS=CARDS*2
70 N=INT(1+CARDS*RND(1))
71 IF INT(N/2)=N/2 THEN N=N-1
72 FOR X=1 TO N
80 READ A$
90 NEXT X
110 READ B$
120 PRINT"What does this word mean:";B$
130 RESTORE
140 INPUT R$
150 IF R$=A$ THEN 190
160 PRINT"Wrong"
170 PRINT"The correct answer is:";A$
175 INPUT "Press <Enter> to see another flash-
    card";HA$:PRINT
180 GOTO 70
190 PRINT"Correct"
195 INPUT "Press <Enter> to see another flash-
    card";HA$:PRINT
200 GOTO 70
```

• • •

Although it would certainly be more user-friendly to enter in both sides of the flashcards during the program's run rather than typing them straight into the code, such entry would seriously bog down **FLASH.BAS**—much easier to enter in the data once, and save the program code instead. Also, because of the randomization of the flashcards, you may end up seeing the same cards repeatedly, while almost never seeing certain others; such is the nature of randomization. But with a little algorithmic maneuvering, that could be changed (see **LOTTERY.BAS**, for instance). In fact, when Apple first introduced the shuffle feature (which plays songs in a random order) on their iPods, users suspected that there was some sort of secret pattern to the playlist—the songs didn't *seem* to be popping up randomly. Apple rigged a new "randomization" algorithm that would give the appearance of randomness—for example, by not playing the same song twice in a row—to quell the anxieties of the conspiracy theorists.

Interactive Fiction
LOAD "FICTION.BAS"

Ok

RUN_

If you've ever read a *Choose Your Own Adventure* book, then you know what interactive fiction is: rather than reading a book straight through from the first page to the last, the reader is permitted to make decisions, affecting characters and plot points.

It wasn't long before interactive fiction migrated to electronic form as text-based stories (or "text adventures") on computer terminals. The first such text-based computer game, called *Adventure*, arrived on the scene in 1975. Perhaps the best of *Adventure*'s descendants was *Pyramid 2000*, based on the earlier *Colossal Cave*. *Pyramid* is scavenger hunt with an Egyptian mythology backdrop and lots left to the imagination.

GW-BASIC offers a great venue to create your own interactive fiction game. After loading up *Desert Sands*, the skeleton game in code form below, you are presented with several options. Navigate your way through its claustrophobic world with the correct choices to avoid peril—or certain death.

• • •

Notice that menu options must be presented one line per option, since selection relies on the **LINE INPUT** function. Also notice that (*) will exit the program—to the BASIC interpreter or to (and here's some ancient mythology) DOS.

• • •

FICTION.BAS

```
10 KEY OFF:SCREEN 9:COLOR 15,1:CLS
15 CLS
20 PRINT"(*)":PRINT"<INTERACTIVE FICTION GAME>"
30 PRINT
40 PRINT"*****************************************
****************************************":PRINT
   "         Files are: ":PRINT"Title":PRINT
   "Help":PRINT"Exit":PRINT
50 PRINT"
   WORDS:"
60 PRINT"
   ******"
70 PRINT" You are stranded in the Sahara Desert
   with no food or water. You see a cave with a
   river flowing from it!!"
80 PRINT "You could go there or wait for help, it
   is your choice."
90 PRINT"1.GO TO THE CAVE"
100 PRINT"2.WAIT FOR HELP"
110 LINE INPUT T$
120 IF T$="Exit" THEN GOTO 190
125 IF T$="Title" THEN GOTO 500
126 IF T$="(*)" THEN GOTO 190
130 IF T$="Help" THEN GOTO 150
132 IF T$="1.GO TO THE CAVE" THEN GOTO 200
134 IF T$="2.WAIT FOR HELP" THEN GOTO 270
135 IF T$="MJL" THEN GOTO 261
140 BEEP:GOTO 110
150 CLS:PRINT:PRINT:PRINT" Point the cursor to the
    choice and press <ENTER>.":PRINT:PRINT"*OK*"
160 LINE INPUT J$
170 IF J$="*OK*" THEN GOTO 15
180 BEEP:GOTO 160
190 CLS:PRINT:PRINT:PRINT"   EXIT TO DOS OR TO
    BASIC?":PRINT"DOS":PRINT"BASIC"
192 LINE INPUT D$
193 IF D$="DOS" THEN SYSTEM
195 IF D$="BASIC" THEN END
197 BEEP:GOTO 192
```

```
200 CLS:PRINT"        Files are:":PRINT"End game,
    YOU LOST!"
210 PRINT:PRINT"
    WORDS:"
220 PRINT"
    ******"
230 PRINT" You try to make it to the cave but see
    it is too far to go to. You drop and as you
    look at the cave with the running water in
    your last few seconds, you realize it was only
    a mirage!!!":PRINT"     -the end!!-"
240 LINE INPUT A$
250 IF A$="End game, YOU LOST!" THEN GOTO 190
260 BEEP:GOTO 240
261 CLS:PRINT:PRINT:PRINT" The name of the Au-
    thor.":PRINT"*OK*"
262 LINE INPUT R$
263 IF R$="*OK*" THEN GOTO 15
264 BEEP:GOTO 262
270 CLS:PRINT"        Files are:":PRINT"Exit":PRINT
280 PRINT"                        WORDS:"
290 PRINT"                        ******"
300 PRINT" You stay where you are and you see an
    woman in the distance.":PRINT"1.RUN
    AWAY":PRINT"2.TALK TO HER"
310 LINE INPUT F$
320 IF F$="Exit" THEN GOTO 190
330 IF F$="1.RUN AWAY" THEN GOTO 350
335 IF F$="2.TALK TO HER" THEN GOTO 420
340 BEEP:GOTO 310
350 CLS:PRINT"        Files are:":PRINT"You lost,
    end game":PRINT
360 PRINT"                        WORDS:"
370 PRINT"                        ******"
380 PRINT" You run away and that is the last per-
    son you ever see again."
390 LINE INPUT U$
400 IF U$="You lost, end game" THEN GOTO 190
410 BEEP:GOTO 390
420 CLS:PRINT"            Files are:":PRINT"End
    game, you WIN!!":PRINT"Restart":PRINT
430 PRINT"                        WORDS:"
440 PRINT"                        ******"
```

```
450 PRINT" She takes you to her village and gives
    you food. You won!!"
460 LINE INPUT L$
470 IF L$="Restart" THEN GOTO 15
480 IF L$="End game, you WIN!!" THEN GOTO 190
490 BEEP:GOTO 460
500 CLS:PRINT:PRINT:PRINT:PRINT:PRINT"
    D E S E R T   S A N D S":PRINT:PRINT"*OK*"
510 LINE INPUT S$
520 IF S$="*OK*" THEN GOTO 15
530 BEEP:GOTO 510
```

• • •

This bare-bones program is ripe for expansion. Build up the story, present more choices, add items that you can collect (or lose)—the possibilities are endless if you're into storytelling.

Word Processing
LOAD "WPB.BAS"

Microsoft Word mostly has a stranglehold on word pro-cessing today, but GW-BASIC still has a couple of I/O (input/output) tricks up its sleeve.

Run **WPB.BAS**, highlight and click the "*OK*" text, and you're presented with a menu of four options: "New File," "Load File," "Options," and "Exit."

Click on "New File," and you're queried for a file name; make sure to append a *.txt* extension. **WPB.BAS** permits twenty paragraphs, each set by a carriage return. Pressing F1 at a new line ends your document and saves your file.

To open a file, select "Load File" and type in the file name. When the file loads, any paragraphs you wish to save as-is you'll need to press ENTER overtop of—at the end of the last lines of the respective paragraphs.

Finally, if you're annoyed at word processing with a black and white display, selecting "Options" in the main menu permits a little text-and-background flexibility.

● ● ●

Line **20** assigns the F1 key to "-1" along with a carriage return (the ASCII code for ENTER is 13).

The I/O statement **OPEN** sets up a new file in line **80**, and opens and reads a preexisting file in line **230**. Observe the distinction: when creating a file, the **"O"** parameter is utilized (for output), whereas when pulling up an already

made file, the **"I"** parameter is used (for input). Every
OPEN must be paired with a **CLOSE**.

For newly created files: Lines **84** to **100** store all of the
user's text into an array, paragraph by paragraph; each paragraph is **PRINT#**ed straight to the *.txt* file. Pressing F1
terminates the entries and sends the user back to the main
menu.

For preexisting files: Lines **220** to **300** open the old file
and store its contents into array, one paragraph at a time,
until either twenty paragraphs have been exceeded or the
file ends (which is caught by the **EOF** function). Afterwards, lines **300** to **340** print the file's contents on-screen
and throw the program back to the text editor (lines **84** to
100).

● ● ●

WPB.BAS

```
10 KEY OFF:CLS:SCREEN 9:SCREEN 0:COLOR
   15:CLS:PRINT:PRINT:PRINT:PRINT "WORD PROCESSOR
   FOR BASIC ----> {WPB}"
20 KEY 1,"-1"+CHR$(13)
30 PRINT:PRINT"*OK*"
40 LINE INPUT K$
50 IF K$="*OK*" THEN GOTO 61
60 BEEP:GOTO 40
61 CLS:PRINT:PRINT"{WPB} MAIN MENU"
62 PRINT"-----------------":PRINT:PRINT"NEW
   FILE":PRINT:PRINT"LOAD FILE"
63 PRINT:PRINT"OPTIONS":PRINT:PRINT"EXIT"
64 LINE INPUT X$
65 IF X$="NEW FILE" THEN GOTO 70
66 IF X$="LOAD FILE" THEN GOTO 200
67 IF X$="OPTIONS" THEN GOTO 500
68 IF X$="EXIT" THEN CLS:END
69 GOTO 64
70 CLS
71 LOCATE 25,1:PRINT"----> {WPB}":LOCATE 1,1
75 INPUT"What would would like to call your text
   file (place a .txt extension)";NAM$
```

```
80 OPEN "O",#1,NAM$
81 PRINT"You can write at most 20 paragraphs.
   Press <ENTER> to end a paragraph.":PRINT"Hit F1
   to close and save your text file."
82 PRINT"Simply start typing to begin your docu-
   ment.":PRINT
84 DIM PAR$(20):N=1
85 WHILE N<21
86 LINE INPUT PAR$(N)
87 IF PAR$(N)="-1" THEN GOTO 100
90 PRINT #1, PAR$(N)
95 N=N+1
98 WEND
100 CLOSE #1
105 PRINT"YOUR FILE HAS BEEN SAVED AS ";NAM$
106 CLEAR
107 INPUT"PRESS F1 TO EXIT BACK TO THE MAIN
    MENU";T$
110 IF T$="-1" THEN GOTO 61 ELSE GOTO 107
200 CLS
210 LOCATE 25,1:PRINT"----> {WPB}":LOCATE 1,1
215 FILES
220 INPUT"What file would you like to open (make
    sure to place the .txt extension)";FL$
230 OPEN "I",#1,FL$
240 DIM PAR2$(20):N=1
250 FOR LOOP=1 TO 20
260 INPUT #1,PAR2$(LOOP)
270 IF EOF(1) THEN GOTO 300
275 N=N+1
280 NEXT LOOP
300 CLOSE #1
305 CLS
307 PRINT"You can write at most 20 paragraphs.
    Press <ENTER> to end a paragraph.":PRINT"Hit
    F1 to close and save your text file."
308 PRINT"NOTE: You will need to hit <ENTER> over-
    top of paragraphs you wish to keep.":PRINT"But
    when hitting <ENTER>, make sure you are at the
    END of the line."
309 LOCATE 25,1:PRINT"----> {WPB} ...";FL$:LOCATE
    5,1
310 FOR LOOP2=1 TO N
315 PRINT PAR2$(LOOP2)
```

```
320 NEXT LOOP2
330 OPEN "O",#1,FL$
335 NAM$=FL$
340 GOTO 84
500 CLS:PRINT:INPUT"TEXT COLOR(1-15) 15 DEFAULT";T
510 IF T=0 THEN T=15
540 PRINT:INPUT"BACKGROUND COLOR(0-15) 0
    DEFAULT";B
550 IF B=0 THEN B=0
580 COLOR T,B:CLS:GOTO 61
```

• • •

The word processor is cumbersome to use, and it doesn't always load files as you would expect. For example, insert a comma into a sentence, save the file, and reopen the text—instead of a comma, you'll find that the comma signaled to GW-BASIC to split the paragraph into two. Fixing these sorts of bugs, as well as handling I/O more efficiently, are doubtless the keys to making a more functional, useful word processing program.

Two Big Numbers
LOAD "ADD.BAS"

Whole numbers can only be of a limited size in GW-BASIC; at a certain point, they become approximated with scientific notation, denoted with an E rather than a ten. With integers, that "certain point" is beyond 32,767, or one subtracted from two to the fifteenth power. So mathematical operations, like addition, become mere approximations when the numbers blow up.

If we just restrict our attention to adding two really large numbers—say, at most seventy-five digits each—perhaps we can get around some of these limitations.

When entering your two numbers to be added, make sure that they have the same number of digits (you'll have to place zeros in front of the smaller numbers, kind of like the *General Lee*'s number in the *Dukes of Hazzard*). Press the ESCAPE key several times to see your sum appear.

● ● ●

As is perhaps becoming a theme, arrays are the linchpin. The two big numbers are entered as a series of single digits into **ARRAY1** and **ARRAY2**, respectively. If seventy-five digits are exceeded, the big number entry is terminated. Lines **210** and onward handle calculating the sum, digit by digit (taking into account carrying, on line **381**), as well as the output of the final result on the screen (lines **382** and **386**).

● ● ●

ADD.BAS

```
10 KEY OFF:SCREEN 9:COLOR 15,0:CLS
20 DIM ARRAY1(100):DIM ARRAY2(100):DIM
   ANSWER(150):DIM DIGITS1(2):T=1
30 PRINT"Adding Machine:   Numbers: Max length of
   75 digits."
35 PRINT"Put zeros in front of numbers not used,
   make sure both are same length."
36 PRINT"Press 'ESC' to end current number entry,
   there are two numbers to enter."
37 PRINT"Do not enter any decimal points. Do addi
   tion of decimals as separate problems."
38 LOCATE 10,3
40 WHILE I$<>CHR$(27)
50 I$=INKEY$
55 IF T>75 THEN PRINT CHR$(27);:GOTO 120
60 IF I$="1" THEN ARRAY1(T)=1:T=T+1
65 IF I$="2" THEN ARRAY1(T)=2:T=T+1
70 IF I$="3" THEN ARRAY1(T)=3:T=T+1
75 IF I$="4" THEN ARRAY1(T)=4:T=T+1
80 IF I$="5" THEN ARRAY1(T)=5:T=T+1
85 IF I$="6" THEN ARRAY1(T)=6:T=T+1
90 IF I$="7" THEN ARRAY1(T)=7:T=T+1
95 IF I$="8" THEN ARRAY1(T)=8:T=T+1
100 IF I$="9" THEN ARRAY1(T)=9:T=T+1
105 IF I$="0" THEN ARRAY1(T)=0:T=T+1
110 PRINT I$;
115 WEND
120 T=1:I$=""
125 LOCATE 11,1:PRINT"+":LOCATE 11,3
130 WHILE I$<>CHR$(27)
135 I$=INKEY$
136 IF T>75 THEN PRINT CHR$(27);:GOTO 200
140 IF I$="1" THEN ARRAY2(T)=1:T=T+1
145 IF I$="2" THEN ARRAY2(T)=2:T=T+1
150 IF I$="3" THEN ARRAY2(T)=3:T=T+1
155 IF I$="4" THEN ARRAY2(T)=4:T=T+1
160 IF I$="5" THEN ARRAY2(T)=5:T=T+1
165 IF I$="6" THEN ARRAY2(T)=6:T=T+1
170 IF I$="7" THEN ARRAY2(T)=7:T=T+1
175 IF I$="8" THEN ARRAY2(T)=8:T=T+1
```

```
180 IF I$="9" THEN ARRAY2(T)=9:T=T+1
185 IF I$="0" THEN ARRAY2(T)=0:T=T+1
190 PRINT I$;
195 WEND
200 FOR DUMMY=1 TO T+3:LOCATE 12,DUMMY:PRINT
    CHR$(196);:NEXT DUMMY
210 FOR AMA=T TO 2 STEP -1
220 TEMP=ARRAY1(AMA)+ARRAY2(AMA)+DIG
230 IF TEMP>9 THEN DIG=1:ANSWER(AMA)=TEMP-10
240 IF TEMP<10 THEN DIG=0:ANSWER(AMA)=TEMP
350 NEXT AMA
360 ANSWER(1)=ARRAY1(1)+ARRAY2(1)+DIG
370 LOCATE 14,5:FOR DUMMY=2 TO T-1:PRINT
    ANSWER(DUMMY);:NEXT DUMMY
380 LOCATE 14,1
381 IF ANSWER(1)>9 THEN PRINT 1:GOTO 386
382 IF ANSWER(1)<10 THEN LOCATE 14,3:PRINT
    ANSWER(1);
383 I$="":GOTO 390
386 I$="":LOCATE 14,3:PRINT(ANSWER(1)-10)
390 WHILE I$<>CHR$(27):I$=INKEY$:WEND
400 LOCATE 18,1:END
```

● ● ●

Although there are obvious limitations with the program—Why only seventy-five digits? Why only addition? Why only two numbers?—the code gives you a nice foundation to expand ADD.BAS's power and flexibility.

Blackjack

LOAD "BJACK.BAS"

Ok

RUN_

Should you hit or stand?

Blackjack is one of the most widely played casino games in the world precisely because it's so simple to play. Blackjack's also one of the most controversial games because of the development of strategies like card counting, which—as first described in the book *Beat the Dealer* by mathematician Edward O. Thorp, and as seen in over-the-top movies like *21*—relies on carefully observing which cards pop out of the shoe.

If you're not familiar with the game, there are several simple rules:

1. You are given two cards to start. If your cards' ranks sum to 21 points, you have blackjack;
2. If not, you can keep asking for more cards (hitting) until you have a score at or below 21 points and, if you beat the dealer's score, you win; or
3. You can hope the dealer goes bust, since he must keep drawing cards until he reaches a sum of at least 17.

A card with a rank of two is worth two points; with a rank of three, three points; and so on, with face cards worth 10 points each and aces worth either 11 points or 1 point, depending on which points scheme doesn't bust the player (or dealer), if either.

```
e dealer now picks two cards randomly. On
ealer shows a Nine of ♦

ou get two cards to start:
ack of ♦
wo of ♦
ould you like to _H_it or _S_tand? S
ow the dealer will keep drawing cards unti
ing of ♦
our card sum is  12
he dealer's card sum is  19
he dealer beat you on this round.
lay again (Y or N)? _
```

Run **BJACK.BAS** to play one hand at a time against the dealer. When prompted, you'll press *H* to hit (ask for another card) or *S* to stand (stop pulling cards and stick with the hand you've got). Can you (repeatedly) beat the dealer?

● ● ●

A number of arrays assign numbers and values to cards—see lines **30** to **40**. Then, ten cards are—not in view of the player or dealer—picked "off stage" randomly by the computer (lines **110** to **118**). Note that the suits don't matter here, although they are shown as each card is drawn, purely for aesthetic reasons. Also note that the same card, both in terms of rank and suit, can be repeatedly drawn in a single round of **BJACK.BAS**; you might want to imagine an infinite number of decks in the shoe, so card counting won't help you at all here. Each card pull is independent of the others.

The trickiest part of the **BJACK.BAS** code is accounting for the aces: "soft" aces, which are valued at 11 apiece, and "hard" aces, valued at 1 apiece. So there are two arrays for the player and two for the dealer: **YOU** and **DEALER**, which treat aces as soft, and **YOUACE** and **DEALACE**, which treat aces as hard. Later on in the code, sums of hands are calculated for the player and dealer twice each, and assigned to the variables **YOURSUM1** and **YOURSUM2**, and **DEALSUM1** and **DEALSUM2**. If *both* sums for the player (or both sums for the dealer) exceed 21, then the player (or dealer) goes bust. (The sum-checks can be found in line **160** as well as in lines **300** to **330**.)

● ● ●

BJACK.BAS

```
10 KEY OFF:SCREEN 9:SCREEN 0:COLOR
   15,1:CLS:RANDOMIZE TIMER
20 PRINT"BLACKJACK v. 1.0"
30 DIM CARDTYPE$(14):DIM CARDVAL(14):DIM
   CARDSUIT(4):DIM DEALER(10):DIM YOU(10):DIM
   DEALACE(10):DIM YOUACE(10)
35 CARDTYPE$(1)="Ace":CARDTYPE$(2)="Two":CARDTYPE$
   (3)="Three":CARDTYPE$(4)="Four":CARDTYPE$(5)="Fi
   ve":CARDTYPE$(6)="Six":CARDTYPE$(7)="Seven":CARD
   TYPE$(8)="Eight":CARDTYPE$(9)="Nine":CARDTYPE$(1
   0)="Ten":CARDTYPE$(11)="Jack"
36 CARDTYPE$(12)="Queen":CARDTYPE$(13)="King"
40 CARDVAL(1)=11:CARDVAL(2)=2:CARDVAL(3)=3:
   CARDVAL(4)=4:CARDVAL(5)=5:CARDVAL(6)=6:CARDVAL(7
   )=7:CARDVAL(8)=8:CARDVAL(9)=9:CARDVAL(10)=10:CAR
   DVAL(11)=10:CARDVAL(12)=10:CARDVAL(13)=10:
   CARDVAL(14)=1    'Cardvalue=14 is for a ACE=1 ra
   ther than ACE=11
100 CLS:PRINT:PRINT"The dealer now picks two cards
    randomly. One will be shown to you."
110 FOR D=1 TO 10:DEALER(D)=INT(1+13*RND(1)):
    YOU(D)=INT(1+13*RND(1))    'Picks ten cards for
    the dealer, and five cards for you
115 IF DEALER(D)=1 THEN DEALACE(D)=14 ELSE
    DEALACE(D)=DEALER(D)    'Sets up lower value
    for ace for dealer
116 IF YOU(D)=1 THEN YOUACE(D)=14 ELSE
    YOUACE(D)=YOU(D)    'Sets up lower value for
    ace for player
118 NEXT D
120 PRINT"Dealer shows a ";CARDTYPE$(DEALER(1));"
    of ";CHR$(INT(1+4*RND(1))+2)
130 PRINT:PRINT"You get two cards to start:"
135 PRINT CARDTYPE$(YOU(1));" of ";CHR$(INT(1+4*
    RND(1))+2)
```

```
136 PRINT CARDTYPE$(YOU(2));" of ";CHR$(INT(1+4*
    RND(1))+2)
138 LOOP=2:P$="":YOURSUM1=0:YOURSUM1=CARDVAL
    (YOU(1))+CARDVAL(YOU(2)):YOURSUM2=0:YOURSUM2=C
    ARDVAL(YOUACE(1))+CARDVAL(YOUACE(2))
139 INPUT"Would you like to _H_it or
    _S_tand";I$:IF I$="S" THEN 200 ELSE 140
140 'Drawing cards for the player
145 PRINT"Okay, let's draw another card for you."
147 LOOP=LOOP+1
150 PRINT CARDTYPE$(YOU(LOOP));" of ";CHR$(INT
    (1+4*RND(1))+2)
155 YOURSUM1=YOURSUM1+CARDVAL(YOU(LOOP))    'Sum
    with ACE=10
156 YOURSUM2=YOURSUM2+CARDVAL(YOUACE(LOOP))   'Sum
    with ACE=1
160 IF (YOURSUM1>21 AND YOURSUM2>21) THEN GOTO 500
170 INPUT"Would you like to _H_it or
    _S_tand";P$:IF P$="S" THEN 200 ELSE 140
200 'Now the dealer draws his remaining cards
205 LOOP=2:DEALSUM1=0:DEALSUM1=CARDVAL(DEALER(1)):
    DEALSUM2=0:DEALSUM2=CARDVAL(DEALACE(1))
210 PRINT"Now the dealer will keep drawing cards
    until hitting or exceeding a sum of 17."
215 'Dealer keeps drawing cards
220 PRINT CARDTYPE$(DEALER(LOOP));" of ";CHR$(INT
    (1+4*RND(1))+2)
225 DEALSUM1=DEALSUM1+CARDVAL(DEALER(LOOP))
227 DEALSUM2=DEALSUM2+CARDVAL(DEALACE(LOOP))
230 LOOP=LOOP+1
240 IF (DEALSUM1<17 AND DEALSUM2<17) THEN 215
300 'Determine who won the round
301 DEALSUM=0:YOURSUM=0     'Set to zero
302 IF DEALSUM1<=21 THEN DEALSUM=DEALSUM1 ELSE
    DEALSUM=DEALSUM2
303 IF YOURSUM1<=21 THEN YOURSUM=YOURSUM1 ELSE
    YOURSUM=YOURSUM2
304 PRINT"Your card sum is ";YOURSUM
305 PRINT"The dealer's card sum is ";DEALSUM
307 IF DEALSUM>21 THEN PRINT"The dealer
    lost.":DEALSUM=0
310 IF YOURSUM>DEALSUM THEN PRINT"You beat the
    dealer this round.":GOTO 510
```

```
320 IF YOURSUM=DEALSUM THEN PRINT"You and the
    dealer tied.":GOTO 510
330 IF YOURSUM<DEALSUM THEN PRINT"The dealer beat
    you on this round.":GOTO 510
500 PRINT:PRINT"Sorry, you lost."
510 INPUT"Play again (Y or N)";Y$
520 IF Y$="Y" THEN 100 ELSE CLS:END
```

● ● ●

Most, but not all, of the basic rules of **BJACK.BAS** are programmed in. The player is not given the option to "split," for instance.

Another problem with **BJACK.BAS** is that there's no narrative; you can't bet, so winning or losing any particular hand has no long-term meaning.

You might want to consider adding another player at the table (either computerized or human). **BJACK.BAS** can have replay value only if there's something to play for—and right now there isn't.

Poker

LOAD "POKER.BAS"

Ok

RUN

The modern card game of poker has its roots in the Mississippi riverboats of the nineteenth century. But its national popularity really took off in the 1970s, right around the time the World Series of Poker (WSOP) began. By the turn of the last century, people were playing poker online (both for real and virtual cash), as well as watching tournaments on television featuring such larger-than-life characters as Chris Moneymaker, who won the WSOP in 2003, and Doyle Brunson, the granddaddy of poker's most played variant today, Texas hold'em.

POKER.BAS presents you with a stripped-down version of the no-limit hold'em game: the only option is heads-up (one-on-one) play versus the computer. You are asked for a starting bankroll—which your computer opponent is given in turn—and then presented with your hole cards (a pair of starting cards, of which there are 169 meaningful different sets—that's thirteen unique card ranks multiplied by thirteen unique card ranks) and a bevy of options. Would you like to bet, fold, see more information (like bankrolls and hole cards), or simply cash your chips and bounce? Your choices might lead you to millions—or you might bust out. (Virtually, of course.)

You should note the differences in rules between POKER.BAS and a real hold'em heads-up game. In the program, all five community cards are shown at once, rather than revealing the flop, turn and river successively; thus, you can only bet at most twice during each hand. But you can bet your entire bankroll at any time—hence it's *no limit* poker.

Big blinds and small blinds are discarded in favor of a uniform fifty dollar entry fee into each pot, with no possibility of simply folding before paying, and you'll always bet before the computer does. In addition, the computer—as you'll see—bets each hand in a *very* simplistic manner. Finally, consider this list of every hand strength, ordered from lowest to highest:

- HIGH CARD—player with highest ranked card wins; for instance, a seven of hearts beats a six of clubs;

- ONE PAIR—player with the higher ranked pair wins; for example, a pair of kings tops a pair of jacks;

- TWO PAIR—player with the higher of two ranked pairs of cards wins; so a pair of kings and eights beats a pair of queens and fives;

- THREE OF A KIND—player with the higher of three cards of the same rank, along with two of unmatched rank, wins; for instance, three fours tops three twos;

- STRAIGHT—player with higher rank of five cards of sequential rank wins; for example, a seven-six-five-four-three beats a six-five-four-three-two;

- FLUSH—player with the higher rank of all five cards of the same suit wins; so a set of five spades, with a king as the highest rank, tops a set of five diamonds, with a jack as the highest rank;

- FULL HOUSE—player with the higher of three cards of the same rank, and two of another rank, wins;

- FOUR OF A KIND—player with higher of four cards of the same rank wins;

- STRAIGHT FLUSH—player with five cards both all of the same suit and of successive ranks;
- ROYAL FLUSH—player with an ace, king, queen, jack, and ten, all of the same suit, wins. (This is a subset of the straight flush.)

There are $\binom{52}{5} = \dfrac{52!}{(52-5)!5!} = 2,598,960$ possible five-card poker hands. Another way to look at this: there are about 2.6 million possible unique sets of five cards in a standard deck. (The numbers in the large set of parentheses above are read as "fifty-two choose five"; the notation is a staple of the mathematical field of combinatorics, which studies counting problems.) So, while there are only four possible royal flushes, there are 123,552 possible two-pair combinations, for instance.

The **POKER.BAS** program recognizes most, but not all, of the hand strengths. You should already sniff some (significant) challenges coming; as always, the challenges are enumerated at the end of the chapter.

• • •

Because of both the length and complexity of the program, it's best that we examine it a chunk of code at a time.

• • •

First, let's set up the display along with defining several arrays, including a string array of hand types called **TYPE$**. Make sure, especially, to note the numbers assigned to each hand (line **12**).

```
10 KEY OFF:RANDOMIZE TIMER:SCREEN 9:CLS
11 DIM HP1(10):DIM HP2(10):DIM TYPE$(10)
12 TYPE$(1)="ROYAL FLUSH":TYPE$(2)="STRAIGHT
   FLUSH":TYPE$(3)="FOUR-OF-A-KIND":TYPE$(4)="FULL
   HOUSE":TYPE$(5)="FLUSH":TYPE$(6)="STRAIGHT":TYPE
   $(7)="THREE-OF-A-KIND":TYPE$(8)="TWO
   PAIR":TYPE$(9)="ONE PAIR":TYPE$(10)="HIGH CARD
   (NO PAIR)"
```

With the hands set, we need to label every card in the deck. The string array **CARD$** has two arguments, the first denoting the rank and the second the suit.

```
15 'DEFINE CARD FACES AND SUITS
20 DIM CARD$(13,4)
30 CARD$(1,1)="DEUCE OF SPADES":CARD$(2,1)="TREY
   OF SPADES":CARD$(3,1)="FOUR OF
   SPADES":CARD$(4,1)="FIVE OF
   SPADES":CARD$(5,1)="SIX OF
   SPADES":CARD$(6,1)="SEVEN OF
   SPADES":CARD$(7,1)="EIGHT OF
   SPADES":CARD$(8,1)="NINE OF SPADES"
35 CARD$(9,1)="TEN OF SPADES":CARD$(10,1)="JACK OF
   SPADES":CARD$(11,1)="QUEEN OF
   SPADES":CARD$(12,1)="KING OF
   SPADES":CARD$(13,1)="ACE OF SPADES"
40 CARD$(1,2)="DEUCE OF HEARTS":CARD$(2,2)="TREY
   OF HEARTS":CARD$(3,2)="FOUR OF
   HEARTS":CARD$(4,2)="FIVE OF
   HEARTS":CARD$(5,2)="SIX OF
   HEARTS":CARD$(6,2)="SEVEN OF
```

```
    HEARTS":CARD$(7,2)="EIGHT OF
    HEARTS":CARD$(8,2)="NINE OF HEARTS"
 45 CARD$(9,2)="TEN OF HEARTS":CARD$(10,2)="JACK OF
    HEARTS":CARD$(11,2)="QUEEN OF
    HEARTS":CARD$(12,2)="KING OF
    HEARTS":CARD$(13,2)="ACE OF HEARTS"
 50 CARD$(1,3)="DEUCE OF DIAMONDS":CARD$(2,3)="TREY
    OF DIAMONDS":CARD$(3,3)="FOUR OF
    DIAMONDS":CARD$(4,3)="FIVE OF
    DIAMONDS":CARD$(5,3)="SIX OF
    DIAMONDS":CARD$(6,3)="SEVEN OF
    DIAMONDS":CARD$(7,3)="EIGHT OF
    DIAMONDS":CARD$(8,3)="NINE OF DIAMONDS"
 55 CARD$(9,3)="TEN OF DIAMONDS":CARD$(10,3)="JACK
    OF DIAMONDS":CARD$(11,3)="QUEEN OF
    DIAMONDS":CARD$(12,3)="KING OF
    DIAMONDS":CARD$(13,3)="ACE OF DIAMONDS"
 60 CARD$(1,4)="DEUCE OF CLUBS":CARD$(2,4)="TREY OF
    CLUBS":CARD$(3,4)="FOUR OF
    CLUBS":CARD$(4,4)="FIVE OF
    CLUBS":CARD$(5,4)="SIX OF
    CLUBS":CARD$(6,4)="SEVEN OF
    CLUBS":CARD$(7,4)="EIGHT OF
    CLUBS":CARD$(8,4)="NINE OF CLUBS"
 65 CARD$(9,4)="TEN OF CLUBS":CARD$(10,4)="JACK OF
    CLUBS":CARD$(11,4)="QUEEN OF
    CLUBS":CARD$(12,4)="KING OF
    CLUBS":CARD$(13,4)="ACE OF CLUBS"
```

Next, an on-screen title is displayed, and the player is queried about a starting bankroll, not to exceed ten thousand dollars (note that instead of dealing with different denominations of chips, a generic cash bankroll is used for simplicity's sake). Both the computer and the player begin with an equal amount of cash.

```
 70 '-----------------------------------------------
 80 COLOR 15,0:LOCATE 12,20:PRINT"NO LIMIT TEXAS
    HOLD'EM: HEADS-UP EDITION"
 85 FOR PAUSE=1 TO 6000:NEXT PAUSE
 90 CLS
```

```
95 LOCATE 14,20:INPUT"STARTING BANKROLL ($100 TO
   $10,000)";YOURBANK
100 IF YOURBANK<100 OR YOURBANK>10000 THEN 90
105 COMPBANK=YOURBANK  'BOTH COMPUTER AND YOU ARE
   ASSIGNED THE SAME STARTING BANKROLL
```

Now we shuffle up and deal the hole cards to the player—and the computer (off-screen, of course). All relevant variables are reset, and the cards are dealt. In addition, an equal amount of cash from each bankroll is procured to build the hundred-dollar pot.

```
110 '---------------------------------------------
115 DIM DEALT(13,4)
200 'DISTRIBUTE HOLE CARDS--NEW HAND
206 'RESET DEALT HAND (SHUFFLE UP AND DEAL)
207 FOR A=1 TO 4:FOR B=1 TO 13:DEALT(B,A)=0:NEXT
   B:NEXT A
210 NEWHAND=0  'THIS IS A NEW HAND!
215 FOR HOLECARDS=1 TO 4
220 FACE=INT(1+13*RND(1)):SUIT=INT(1+4*RND(1))
230 IF DEALT(FACE,SUIT)<>0 THEN 220
240 DEALT(FACE,SUIT)=HOLECARDS 'TELLS WHICH PLAYER
   HAS WHAT HOLE CARDS (YOU=1 AND 2, THE COMPUTER
   HAS 3 AND 4)
250 NEXT HOLECARDS
260 'TAKE $50 FROM EACH PLAYER TO START THE POT
   WITH
270 POTAMOUNT=100:YOURBANK=YOURBANK-50:COMPBANK=
   COMPBANK-50
```

A subroutine designed to print out the player's hole cards is called before displaying the main menu. GW-BASIC waits for you to enter a menu option, at which point a subroutine (or subroutines) is called to execute the option you selected.

```
300 GOSUB 1000    'START GAME WITH HOLE CARDS
   AUTOMATICALLY SHOWN
310 PRINT:PRINT"Menu:":PRINT"1.See Hole Cards,
   2.See the Bankrolls, 3.Make a bet, 4.Fold Your
```

```
      Hand, 5.Check Pot Amount, 6.Cash Your Chips
      and Exit"
320 INPUT"TYPE THE NUMBER AND YOUR CHOICE, AND HIT
      <ENTER>";CHOICE
325 IF CHOICE=1 THEN GOSUB 1000
327 IF CHOICE=2 THEN PRINT"You have $";YOURBANK;"
      and the computer has $";COMPBANK;"."
334 IF CHOICE=3 THEN GOSUB 9600:GOSUB 9800
335 IF CHOICE=4 THEN GOTO 9500
337 IF CHOICE=5 THEN PRINT"The Pot has
      $";POTAMOUNT
339 IF CHOICE=6 THEN PRINT"You just cashed out.
      Hope you enjoyed the game!":END
400 IF NEWHAND=1 THEN GOTO 200 ELSE GOTO 310
```

An algorithm to display the player's hole cards makes use of several **FOR/NEXT** loops; the **RETURN** statement, of course, throws the program back to where the subroutine was called.

```
1000 'SUBROUTINE PRINTS OUT PLAYER 1'S HOLE CARDS
1010 PRINT
1020 PRINT "YOUR HOLE CARDS ARE ":
      PRINT"********************"
1030 FOR SEARCHS=1 TO 4:FOR SEARCHF=1 TO 13
1040 IF (DEALT(SEARCHF,SEARCHS)=1 OR
      DEALT(SEARCHF,SEARCHS)=2) THEN PRINT
      CARD$(SEARCHF,SEARCHS)
1050 NEXT SEARCHF:NEXT SEARCHS
1060 PRINT"********************"
1100 RETURN
```

The five community cards—the flop (three cards), the turn (one card), and the river (one card)—are selected randomly. Notice the comments below: the flop is denoted by the **DEALT** array elements **10**, **11**, and **12**, while the turn is assigned to **20** and the river to **30**.

```
2000 'SUBROUTINE PICKS THE FLOP, TURN, AND THE
      RIVER
2010 FOR FLOP=1 TO 3
```

```
2020 FACE=INT(1+13*RND(1)):SUIT=INT(1+4*RND(1))
2030 IF DEALT(FACE,SUIT)<>0 THEN 2020
2040 DEALT(FACE,SUIT)=9+FLOP  'FLOP CARDS DENOTED
     BY DEALT=10, 11 AND 12
2050 NEXT FLOP
2060 FOR TURN=1 TO 1
2070 FACE=INT(1+13*RND(1)):SUIT=INT(1+4*RND(1))
2080 IF DEALT(FACE,SUIT)<>0 THEN 2060
2090 DEALT(FACE,SUIT)=20  'TURN CARD DENOTED BY
     DEALT=20
2100 NEXT TURN
2110 FOR RIVER=1 TO 1
2120 FACE=INT(1+13*RND(1)):SUIT=INT(1+4*RND(1))
2130 IF DEALT(FACE,SUIT)<>0 THEN 2110
2140 DEALT(FACE,SUIT)=30  'RIVER CARD DENOTED BY
     DEALT=30
2150 NEXT RIVER
2200 RETURN
```

Here's where the meat and potatoes of the program lies. There are two significant challenges when simulating a game like poker: coding the rules and creating the AI (artificial intelligence) of the computerized opponent(s). Much ink is about to be spilled on the former.

First, take careful note of how the variables, "defined" (I mean that in the loosest possible sense; after all, this is free-stylin' GW-BASIC) in lines **3015** to **2026**, are assigned values thereafter. These particular variables are set to equal the ranks and suits of the player's (**P1**), the computer's (**P2**), and the community cards, and all will be used for conditional comparisons later on.

```
3000 'SUBROUTINE--FINDS WHICH PLAYER HAS THE BEST
     FIVE-CARD HAND
3010 'THROUGH EACH SEARCH, ONE OF THE TWO PLAYERS
     WILL BE IN THE LEAD
3015 P1SCORE=0:P2SCORE=0
3020 P1FACE1=0:P1FACE2=0:P1SUIT1=0:P1SUIT2=0
3025 P2FACE1=0:P2FACE2=0:P2SUIT1=0:P2SUIT2=0
3026 F1FACE=0:F1SUIT=0:F2FACE=0:F2SUIT=0:F3FACE=0:
     F3SUIT=0:TFACE=0:TSUIT=0:RFACE=0:RSUIT=0
```

```
3030 FOR SEARCHS=1 TO 4:FOR SEARCHF=1 TO 13
3040 IF DEALT(SEARCHF,SEARCHS)=1 THEN P1FACE1=
     SEARCHF:P1SUIT1=SEARCHS
3050 IF DEALT(SEARCHF,SEARCHS)=2 THEN P1FACE2=
     SEARCHF:P1SUIT2=SEARCHS
3060 IF DEALT(SEARCHF,SEARCHS)=3 THEN P2FACE1=
     SEARCHF:P2SUIT1=SEARCHS
3070 IF DEALT(SEARCHF,SEARCHS)=4 THEN P2FACE2=
     SEARCHF:P2SUIT2=SEARCHS
3080 IF DEALT(SEARCHF,SEARCHS)=10 THEN F1FACE=
     SEARCHF:F1SUIT=SEARCHS
3090 IF DEALT(SEARCHF,SEARCHS)=11 THEN F2FACE=
     SEARCHF:F2SUIT=SEARCHS
3100 IF DEALT(SEARCHF,SEARCHS)=12 THEN F3FACE=
     SEARCHF:F3SUIT=SEARCHS
3110 IF DEALT(SEARCHF,SEARCHS)=20 THEN TFACE=
     SEARCHF:TSUIT=SEARCHS
3120 IF DEALT(SEARCHF,SEARCHS)=30 THEN RFACE=
     SEARCHF:RSUIT=SEARCHS
3130 NEXT SEARCHF:NEXT SEARCHS
```

The initial comparison: determine who has the higher hole
card, the player or the computer. HP1(10) and HP2(10)
are the array elements assigned to the hole card; the subroutine sets the corresponding higher-hole-card array element to 1.

```
3140 'NOW THAT THE CARDS HAVE BEEN ASSIGNED
     VARIABLES, LET'S SEE WHO HAS THE BEST HAND
3150 FOR Q=1 TO 10
3155 HP1(Q)=0:HP2(Q)=0
3160 NEXT Q
3200 'SEARCH #1: THE HIGHER HOLE CARD
3210 IF (P1FACE1>P2FACE1 AND P1FACE1>P2FACE2) THEN
     HP1(10)=1:GOTO 3300
3220 IF (P1FACE2>P2FACE1 AND P1FACE2>P2FACE2) THEN
     HP1(10)=1:GOTO 3300
3230 IF (P2FACE1>P1FACE1 AND P2FACE1>P1FACE2) THEN
     HP2(10)=1:GOTO 3300
3240 IF (P2FACE2>P1FACE1 AND P2FACE2>P1FACE2) THEN
     HP2(10)=1:GOTO 3300
```

Next, pairs of cards are accounted for. There are $\binom{13}{1}\binom{4}{2}\binom{12}{3}\binom{4}{1}\binom{4}{1}\binom{4}{1}$ = 1,098,240 single pairs of cards from a five-card hand, but we don't need to check for every *unique* pair on the board; that would take too much computer-processing time in addition to being a coding nightmare. Instead, we need to see if *sets* of two cards are equal in rank. For instance, do the player's hole cards have the same rank? How about one of the player's hole cards, along with one of the community cards—do they match rank?

At most, the player (or computer) can snag two pair. Every possible combination of pairs must be searched for—brute force is the order of the day, no matter how you optimize the search. (Nevertheless, notice that *only* pairs involving hole cards are accounted for below, of which there are only eleven combinations per player; more possibilities remain for you to code.) The program keeps a running tally of card pairs with two counters: **COMPPAIR** and **YOURPAIR**. If the player (or the computer) ends up having more than one pair, the eighth element of the **HP** array is set to **1**. The computer's cards are examined first.

```
3300 'SEARCH #2: THE HIGHER PAIR (OR PAIRS)
3310 'SEE IF THE COMPUTER HAS AT LEAST ONE PAIR
3315 COMPPAIR=0   'A COUNTER TO TELL HOW MANY PAIRS
     THE COMPUTER HAS
3320 IF (P2FACE1=P2FACE2) THEN COMPPAIR=COMPPAIR+1
     :HP2(9)=P2FACE2
3330 IF (P2FACE1=F1FACE) THEN COMPPAIR=COMPPAIR+1:
     HP2(9)=F1FACE
3340 IF (P2FACE1=F2FACE) THEN COMPPAIR=COMPPAIR+1:
     HP2(9)=F2FACE
3345 IF (P2FACE1=F3FACE) THEN COMPPAIR=COMPPAIR+1:
     HP2(9)=F3FACE
3350 IF (P2FACE1=TFACE) THEN COMPPAIR=COMPPAIR+1:
     HP2(9)=TFACE
```

```
3360 IF (P2FACE1=RFACE) THEN COMPPAIR=COMPPAIR+1:
     HP2(9)=RFACE
3370 IF (P2FACE2=F1FACE) THEN COMPPAIR=COMPPAIR+1:
     HP2(9)=F1FACE
3380 IF (P2FACE2=F2FACE) THEN COMPPAIR=COMPPAIR+1:
     HP2(9)=F2FACE
3385 IF (P2FACE2=F3FACE) THEN COMPPAIR=COMPPAIR+1:
     HP2(9)=F3FACE
3390 IF (P2FACE2=TFACE) THEN COMPPAIR=COMPPAIR+1:
     HP2(9)=TFACE
3400 IF (P2FACE2=RFACE) THEN COMPPAIR=COMPPAIR+1:
     HP2(9)=RFACE
3410 IF COMPPAIR>1 THEN HP2(8)=1  'CHECK TO SEE IF
     THE COMPUTER HAD >1 PAIR

3415 'SEE IF YOU HAVE AT LEAST ONE PAIR
3420 YOURPAIR=0  'A COUNTER TO TELL HOW MANY PAIRS
     YOUR HAVE
3430 IF (P1FACE1=P1FACE2) THEN YOURPAIR=YOURPAIR+1
     :HP1(9)=P1FACE2
3440 IF (P1FACE1=F1FACE) THEN YOURPAIR=YOURPAIR+1
     :HP1(9)=F1FACE
3450 IF (P1FACE1=F2FACE) THEN YOURPAIR=YOURPAIR+1
     :HP1(9)=F2FACE
3455 IF (P1FACE1=F3FACE) THEN YOURPAIR=YOURPAIR+1
     :HP1(9)=F3FACE
3460 IF (P1FACE1=TFACE) THEN YOURPAIR=YOURPAIR+1
     :HP1(9)=TFACE
3470 IF (P1FACE1=RFACE) THEN YOURPAIR=YOURPAIR+1
     :HP1(9)=RFACE
3480 IF (P1FACE2=F1FACE) THEN YOURPAIR=YOURPAIR+1
     :HP1(9)=F1FACE
3490 IF (P1FACE2=F2FACE) THEN YOURPAIR=YOURPAIR+1
     :HP1(9)=F2FACE
3495 IF (P1FACE2=F3FACE) THEN YOURPAIR=YOURPAIR+1
     :HP1(9)=F3FACE
3500 IF (P1FACE2=TFACE) THEN YOURPAIR=YOURPAIR+1
     :HP1(9)=TFACE
3510 IF (P1FACE2=RFACE) THEN YOURPAIR=YOURPAIR+1
     :HP1(9)=RFACE
3520 IF YOURPAIR>1 THEN HP1(8)=1 'CHECK TO SEE IF
     YOU HAD >1 PAIR
```

Analogous to searching for pairs, accounting for three cards of the same rank (along with two other unmatched cards) is tedious work. Although there are $\binom{13}{1}\binom{4}{3}\binom{12}{2}\binom{4}{1}\binom{4}{1}$ = 54,912 possible three-of-a-kind hands in a five-card hand, each *unique* hand doesn't need to be searched for—though almost every possible set of three cards must be checked (the exceptions include sets of three cards matching ranks out of the five community cards, which benefits the player and computer equally). If a match is found, the variable **P1STATUS** or **P2STATUS** is set to a certain value for the player and the computer, respectively, to later serve as a springboard for the full house search. The player's cards are examined by the algorithm first.

```
3600 'SEARCH #3: THREE-OF-A-KIND
3605 'CHECK TO SEE IF YOU HAVE THREE-OF-A-KIND
     (ALSO SET IT UP FOR LATER CHECKING FULL
     HOUSE)
3607 P1STATUS=0    'FOR CHECKING IF YOU HAVE A FULL
     HOUSE...LATER
3610 IF (P1FACE1=P1FACE2) AND (P1FACE2=F1FACE)
     THEN HP1(7)=F1FACE:P1STATUS=1
3620 IF (P1FACE1=P1FACE2) AND (P1FACE2=F2FACE)
     THEN HP1(7)=F2FACE:P1STATUS=2
3630 IF (P1FACE1=P1FACE2) AND (P1FACE2=F3FACE)
     THEN HP1(7)=F3FACE:P1STATUS=3
3640 IF (P1FACE1=P1FACE2) AND (P1FACE2=TFACE) THEN
     HP1(7)=TFACE:P1STATUS=4
3650 IF (P1FACE1=P1FACE2) AND (P1FACE2=RFACE) THEN
     HP1(7)=RFACE:P1STATUS=5
3660 IF (P1FACE1=F1FACE) AND (P1FACE1=TFACE) THEN
     HP1(7)=TFACE:P1STATUS=8
3670 IF (P1FACE1=F1FACE) AND (P1FACE1=RFACE) THEN
     HP1(7)=RFACE:P1STATUS=9
3680 IF (P1FACE1=F2FACE) AND (P1FACE1=F3FACE) THEN
     HP1(7)=F3FACE:P1STATUS=10
3690 IF (P1FACE1=F2FACE) AND (P1FACE1=TFACE) THEN
     HP1(7)=TFACE:P1STATUS=11
```

```
3700 IF (P1FACE1=F2FACE) AND (P1FACE1=RFACE) THEN
     HP1(7)=RFACE:P1STATUS=12
3710 IF (P1FACE1=F3FACE) AND (P1FACE1=TFACE) THEN
     HP1(7)=TFACE:P1STATUS=13
3720 IF (P1FACE1=F3FACE) AND (P1FACE1=RFACE) THEN
     HP1(7)=RFACE:P1STATUS=14
3730 IF (P1FACE1=TFACE) AND (P1FACE1=RFACE) THEN
     HP1(7)=RFACE:P1STATUS=15
3740 IF (P1FACE2=F1FACE) AND (P1FACE2=F2FACE) THEN
     HP1(7)=F2FACE:P1STATUS=16
3750 IF (P1FACE2=F1FACE) AND (P1FACE2=F3FACE) THEN
     HP1(7)=F3FACE:P1STATUS=17
3760 IF (P1FACE2=F1FACE) AND (P1FACE2=TFACE) THEN
     HP1(7)=TFACE:P1STATUS=18
3770 IF (P1FACE2=F1FACE) AND (P1FACE2=RFACE) THEN
     HP1(7)=RFACE:P1STATUS=19
3780 IF (P1FACE2=F2FACE) AND (P1FACE2=F3FACE) THEN
     HP1(7)=F3FACE:P1STATUS=20
3790 IF (P1FACE2=F2FACE) AND (P1FACE2=TFACE) THEN
     HP1(7)=TFACE:P1STATUS=21
3800 IF (P1FACE2=F2FACE) AND (P1FACE2=RFACE) THEN
     HP1(7)=RFACE:P1STATUS=22
3810 IF (P1FACE2=F3FACE) AND (P1FACE2=TFACE) THEN
     HP1(7)=TFACE:P1STATUS=23
3820 IF (P1FACE2=F3FACE) AND (P1FACE2=RFACE) THEN
     HP1(7)=RFACE:P1STATUS=24
3830 IF (P1FACE2=TFACE) AND (P1FACE2=RFACE) THEN
     HP1(7)=RFACE:P1STATUS=25

3840 'CHECK TO SEE IF THE COMPUTER HAS THREE-OF-A-
     KIND
3845 P2STATUS=0   'FOR CHECKING IF COMPUTER HAS A
     FULL HOUSE...LATER
3850 IF (P2FACE1=P2FACE2) AND (P2FACE2=F1FACE)
     THEN HP2(7)=F1FACE:P2STATUS=1
3860 IF (P2FACE1=P2FACE2) AND (P2FACE2=F2FACE)
     THEN HP2(7)=F2FACE:P2STATUS=2
3870 IF (P2FACE1=P2FACE2) AND (P2FACE2=F3FACE)
     THEN HP2(7)=F3FACE:P2STATUS=3
3880 IF (P2FACE1=P2FACE2) AND (P2FACE2=TFACE) THEN
     HP2(7)=TFACE:P2STATUS=4
3890 IF (P2FACE1=P2FACE2) AND (P2FACE2=RFACE) THEN
     HP2(7)=RFACE:P2STATUS=5
```

```
3900 IF (P2FACE1=F1FACE) AND (P2FACE1=F2FACE) THEN
     HP2(7)=F2FACE:P2STATUS=6
3910 IF (P2FACE1=F1FACE) AND (P2FACE1=F3FACE) THEN
     HP2(7)=F3FACE:P2STATUS=7
3920 IF (P2FACE1=F1FACE) AND (P2FACE1=TFACE) THEN
     HP2(7)=TFACE:P2STATUS=8
3930 IF (P2FACE1=F1FACE) AND (P2FACE1=RFACE) THEN
     HP2(7)=RFACE:P2STATUS=9
3940 IF (P2FACE1=F2FACE) AND (P2FACE1=F3FACE) THEN
     HP2(7)=F3FACE:P2STATUS=10
3950 IF (P2FACE1=F2FACE) AND (P2FACE1=TFACE) THEN
     HP2(7)=TFACE:P2STATUS=11
3960 IF (P2FACE1=F2FACE) AND (P2FACE1=RFACE) THEN
     HP2(7)=RFACE:P2STATUS=12
3970 IF (P2FACE1=F3FACE) AND (P2FACE1=TFACE) THEN
     HP2(7)=TFACE:P2STATUS=13
3980 IF (P2FACE1=F3FACE) AND (P2FACE1=RFACE) THEN
     HP2(7)=RFACE:P2STATUS=14
3990 IF (P2FACE1=TFACE) AND (P2FACE1=RFACE) THEN
     HP2(7)=RFACE:P2STATUS=15
4000 IF (P2FACE2=F1FACE) AND (P2FACE1=F2FACE) THEN
     HP2(7)=F2FACE:P2STATUS=16
```

There are $\binom{13}{1}\binom{4}{3}\binom{12}{1}\binom{4}{2} = 3{,}744$ possible full houses among all five-card hands. Only if the player (or computer) has (temporarily) hit three-of-a-kind is a full house—three cards of one rank, two cards of another—a possibility.

The variables **P1STATUS** and **P2STATUS** tell the program not only whether or not the player and computer, respectively, (so far in the search) have three cards of the same rank; the variables also identify *which three cards*. That way, each conditional statement checks for pairs among the remaining cards on the table.

You first thought might be: why do we need to check for pairs *again*? Can't we just combine the results of the pairs' search with the three-of-a-kind search and call it a day? Unfortunately, this won't work—there is the possibility of cards overlapping between the searches.

Fifty distinct searches for pairs need to be conducted for both the player (done first) and the computer (done second): $2\left[\binom{7}{3}-\binom{5}{2}\right]=50$. Although brute force is again required, make sure to examine the code systematically to find the patterns.

```
4500 'SEARCH #5: A FULL HOUSE
4510 'CHECK TO SEE IF YOU HAVE A FULL HOUSE (YOU
     MUST ALREADY HAVE THREE-OF-A-KIND)
4520 IF P1STATUS=1 AND ((F2FACE=F3FACE) OR
     (F2FACE=TFACE) OR (F2FACE=RFACE)) THEN
     HP1(4)=F1FACE
4525 IF P1STATUS=1 AND ((F3FACE=TFACE) OR
     (F3FACE=RFACE)) THEN HP1(4)=F1FACE
4530 IF P1STATUS=1 AND (TFACE=RFACE) THEN
     HP1(4)=F1FACE
4535 IF P1STATUS=2 AND ((F1FACE=F3FACE) OR
     (F1FACE=TFACE) OR (F1FACE=RFACE)) THEN
     HP1(4)=F2FACE
4540 IF P1STATUS=2 AND ((F3FACE=TFACE) OR
     (F3FACE=RFACE)) THEN HP1(4)=F2FACE
4545 IF P1STATUS=2 AND (TFACE=RFACE) THEN
     HP1(4)=F2FACE
4550 IF P1STATUS=3 AND ((F1FACE=F2FACE) OR
     (F1FACE=TFACE) OR (F1FACE=RFACE)) THEN
     HP1(4)=F3FACE
4555 IF P1STATUS=3 AND ((F2FACE=TFACE) OR
     (F2FACE=RFACE)) THEN HP1(4)=F3FACE
4560 IF P1STATUS=3 AND (TFACE=RFACE) THEN
     HP1(4)=F3FACE
4565 IF PSTATUS=4 AND ((F1FACE=F2FACE) OR
     (F1FACE=F3FACE) OR (F1FACE=RFACE)) THEN
     HP1(4)=TFACE
4570 IF PSTATUS=4 AND ((F2FACE=F3FACE) OR
     (F2FACE=RFACE)) THEN HP1(4)=TFACE
4575 IF PSTATUS=4 AND (F3FACE=RFACE) THEN
     HP1(4)=TFACE
4580 IF PSTATUS=5 AND ((F1FACE=F2FACE) OR
     (F1FACE=F3FACE) OR (F1FACE=TFACE)) THEN
     HP1(4)=RFACE
```

```
4585 IF PSTATUS=5 AND ((F2FACE=F3FACE) OR
     (F2FACE=TFACE)) THEN HP1(4)=RFACE
4590 IF PSTATUS=5 AND (F3FACE=TFACE) THEN
     HP1(4)=RFACE
4595 IF PSTATUS=6 AND ((P1FACE2=F3FACE) OR
     (P1FACE2=TFACE) OR (P1FACE2=RFACE)) THEN
     HP1(4)=F2FACE
4600 IF PSTATUS=6 AND ((F3FACE=TFACE) OR
     (F3FACE=RFACE)) THEN HP1(4)=F2FACE
4605 IF PSTATUS=6 AND (TFACE=RFACE) THEN
     HP1(4)=F2FACE
4610 IF PSTATUS=7 AND ((P1FACE2=F2FACE) OR
     (P1FACE2=RFACE) OR (P1FACE2=TFACE)) THEN
     HP1(4)=F3FACE
4615 IF PSTATUS=7 AND ((F2FACE=RFACE) OR
     (F2FACE=TFACE)) THEN HP1(4)=F3FACE
4620 IF PSTATUS=7 AND (RFACE=TFACE) THEN
     HP1(4)=F3FACE
4625 IF PSTATUS=8 AND ((P1FACE2=F2FACE) OR
     (P1FACE2=F3FACE) OR (P1FACE2=RFACE)) THEN
     HP1(4)=TFACE
4630 IF PSTATUS=8 AND ((F2FACE=F3FACE) OR
     (F2FACE=RFACE)) THEN HP1(4)=TFACE
4635 IF PSTATUS=8 AND (F3FACE=RFACE) THEN
     HP1(4)=TFACE
4640 IF PSTATUS=9 AND ((P1FACE2=F2FACE) OR
     (P1FACE2=F3FACE) OR (P1FACE2=TFACE)) THEN
     HP1(4)=RFACE
4645 IF PSTATUS=9 AND ((F2FACE=F3FACE) OR
     (F2FACE=TFACE)) THEN HP1(4)=RFACE
4650 IF PSTATUS=9 AND (F3FACE=TFACE) THEN
     HP1(4)=RFACE
4655 IF PSTATUS=10 AND ((P1FACE2=F1FACE) AND
     (P1FACE2=TFACE) AND (P1FACE2=RFACE)) THEN
     HP1(4)=F3FACE
4660 IF PSTATUS=10 AND ((F1FACE=TFACE) AND
     (F1FACE=RFACE)) THEN HP1(4)=F3FACE
4665 IF PSTATUS=10 AND (TFACE=RFACE) THEN
     HP1(4)=F3FACE
4670 IF PSTATUS=11 AND ((P1FACE2=F1FACE) OR
     (P1FACE2=F3FACE) OR (P1FACE2=RFACE)) THEN
     HP1(4)=TFACE
4675 IF PSTATUS=11 AND ((F1FACE=F3FACE) OR
     (F1FACE=RFACE)) THEN HP1(4)=TFACE
```

```
4680 IF PSTATUS=11 AND (F3FACE=RFACE) THEN
     HP1(4)=TFACE
4685 IF PSTATUS=12 AND ((P1FACE2=F1FACE) OR
     (P1FACE2=F3FACE) OR (P1FACE2=TFACE)) THEN
     HP1(4)=RFACE
4690 IF PSTATUS=12 AND ((F1FACE=F3FACE) OR
     (F1FACE=TFACE)) THEN HP1(4)=RFACE
4695 IF PSTATUS=12 AND (F3FACE=TFACE) THEN
     HP1(4)=RFACE
4700 IF PSTATUS=13 AND ((P1FACE2=F1FACE) OR
     (P1FACE2=F2FACE) OR (P1FACE2=RFACE)) THEN
     HP1(4)=TFACE
4705 IF PSTATUS=13 AND ((F1FACE=F2FACE) OR
     (F1FACE=RFACE)) THEN HP1(4)=TFACE
4710 IF PSTATUS=13 AND (F2FACE=RFACE) THEN
     HP1(4)=TFACE
4715 IF PSTATUS=14 AND ((P1FACE2=F1FACE) OR
     (P1FACE2=F2FACE) OR (P1FACE2=TFACE)) THEN
     HP1(4)=RFACE
4720 IF PSTATUS=14 AND ((F1FACE=F2FACE) OR
     (F1FACE=TFACE)) THEN HP1(4)=RFACE
4725 IF PSTATUS=14 AND (F2FACE=TFACE) THEN
     HP1(4)=RFACE
4730 IF PSTATUS=15 AND ((P1FACE2=F1FACE) OR
     (P1FACE2=F2FACE) OR (P1FACE2=F3FACE)) THEN
     HP1(4)=RFACE
4735 IF PSTATUS=15 AND ((F1FACE=F2FACE) OR
     (F1FACE=F3FACE)) THEN HP1(4)=RFACE
4740 IF PSTATUS=15 AND (F2FACE=F3FACE) THEN
     HP1(4)=RFACE
4745 IF PSTATUS=16 AND ((P1FACE1=F3FACE) OR
     (P1FACE1=TFACE) OR (P1FACE1=RFACE)) THEN
     HP1(4)=F2FACE
4750 IF PSTATUS=16 AND ((F3FACE=TFACE) OR
     (F3FACE=RFACE)) THEN HP1(4)=F2FACE
4755 IF PSTATUS=16 AND (TFACE=RFACE) THEN
     HP1(4)=F2FACE
4760 IF PSTATUS=17 AND ((P1FACE1=F2FACE) OR
     (P1FACE1=TFACE) OR (P1FACE1=RFACE)) THEN
     HP1(4)=F3FACE
4765 IF PSTATUS=17 AND ((F2FACE=TFACE) OR
     (F2FACE=RFACE)) THEN HP1(4)=F3FACE
4770 IF PSTATUS=17 AND (TFACE=RFACE) THEN
     HP1(4)=F3FACE
```

```
4775 IF PSTATUS=18 AND ((P1FACE1=F2FACE) OR
     (P1FACE1=F3FACE) OR (P1FACE1=RFACE)) THEN
     HP1(4)=TFACE
4780 IF PSTATUS=18 AND ((F2FACE=F3FACE) OR
     (F2FACE=RFACE)) THEN HP1(4)=TFACE
4785 IF PSTATUS=18 AND (F3FACE=RFACE) THEN
     HP1(4)=TFACE
4790 IF PSTATUS=19 AND ((P1FACE1=F2FACE) OR
     (P1FACE1=F3FACE) OR (P1FACE1=TFACE)) THEN
     HP1(4)=RFACE
4795 IF PSTATUS=19 AND ((F2FACE=F3FACE) OR
     (F2FACE=TFACE)) THEN HP1(4)=RFACE
4800 IF PSTATUS=19 AND (F3FACE=TFACE) THEN
     HP1(4)=RFACE
4805 IF PSTATUS=20 AND ((P1FACE1=F1FACE) OR
     (P1FACE1=TFACE) OR (P1FACE1=RFACE)) THEN
     HP1(4)=F3FACE
4810 IF PSTATUS=20 AND ((F1FACE=TFACE) OR
     (F1FACE=RFACE)) THEN HP1(4)=F3FACE
4815 IF PSTATUS=20 AND (TFACE=RFACE) THEN
     HP1(4)=F3FACE
4820 IF PSTATUS=21 AND ((P1FACE1=F1FACE) OR
     (P1FACE1=F3FACE) OR (P1FACE1=RFACE)) THEN
     HP1(4)=TFACE
4825 IF PSTATUS=21 AND ((F1FACE=F3FACE) OR
     (F1FACE=RFACE)) THEN HP(4)=TFACE
4830 IF PSTATUS=21 AND (F3FACE=RFACE) THEN
     HP(4)=TFACE
4835 IF PSTATUS=22 AND ((P1FACE1=F1FACE) OR
     (P1FACE1=F3FACE) OR (P1FACE1=TFACE)) THEN
     HP1(4)=RFACE
4840 IF PSTATUS=22 AND ((F1FACE=F3FACE) OR
     (F1FACE=TFACE)) THEN HP1(4)=RFACE
4845 IF PSTATUS=22 AND (F3FACE=TFACE) THEN
     HP1(4)=RFACE
4850 IF PSTATUS=23 AND ((P1FACE1=F1FACE) OR
     (P1FACE1=F2FACE) OR (P1FACE1=RFACE)) THEN
     HP1(4)=TFACE
4855 IF PSTATUS=23 AND ((F1FACE=F2FACE) OR
     (F1FACE=RFACE)) THEN HP1(4)=TFACE
4860 IF PSTATUS=23 AND (F2FACE=RFACE) THEN
     HP1(4)=TFACE
```

```
4865 IF PSTATUS=24 AND ((P1FACE1=F1FACE) OR
     (P1FACE1=F2FACE) OR (P1FACE1=TFACE)) THEN
     HP1(4)=RFACE
4870 IF PSTATUS=24 AND ((F1FACE=F2FACE) OR
     (F1FACE=TFACE)) THEN HP1(4)=RFACE
4875 IF PSTATUS=24 AND (F2FACE=TFACE) THEN
     HP1(4)=RFACE
4880 IF PSTATUS=25 AND ((P1FACE1=F1FACE) OR
     (P1FACE1=F2FACE) OR (P1FACE1=F3FACE)) THEN
     HP1(4)=RFACE
4885 IF PSTATUS=25 AND ((F1FACE=F2FACE) OR
     (F1FACE=F3FACE)) THEN HP1(4)=RFACE
4890 IF PSTATUS=25 AND (F2FACE=F3FACE) THEN
     HP1(4)=RFACE

5510 'CHECK TO SEE IF COMPUTER HAS A FULL HOUSE
     (COMPUTER MUST ALREADY HAVE THREE-OF-A-KIND)
5520 IF P1STATUS=1 AND ((F2FACE=F3FACE) OR
     (F2FACE=TFACE) OR (F2FACE=RFACE)) THEN
     HP2(4)=F1FACE
5525 IF P1STATUS=1 AND ((F3FACE=TFACE) OR
     (F3FACE=RFACE)) THEN HP2(4)=F1FACE
5530 IF P1STATUS=1 AND (TFACE=RFACE) THEN
     HP2(4)=F1FACE
5535 IF P1STATUS=2 AND ((F1FACE=F3FACE) OR
     (F1FACE=TFACE) OR (F1FACE=RFACE)) THEN
     HP2(4)=F2FACE
5540 IF P1STATUS=2 AND ((F3FACE=TFACE) OR
     (F3FACE=RFACE)) THEN HP2(4)=F2FACE
5545 IF P1STATUS=2 AND (TFACE=RFACE) THEN
     HP2(4)=F2FACE
5550 IF P1STATUS=3 AND ((F1FACE=F2FACE) OR
     (F1FACE=TFACE) OR (F1FACE=RFACE)) THEN
     HP2(4)=F3FACE
5555 IF P1STATUS=3 AND ((F2FACE=TFACE) OR
     (F2FACE=RFACE)) THEN HP2(4)=F3FACE
5560 IF P1STATUS=3 AND (TFACE=RFACE) THEN
     HP2(4)=F3FACE
5565 IF PSTATUS=4 AND ((F1FACE=F2FACE) OR
     (F1FACE=F3FACE) OR (F1FACE=RFACE)) THEN
     HP2(4)=TFACE
5570 IF PSTATUS=4 AND ((F2FACE=F3FACE) OR
     (F2FACE=RFACE)) THEN HP2(4)=TFACE
```

```
5575 IF PSTATUS=4 AND (F3FACE=RFACE) THEN
     HP2(4)=TFACE
5580 IF PSTATUS=5 AND ((F1FACE=F2FACE) OR
     (F1FACE=F3FACE) OR (F1FACE=TFACE)) THEN
     HP2(4)=RFACE
5585 IF PSTATUS=5 AND ((F2FACE=F3FACE) OR
     (F2FACE=TFACE)) THEN HP2(4)=RFACE
5590 IF PSTATUS=5 AND (F3FACE=TFACE) THEN
     HP2(4)=RFACE
5595 IF PSTATUS=6 AND ((P2FACE2=F3FACE) OR
     (P2FACE2=TFACE) OR (P2FACE2=RFACE)) THEN
     HP2(4)=F2FACE
5600 IF PSTATUS=6 AND ((F3FACE=TFACE) OR
     (F3FACE=RFACE)) THEN HP2(4)=F2FACE
5605 IF PSTATUS=6 AND (TFACE=RFACE) THEN
     HP2(4)=F2FACE
5610 IF PSTATUS=7 AND ((P2FACE2=F2FACE) OR
     (P2FACE2=RFACE) OR (P2FACE2=TFACE)) THEN
     HP2(4)=F3FACE
5615 IF PSTATUS=7 AND ((F2FACE=RFACE) OR
     (F2FACE=TFACE)) THEN HP2(4)=F3FACE
5620 IF PSTATUS=7 AND (RFACE=TFACE) THEN
     HP2(4)=F3FACE
5625 IF PSTATUS=8 AND ((P2FACE2=F2FACE) OR
     (P2FACE2=F3FACE) OR (P2FACE2=RFACE)) THEN
     HP2(4)=TFACE
5630 IF PSTATUS=8 AND ((F2FACE=F3FACE) OR
     (F2FACE=RFACE)) THEN HP2(4)=TFACE
5635 IF PSTATUS=8 AND (F3FACE=RFACE) THEN
     HP2(4)=TFACE
5640 IF PSTATUS=9 AND ((P2FACE2=F2FACE) OR
     (P2FACE2=F3FACE) OR (P2FACE2=TFACE)) THEN
     HP2(4)=RFACE
5645 IF PSTATUS=9 AND ((F2FACE=F3FACE) OR
     (F2FACE=TFACE)) THEN HP2(4)=RFACE
5650 IF PSTATUS=9 AND (F3FACE=TFACE) THEN
     HP2(4)=RFACE
5655 IF PSTATUS=10 AND ((P2FACE2=F1FACE) AND
     (P2FACE2=TFACE) AND (P2FACE2=RFACE)) THEN
     HP2(4)=F3FACE
5660 IF PSTATUS=10 AND ((F1FACE=TFACE) AND
     (F1FACE=RFACE)) THEN HP2(4)=F3FACE
5665 IF PSTATUS=10 AND (TFACE=RFACE) THEN
     HP2(4)=F3FACE
```

```
5670 IF PSTATUS=11 AND ((P2FACE2=F1FACE) OR
     (P2FACE2=F3FACE) OR (P2FACE2=RFACE)) THEN
     HP2(4)=TFACE
5675 IF PSTATUS=11 AND ((F1FACE=F3FACE) OR
     (F1FACE=RFACE)) THEN HP2(4)=TFACE
5680 IF PSTATUS=11 AND (F3FACE=RFACE) THEN
     HP2(4)=TFACE
5685 IF PSTATUS=12 AND ((P2FACE2=F1FACE) OR
     (P2FACE2=F3FACE) OR (P2FACE2=TFACE)) THEN
     HP2(4)=RFACE
5690 IF PSTATUS=12 AND ((F1FACE=F3FACE) OR
     (F1FACE=TFACE)) THEN HP2(4)=RFACE
5695 IF PSTATUS=12 AND (F3FACE=TFACE) THEN
     HP2(4)=RFACE
5700 IF PSTATUS=13 AND ((P2FACE2=F1FACE) OR
     (P2FACE2=F2FACE) OR (P2FACE2=RFACE)) THEN
     HP2(4)=TFACE
5705 IF PSTATUS=13 AND ((F1FACE=F2FACE) OR
     (F1FACE=RFACE)) THEN HP2(4)=TFACE
5710 IF PSTATUS=13 AND (F2FACE=RFACE) THEN
     HP2(4)=TFACE
5715 IF PSTATUS=14 AND ((P2FACE2=F1FACE) OR
     (P2FACE2=F2FACE) OR (P2FACE2=TFACE)) THEN
     HP2(4)=RFACE
5720 IF PSTATUS=14 AND ((F1FACE=F2FACE) OR
     (F1FACE=TFACE)) THEN HP2(4)=RFACE
5725 IF PSTATUS=14 AND (F2FACE=TFACE) THEN
     HP2(4)=RFACE
5730 IF PSTATUS=15 AND ((P2FACE2=F1FACE) OR
     (P2FACE2=F2FACE) OR (P2FACE2=F3FACE)) THEN
     HP2(4)=RFACE
5735 IF PSTATUS=15 AND ((F1FACE=F2FACE) OR
     (F1FACE=F3FACE)) THEN HP2(4)=RFACE
5740 IF PSTATUS=15 AND (F2FACE=F3FACE) THEN
     HP2(4)=RFACE
5745 IF PSTATUS=16 AND ((P2FACE1=F3FACE) OR
     (P2FACE1=TFACE) OR (P2FACE1=RFACE)) THEN
     HP2(4)=F2FACE
5750 IF PSTATUS=16 AND ((F3FACE=TFACE) OR
     (F3FACE=RFACE)) THEN HP2(4)=F2FACE
5755 IF PSTATUS=16 AND (TFACE=RFACE) THEN
     HP2(4)=F2FACE
```

```
5760 IF PSTATUS=17 AND ((P2FACE1=F2FACE) OR
     (P2FACE1=TFACE) OR (P2FACE1=RFACE)) THEN
     HP2(4)=F3FACE
5765 IF PSTATUS=17 AND ((F2FACE=TFACE) OR
     (F2FACE=RFACE)) THEN HP2(4)=F3FACE
5770 IF PSTATUS=17 AND (TFACE=RFACE) THEN
     HP2(4)=F3FACE
5775 IF PSTATUS=18 AND ((P2FACE1=F2FACE) OR
     (P2FACE1=F3FACE) OR (P2FACE1=RFACE)) THEN
     HP2(4)=TFACE
5780 IF PSTATUS=18 AND ((F2FACE=F3FACE) OR
     (F2FACE=RFACE)) THEN HP2(4)=TFACE
5785 IF PSTATUS=18 AND (F3FACE=RFACE) THEN
     HP2(4)=TFACE
5790 IF PSTATUS=19 AND ((P2FACE1=F2FACE) OR
     (P2FACE1=F3FACE) OR (P2FACE1=TFACE)) THEN
     HP2(4)=RFACE
5795 IF PSTATUS=19 AND ((F2FACE=F3FACE) OR
     (F2FACE=TFACE)) THEN HP2(4)=RFACE
5800 IF PSTATUS=19 AND (F3FACE=TFACE) THEN
     HP2(4)=RFACE
5805 IF PSTATUS=20 AND ((P2FACE1=F1FACE) OR
     (P2FACE1=TFACE) OR (P2FACE1=RFACE)) THEN
     HP2(4)=F3FACE
5810 IF PSTATUS=20 AND ((F1FACE=TFACE) OR
     (F1FACE=RFACE)) THEN HP2(4)=F3FACE
5815 IF PSTATUS=20 AND (TFACE=RFACE) THEN
     HP2(4)=F3FACE
5820 IF PSTATUS=21 AND ((P2FACE1=F1FACE) OR
     (P2FACE1=F3FACE) OR (P2FACE1=RFACE)) THEN
     HP2(4)=TFACE
5825 IF PSTATUS=21 AND ((F1FACE=F3FACE) OR
     (F1FACE=RFACE)) THEN HP(4)=TFACE
5830 IF PSTATUS=21 AND (F3FACE=RFACE) THEN
     HP(4)=TFACE
5835 IF PSTATUS=22 AND ((P2FACE1=F1FACE) OR
     (P2FACE1=F3FACE) OR (P2FACE1=TFACE)) THEN
     HP2(4)=RFACE
5840 IF PSTATUS=22 AND ((F1FACE=F3FACE) OR
     (F1FACE=TFACE)) THEN HP2(4)=RFACE
5845 IF PSTATUS=22 AND (F3FACE=TFACE) THEN
     HP2(4)=RFACE
```

```
5850 IF PSTATUS=23 AND ((P2FACE1=F1FACE) OR
     (P2FACE1=F2FACE) OR (P2FACE1=RFACE)) THEN
     HP2(4)=TFACE
5855 IF PSTATUS=23 AND ((F1FACE=F2FACE) OR
     (F1FACE=RFACE)) THEN HP2(4)=TFACE
5860 IF PSTATUS=23 AND (F2FACE=RFACE) THEN
     HP2(4)=TFACE
5865 IF PSTATUS=24 AND ((P2FACE1=F1FACE) OR
     (P2FACE1=F2FACE) OR (P2FACE1=TFACE)) THEN
     HP2(4)=RFACE
5870 IF PSTATUS=24 AND ((F1FACE=F2FACE) OR
     (F1FACE=TFACE)) THEN HP2(4)=RFACE
5875 IF PSTATUS=24 AND (F2FACE=TFACE) THEN
     HP2(4)=RFACE
5880 IF PSTATUS=25 AND ((P2FACE1=F1FACE) OR
     (P2FACE1=F2FACE) OR (P2FACE1=F3FACE)) THEN
     HP2(4)=RFACE
5885 IF PSTATUS=25 AND ((F1FACE=F2FACE) OR
     (F1FACE=F3FACE)) THEN HP2(4)=RFACE
5890 IF PSTATUS=25 AND (F2FACE=F3FACE) THEN
     HP2(4)=RFACE
```

Next up: four-of-a-kind, or all four cards of the same rank. Although standard poker five-card hands contain $\binom{13}{1}\binom{4}{4}\binom{12}{1}\binom{4}{1} = 624$ possible four-of-a-kind hands, we don't have to check for each unique hand. Instead, we need to examine possible sets of four cards among the seven, making sure to include at least one hole card in the set (since if we find a four-of-a-kind *exclusively* among the five community cards, the set benefits both the player and the computer equally). Take a look at the possibilities below; for simplicity's sake, the seven cards on the table are labeled with the letters "A" to "G":

Card Rank	FACE1	FACE2	F1FACE	F2FACE
Label	"A"	"B"	"C"	"D"

Card Rank	F3FACE	TFACE	RFACE
Label	"E"	"F"	"G"

Relevant Sets:	ABCD	ACDE	BCDE
	ABCE	ACDF	BCDF
	ABCF	ACDG	BCDG
	ABCG	ACEF	BCEF
	ABDE	ACEG	BCEG
	ABDF	ACFG	BCFG
	ABDG	ADEF	BDEF
	ABEF	ADEG	BDEG
	ABEG	AEFG	BEFG
	ABFG	ADFG	BDFG

Irrelevant Sets:	CDEF
	CDEG
	CEFG
	CDFG
	DEFG

Combinatorially, this works out to thirty "relevant" fours-of-a-kind, and five "irrelevant" card sets which should not be coded. Mathematically, $\binom{7}{4} - \binom{5}{4} = 35 - 5 = 30$.

Back to the program: If a four-of-a-kind is found, the associated **HP** array should be assigned to the card set's rank. The search begins with the player's cards, with the computer's then following suit; but realize that all thirty combinations are purposely *not* listed below. You should be able to take up the cause and finish the coding yourself, if you are sufficiently inclined.

```
4010 'CHECK TO SEE IF YOU HAVE FOUR-OF-A-KIND
4020 IF (P1FACE1=P1FACE2) AND (P1FACE1=F1FACE) AND
     (P1FACE1=F2FACE) THEN HP1(3)=F2FACE
4030 IF (P1FACE1=P1FACE2) AND (P1FACE1=F1FACE) AND
     (P1FACE1=F3FACE) THEN HP1(3)=F3FACE
4040 IF (P1FACE1=P1FACE2) AND (P1FACE1=F1FACE) AND
     (P1FACE1=TFACE) THEN HP1(3)=TFACE
4050 IF (P1FACE1=P1FACE2) AND (P1FACE1=F1FACE) AND
     (P1FACE1=RFACE) THEN HP1(3)=RFACE
4060 IF (P1FACE1=P1FACE2) AND (P1FACE1=F2FACE) AND
     (P1FACE1=F3FACE) THEN HP1(3)=F3FACE
4070 IF (P1FACE1=P1FACE2) AND (P1FACE1=F2FACE) AND
     (P1FACE1=TFACE) THEN HP1(3)=TFACE
4080 IF (P1FACE1=P1FACE2) AND (P1FACE1=F2FACE) AND
     (P1FACE1=RFACE) THEN HP1(3)=RFACE



4200 'CHECK TO SEE IF COMPUTER HAS FOUR-OF-A-KIND
4220 IF (P2FACE1=P2FACE2) AND (P2FACE1=F1FACE) AND
     (P2FACE1=F2FACE) THEN HP2(3)=F2FACE
4230 IF (P2FACE1=P2FACE2) AND (P2FACE1=F1FACE) AND
     (P2FACE1=F3FACE) THEN HP2(3)=F3FACE
4240 IF (P2FACE1=P2FACE2) AND (P2FACE1=F1FACE) AND
     (P2FACE1=TFACE) THEN HP2(3)=TFACE
4250 IF (P2FACE1=P2FACE2) AND (P2FACE1=F1FACE) AND
     (P2FACE1=RFACE) THEN HP2(3)=RFACE
4260 IF (P2FACE1=P2FACE2) AND (P2FACE1=F2FACE) AND
     (P2FACE1=F3FACE) THEN HP2(3)=F3FACE
4270 IF (P2FACE1=P2FACE2) AND (P2FACE1=F2FACE) AND
     (P2FACE1=TFACE) THEN HP2(3)=TFACE
4280 IF (P2FACE1=P2FACE2) AND (P2FACE1=F2FACE) AND
     (P2FACE1=RFACE) THEN HP2(3)=RFACE
```

Although this doesn't exhaust the types of hands (more on that later), looking for flushes is the last card search we'll perform. There are $\binom{7}{5} = 21$ possible sets of five cards among seven—but one of those possible sets, the five community cards, can safely be ignored, since if all five community cards have their own, non-overlapping-with-any-hole-cards suit, the community flush benefits the computer and player equally—and thus comes out in the wash.

```
6000 'SEARCH #6: A FLUSH
6002 'THERE ARE (7 CHOOSE 5) = 21 POSSIBILITIES,
     BUT REALLY 20--ONE POSSIBILITY DOESN'T COUNT,
     THE FIVE COMMUNITY CARDS HAVING SAME SUIT
6005 'CHECK TO SEE IF YOU HAVE A FLUSH (FIVE CARDS
     = SAME SUIT); IF SO, INPUT A 1 PLUS ANOTHER 1
     -- IF YOU HAD A HIGH HOLE CARD
6010 IF ((P1SUIT1=P1SUIT2) AND (P1SUIT1=F1SUIT)
     AND (P1SUIT1=F2SUIT) AND (P1SUIT1=F3SUIT))
     THEN HP1(5)=1+HP1(10)
6015 IF ((P1SUIT1=P1SUIT2) AND (P1SUIT1=F1SUIT)
     AND (P1SUIT1=F2SUIT) AND (P1SUIT1=TSUIT))
     THEN HP1(5)=1+HP1(10)
6020 IF ((P1SUIT1=P1SUIT2) AND (P1SUIT1=F1SUIT)
     AND (P1SUIT1=F2SUIT) AND (P1SUIT1=RSUIT))
     THEN HP1(5)=1+HP1(10)
6025 IF ((P1SUIT1=P1SUIT2) AND (P1SUIT1=F1SUIT)
     AND (P1SUIT1=TSUIT) AND (P1SUIT1=RSUIT)) THEN
     HP1(5)=1+HP1(10)
6030 IF ((P1SUIT1=P1SUIT2) AND (P1SUIT1=F1SUIT)
     AND (P1SUIT1=F3SUIT) AND (P1SUIT1=TSUIT))
     THEN HP1(5)=1+HP1(10)
6035 IF ((P1SUIT1=P1SUIT2) AND (P1SUIT1=F1SUIT)
     AND (P1SUIT1=F3SUIT) AND (P1SUIT1=RSUIT))
     THEN HP1(5)=1+HP1(10)
6040 IF ((P1SUIT1=P1SUIT2) AND (P1SUIT1=F2SUIT)
     AND (P1SUIT1=F3SUIT) AND (P1SUIT1=TSUIT))
     THEN HP1(5)=1+HP1(10)
6045 IF ((P1SUIT1=P1SUIT2) AND (P1SUIT1=F2SUIT)
     AND (P1SUIT1=F3SUIT) AND (P1SUIT1=RSUIT))
     THEN HP1(5)=1+HP1(10)
```

```
6050 IF ((P1SUIT1=P1SUIT2) AND (P1SUIT1=F3SUIT)
     AND (P1SUIT1=TSUIT) AND (P1SUIT1=RSUIT)) THEN
     HP1(5)=1+HP1(10)
6055 IF ((P1SUIT1=P1SUIT2) AND (P1SUIT1=F2SUIT)
     AND (P1SUIT1=TSUIT) AND (P1SUIT1=RSUIT)) THEN
     HP1(5)=1+HP1(10)
6060 IF ((P1SUIT1=F1SUIT) AND (P1SUIT1=F2SUIT) AND
     (P1SUIT1=F3SUIT) AND (P1SUIT1=TSUIT)) THEN
     HP1(5)=1+HP1(10)
6065 IF ((P1SUIT1=F1SUIT) AND (P1SUIT1=F2SUIT) AND
     (P1SUIT1=F3SUIT) AND (P1SUIT1=RSUIT)) THEN
     HP1(5)=1+HP1(10)
6070 IF ((P1SUIT1=F1SUIT) AND (P1SUIT1=F2SUIT) AND
     (P1SUIT1=TSUIT) AND (P1SUIT1=RSUIT)) THEN
     HP1(5)=1+HP1(10)
6075 IF ((P1SUIT1=F1SUIT) AND (P1SUIT1=F3SUIT) AND
     (P1SUIT1=TSUIT) AND (P1SUIT1=RSUIT)) THEN
     HP1(5)=1+HP1(10)
6080 IF ((P1SUIT1=F2SUIT) AND (P1SUIT1=F3SUIT) AND
     (P1SUIT1=TSUIT) AND (P1SUIT1=RSUIT)) THEN
     HP1(5)=1+HP1(10)
6085 IF ((P1SUIT2=F1SUIT) AND (P1SUIT2=F2SUIT) AND
     (P1SUIT2=F3SUIT) AND (P1SUIT2=TSUIT)) THEN
     HP1(5)=1+HP1(10)
6090 IF ((P1SUIT2=F1SUIT) AND (P1SUIT2=F2SUIT) AND
     (P1SUIT2=F3SUIT) AND (P1SUIT2=RSUIT)) THEN
     HP1(5)=1+HP1(10)
6100 IF ((P1SUIT2=F1SUIT) AND (P1SUIT2=F2SUIT) AND
     (P1SUIT2=TSUIT) AND (P1SUIT2=RSUIT)) THEN
     HP1(5)=1+HP1(10)
6110 IF ((P1SUIT2=F1SUIT) AND (P1SUIT2=F2SUIT) AND
     (P1SUIT2=TSUIT) AND (P1SUIT2=RSUIT)) THEN
     HP1(5)=1+HP1(10)
6120 IF ((P1SUIT2=F1SUIT) AND (P1SUIT2=F3SUIT) AND
     (P1SUIT2=TSUIT) AND (P1SUIT2=RSUIT)) THEN
     HP1(5)=1+HP1(10)
6130 IF ((P1SUIT2=F2SUIT) AND (P1SUIT2=F3SUIT) AND
     (P1SUIT2=TSUIT) AND (P1SUIT2=RSUIT)) THEN
     HP1(5)=1+HP1(10)

6205 'CHECK TO SEE IF COMPUTER HAS A FLUSH (FIVE
     CARDS = SAME SUIT); IF SO, INPUT A 1 PLUS
     ANOTHER 1 -- IF COMPUTER HAD A HIGH HOLE CARD
```

```
6210 IF ((P2SUIT1=P2SUIT2) AND (P2SUIT1=F1SUIT)
     AND (P2SUIT1=F2SUIT) AND (P2SUIT1=F3SUIT))
     THEN HP2(5)=1+HP2(10)
6215 IF ((P2SUIT1=P2SUIT2) AND (P2SUIT1=F1SUIT)
     AND (P2SUIT1=F2SUIT) AND (P2SUIT1=TSUIT))
     THEN HP2(5)=1+HP2(10)
6220 IF ((P2SUIT1=P2SUIT2) AND (P2SUIT1=F1SUIT)
     AND (P2SUIT1=F2SUIT) AND (P2SUIT1=RSUIT))
     THEN HP2(5)=1+HP2(10)
6225 IF ((P2SUIT1=P2SUIT2) AND (P2SUIT1=F1SUIT)
     AND (P2SUIT1=TSUIT) AND (P2SUIT1=RSUIT)) THEN
     HP2(5)=1+HP2(10)
6230 IF ((P2SUIT1=P2SUIT2) AND (P2SUIT1=F1SUIT)
     AND (P2SUIT1=F3SUIT) AND (P2SUIT1=TSUIT))
     THEN HP2(5)=1+HP2(10)
6235 IF ((P2SUIT1=P2SUIT2) AND (P2SUIT1=F1SUIT)
     AND (P2SUIT1=F3SUIT) AND (P2SUIT1=RSUIT))
     THEN HP2(5)=1+HP2(10)
6240 IF ((P2SUIT1=P2SUIT2) AND (P2SUIT1=F2SUIT)
     AND (P2SUIT1=F3SUIT) AND (P2SUIT1=TSUIT))
     THEN HP2(5)=1+HP2(10)
6245 IF ((P2SUIT1=P2SUIT2) AND (P2SUIT1=F2SUIT)
     AND (P2SUIT1=F3SUIT) AND (P2SUIT1=RSUIT))
     THEN HP2(5)=1+HP2(10)
6250 IF ((P2SUIT1=P2SUIT2) AND (P2SUIT1=F3SUIT)
     AND (P2SUIT1=TSUIT) AND (P2SUIT1=RSUIT)) THEN
     HP2(5)=1+HP2(10)
6255 IF ((P2SUIT1=P2SUIT2) AND (P2SUIT1=F2SUIT)
     AND (P2SUIT1=TSUIT) AND (P2SUIT1=RSUIT)) THEN
     HP2(5)=1+HP2(10)
6260 IF ((P2SUIT1=F1SUIT) AND (P2SUIT1=F2SUIT) AND
     (P2SUIT1=F3SUIT) AND (P2SUIT1=TSUIT)) THEN
     HP2(5)=1+HP2(10)
6265 IF ((P2SUIT1=F1SUIT) AND (P2SUIT1=F2SUIT) AND
     (P2SUIT1=F3SUIT) AND (P2SUIT1=RSUIT)) THEN
     HP2(5)=1+HP2(10)
6270 IF ((P2SUIT1=F1SUIT) AND (P2SUIT1=F2SUIT) AND
     (P2SUIT1=TSUIT) AND (P2SUIT1=RSUIT)) THEN
     HP2(5)=1+HP2(10)
6275 IF ((P2SUIT1=F1SUIT) AND (P2SUIT1=F3SUIT) AND
     (P2SUIT1=TSUIT) AND (P2SUIT1=RSUIT)) THEN
     HP2(5)=1+HP2(10)
```

```
6280 IF ((P2SUIT1=F2SUIT) AND (P2SUIT1=F3SUIT) AND
     (P2SUIT1=TSUIT) AND (P2SUIT1=RSUIT)) THEN
     HP2(5)=1+HP2(10)
6285 IF ((P2SUIT2=F1SUIT) AND (P2SUIT2=F2SUIT) AND
     (P2SUIT2=F3SUIT) AND (P2SUIT2=TSUIT)) THEN
     HP2(5)=1+HP2(10)
6290 IF ((P2SUIT2=F1SUIT) AND (P2SUIT2=F2SUIT) AND
     (P2SUIT2=F3SUIT) AND (P2SUIT2=RSUIT)) THEN
     HP2(5)=1+HP2(10)
6200 IF ((P2SUIT2=F1SUIT) AND (P2SUIT2=F2SUIT) AND
     (P2SUIT2=TSUIT) AND (P2SUIT2=RSUIT)) THEN
     HP2(5)=1+HP2(10)
6210 IF ((P2SUIT2=F1SUIT) AND (P2SUIT2=F2SUIT) AND
     (P2SUIT2=TSUIT) AND (P2SUIT2=RSUIT)) THEN
     HP2(5)=1+HP2(10)
6220 IF ((P2SUIT2=F1SUIT) AND (P2SUIT2=F3SUIT) AND
     (P2SUIT2=TSUIT) AND (P2SUIT2=RSUIT)) THEN
     HP2(5)=1+HP2(10)
6230 IF ((P2SUIT2=F2SUIT) AND (P2SUIT2=F3SUIT) AND
     (P2SUIT2=TSUIT) AND (P2SUIT2=RSUIT)) THEN
     HP2(5)=1+HP2(10)
```

Now it's time to figure out who won the hand. First, since all possible bets have been taken, the computer is required to reveal its hand on-screen.

The **HP** arrays' elements are assigned to hand ranks, but in descending order. Since a **FOR/NEXT** loop cycles through the **HP** arrays in ascending order, the highest-ranked hands are caught first—and once a ranked hand of the player is termed greater than a hand of the computer (or vice versa), the hand is over, a winner is declared (unless it's a tie, which is instead displayed on the screen), and pot winnings are distributed appropriately.

```
9000 'DETERMINE THE WINNER OF THE HAND--BUT FIRST
     SHOW THE COMPUTER'S HOLE CARDS
9001 PRINT "COMPUTER'S HOLE CARDS
     ARE:":PRINT"***************"
9002 FOR SEARCHS=1 TO 4:FOR SEARCHF=1 TO 13
```

```
9004 IF(DEALT(SEARCHF,SEARCHS)=3 OR
     DEALT(SEARCHF,SEARCHS)=4) THEN PRINT
     CARD$(SEARCHF,SEARCHS)
9006 NEXT SEARCHF:NEXT SEARCHS
9010 FOR Q=1 TO 10
9020 IF HP1(Q)>HP2(Q) THEN PRINT"YOU TAKE THE POT
     WITH A ";TYPE$(Q):GOTO 9060
9030 IF HP2(Q)>HP1(Q) THEN PRINT"COMPUTER TAKES
     THE POT WITH A ";TYPE$(Q):GOTO 9062
9040 IF (HP1(Q)=HP2(Q) AND HP1(Q)<>0) THEN
     PRINT"SPLIT POT":GOTO 9064
9050 NEXT Q
9060 YOURBANK=YOURBANK+POTAMOUNT:POTAMOUNT=0:FOR
     A=1 TO 4:FOR B=1 TO 13:DEALT(B,A)=0:NEXT
     B:NEXT A:GOTO 9100
9062 COMPBANK=COMPBANK+POTAMOUNT:POTAMOUNT=0:FOR
     A=1 TO 4:FOR B=1 TO 13:DEALT(B,A)=0:NEXT
     B:NEXT A:GOTO 9100
9064 YOURBANK=YOURBANK+(POTAMOUNT/2):COMPBANK=
     COMPBANK+(POTAMOUNT/2):POTAMOUNT=0:FOR A=1 TO
     4:FOR B=1 TO 13:DEALT(B,A)=0:NEXT B:NEXT
     A:GOTO 9100
9100 RETURN
```

After the hole cards are dealt, but before any bets are taken, the player has the option of folding. A hand folded means an entire pot lost to the computer. If the player has fewer than fifty dollars remaining then the game is over, since the buy-in for additional hands cannot be covered.

```
9500 'SUBROUTINE FOR FOLDING YOUR HAND
9510 PRINT"YOU HAVE FOLDED YOUR HAND; THE COMPUTER
     GETS ALL THE CHIPS IN THE POT."
9520 COMPBANK=COMPBANK+POTAMOUNT
9530 IF (YOURBANK-50)<50 THEN PRINT"You don't have
     enough chips to continue. Nice game, player."
     :END
9540 IF (COMPBANK-50)<50 THEN PRINT"Computer
     doesn't have enough chips to continue. You
     have won!":END
9550 GOTO 200
```

Several times during the course of a hand, the player is queried for a bet. The computer bets in turn, and bets in a very simple manner: if the computer's bankroll exceeds the player's, then it bets half of its current holdings; otherwise, the computer goes all in. The computer pays no attention to its hole cards, the community cards, the player's prospective hole cards, or any other extraneous factors when placing bets.

```
9600 'SUBROUTINE FOR GETTING YOUR BET AMOUNT
9700 PRINT:PRINT"You have
     $";YOURBANK;".":INPUT"How much do you wish to
     bet";YOURBET
9710 IF YOURBET>YOURBANK THEN 9700
9715 IF YOURBET<0 THEN 9700
9716 POTAMOUNT=POTAMOUNT+YOURBET:YOURBANK=
     YOURBANK-YOURBET
9717 COMPBET=0:IF YOURBET>COMPBANK THEN
     COMPBET=COMPBANK ELSE COMPBET=INT(COMPBANK/2)
9718 PRINT"The computer has bet
     $";COMPBET:POTAMOUNT=POTAMOUNT+COMPBET:COMPBA
     NK=COMPBANK-COMPBET
9720 RETURN
```

Once the first set of bets are placed, all of the community cards are shown (unlike in real hold'em, where the flop, turn, and river are revealed successively, with betting opportunities in between). Multiple **FOR/NEXT** loops take care of displaying the community cards on the screen.

Afterwards, the player is queried for a bet, and the computer places one as well; the code here is very similar to the placing-bets code above.

```
9800 'SUBROUTINE FOR FINDING AND REVEALING THE
     FLOP, TURN, AND RIVER (ALL AT ONCE, UNLIKE IN
     ACTUAL HOLD 'EM) AS WELL AS PLACING BETS
9810 GOSUB 2000
9812 PRINT "YOUR HOLE CARDS:     ";
9814 FOR SEARCHS=1 TO 4:FOR SEARCHF=1 TO 13
```

```
9816 IF (DEALT(SEARCHF,SEARCHS)=1 OR
     DEALT(SEARCHF,SEARCHS)=2) THEN PRINT
     CARD$(SEARCHF,SEARCHS),
9818 NEXT SEARCHF:NEXT SEARCHS
9820 PRINT:PRINT "THE FLOP IS
     ":PRINT"*******************"
9830 FOR SEARCHS=1 TO 4:FOR SEARCHF=1 TO 13
9840 IF (DEALT(SEARCHF,SEARCHS)=10 OR
     DEALT(SEARCHF,SEARCHS)=11 OR
     DEALT(SEARCHF,SEARCHS)=12) THEN PRINT
     CARD$(SEARCHF,SEARCHS)
9850 NEXT SEARCHF:NEXT SEARCHS
9855 PRINT:PRINT "THE TURN IS
     ":PRINT"*******************"
9860 FOR SEARCHS=1 TO 4:FOR SEARCHF=1 TO 13
9870 IF DEALT(SEARCHF,SEARCHS)=20 THEN PRINT
     CARD$(SEARCHF,SEARCHS)
9880 NEXT SEARCHF:NEXT SEARCHS
9890 PRINT:PRINT "THE RIVER IS
     ":PRINT"*******************"
9900 FOR SEARCHS=1 TO 4:FOR SEARCHF=1 TO 13
9910 IF DEALT(SEARCHF,SEARCHS)=30 THEN PRINT
     CARD$(SEARCHF,SEARCHS)
9920 NEXT SEARCHF:NEXT SEARCHS
9940 PRINT "How much to bet (anywhere from $0 to
     $";YOURBANK;")";:INPUT YOURBET
9950 IF YOURBET<0 THEN 9940
9955 IF YOURBET>YOURBANK THEN 9940
9958 POTAMOUNT=POTAMOUNT+YOURBET:YOURBANK=
     YOURBANK-YOURBET
9960 COMPBET=0:IF YOURBET>COMPBANK THEN
     COMPBET=COMPBANK ELSE COMPBET=INT(COMPBANK/2)
9962 PRINT"The computer has bet
     $";COMPBET:POTAMOUNT=POTAMOUNT+COMPBET:COMPBA
     NK=COMPBANK-COMPBET
```

Finally (at long last!), the program checks to see who won the pot—and if the player or the computer consequently busted out.

```
9970 'CHECK TO SEE WHO WINS POT
9975 GOSUB 3000
```

```
9980 'CHECK TO SEE IF THE GAME'S ALL OVER FOR YOU-
     -OR THE COMPUTER
9982 IF (YOURBANK-50)<50 THEN PRINT"You don't have
     enough chips to continue. Nice game, player."
     :END
9984 IF (COMPBANK-50)<50 THEN PRINT"Computer
     doesn't have enough chips to continue. You
     have won!":END
9985 FOR A=1 TO 4:FOR B=1 TO 13:DEALT(B,A)=0:NEXT
     B:NEXT A
9986 NEWHAND=1
9990 RETURN
```

• • •

When sketching out improvements to POKER.BAS, there are four key areas to consider.

(1) All possible ranked poker hands are not, as of now, being checked by the program. For instance, not all sets of two pairs will be accounted for, since the pairs' algorithm currently only checks for pairs that have at least one hole card in the mix. Also, not all possible combinations of a four-of-a-kind are coded. In addition, straights and straight flushes (including the king of them all, the royal flush) won't register a peep from the program. The straight is the most complex of all searches because you must first sort the ranks in order, and then determine if there are five cards that rank successively (i.e., with no gaps in between). Hint: Re-familiarize yourself with the bubble sorting technique presented earlier.

(2) Many liberties were taken with hold'em rules. For instance, varying betting order, big and small blinds (bet amounts), chip denominations, presentation of community cards, and the like are either not standard or not included in the code. Improving the program certainly means a much stricter adherence to

traditional hold'em rules. In addition, only heads-up play is permitted; it is complicated, but not impossible, to set a table with more than one computerized opponent.

(3) The computer's betting scheme needs to be much more reflective of a live human being's. Right now, the computer places bets irrespective of the cards on the table.

(4) Graphics would spice things up. In PART 2: GRAPHICS-AND-TEXT PROGRAMS, we will examine graphical techniques in detail. Perhaps then you'll arrive at some fruitful ideas.

●●

● PART 2: GRAPHICS-AND-TEXT PROGRAMS ●

●●

Introduction to Graphics
LOAD "INTROGR.BAS"

Ok

RUN_

GW-BASIC has a number of graphics options. Before really delving into graphics-themed programs, run
INTROGR.BAS to see the basics.

• • •

It's best that we examine the code in segments.

• • •

INTROGR.BAS

Effectively, **INTROGR.BAS** is a (slightly interactive)
slideshow of some basic graphics manipulations. Right
away, the screen is set to **SCREEN 0**—a default text-only
mode. However, the user is asked which screen—**SCREEN
7** (lower resolution graphics) or **SCREEN 9** (higher resolution graphics)—in which to run the slideshow. Pay attention to the maximum number of pixels on each row (given
by **MAXX**) and column (given by **MAXY**) in lines **5** and **6**.
Although these two screens are not the only two graphics
modes available, they are by far the most utilized in the
book's graphics-themed programs.

```
0 KEY OFF:SCREEN 9:SCREEN 0:COLOR 15,0:CLS
3 PRINT"INTRODUCTION TO BASIC GRAPHICS"
4 INPUT"SCREEN 7 OR 9";SCR
```

```
5 IF SCR=7 THEN MAXX=320:MAXY=200
6 IF SCR=9 THEN MAXX=640:MAXY=350
7 IF SCR<7 OR SCR>9 THEN 0
```

The first demo: a blue dot, placed by the **PSET** statement, quickly flashes through every available pixel of screen space. Each time the blue dot is placed, the **PRESET** statement, after a short **PAUSE**, deletes it. By pressing the + or − keys, you can cycle through the available colors for the dot (of which there are fifteen).

```
10 SCREEN SCR:COLOR 15,0:CLS
11 'SEE A BLUE DOT MOVE THROUGH SCREEN
13 FOR Y=1 TO MAXY
15 FOR X=1 TO MAXX
20 PSET(X,Y),C
21 I$=INKEY$
22 IF I$=CHR$(27) THEN 50
24 IF I$="+" THEN C=C+1
25 IF I$="-" THEN C=C-1
26 IF C<1 THEN C=15
27 IF C>15 THEN C=1
29 FOR PAUSE=1 TO 50:NEXT PAUSE
30 PRESET(X,Y)
31 LOCATE 25,1:PRINT MAXX;" by ";MAXY
32 LOCATE 25,22:PRINT"(";X;",";Y;")",";C
35 NEXT X
40 NEXT Y
```

Next demo: a circle grows and shrinks and grows and shrinks and.... The **CIRCLE** statement handles the heavy lifting here, depending on a **FOR/NEXT** loop to change **SIZE**. Analogous to the moving dot, tapping + or − changes the circle's color.

```
50 CLS
60 'THE CIRCLE FUNCTION - BIGGER AND SMALLER
65 C=9
68 FOR LOOP=1 TO 10
70 FOR SIZE=1 TO 50
80 CIRCLE(100,100),SIZE,C
```

```
81 I$=INKEY$
82 IF I$=CHR$(27) THEN 200
84 IF I$="+" THEN C=C+1
85 IF I$="-" THEN C=C-1
86 IF C<1 THEN C=15
87 IF C>15 THEN C=1
90 FOR PAUSE=1 TO 50:NEXT PAUSE
100 CLS
110 NEXT SIZE
120 FOR SIZE=50 TO 1 STEP -1
130 CIRCLE(100,100),SIZE,C
141 I$=INKEY$
142 IF I$=CHR$(27) THEN 200
143 IF I$="+" THEN C=C+1
144 IF I$="-" THEN C=C-1
145 IF C<1 THEN C=15
147 IF C>15 THEN C=1
150 FOR PAUSE=1 TO 50:NEXT PAUSE
160 CLS
170 NEXT SIZE
180 NEXT LOOP
```

The third demo focuses on the **DRAW** statement which, unsurprisingly, permits lines to be drawn on-screen. From whatever position the cursor starts at—the **PSET** statement below centers the cursor at **(50,50)**—lines are constructed in each of eight possible directions, all separated by forty-five degree angles. (This bares the faintest resemblance to the famed Turtle of the LOGO programming language.)

After a blue octagon is sketched out, the **PAINT** statement fills the *enclosed* area with a single color, as long as the boarder of the shape is of a uniform color (in this case, the boarder is of color **9**: i.e., blue).

```
200 'The DRAW statement
205 CLS
210 PRINT"DRAW can move up, down, left, right, or
    diagonally:"
215 PSET(50,50),9
220 DRAW"U10 E10 R10 F10 D10 G10 L10 H10 U10"
```

```
230 LOCATE 15,1:PRINT"Press <ESC> to continue..."
240 IF INKEY$=CHR$(27) THEN GOTO 241 ELSE GOTO 240
241 LOCATE 20,1:PRINT"And PAINT will fill an en
    closed area."
242 PAINT(55,51),15,9
244 FOR PAUSE=1 TO 15000:NEXT PAUSE
250 CLS
```

Finally, a demonstration of a more robust **DRAW** feature: the **DRAW** statement can construct lines to specific coordinates, rather than just in eight predefined directions (similarly to the **LINE** statement, which we will make use of in later programs).

```
260 PRINT"DRAW can also move to specific points"
270 PRINT"on the screen, rather than just moving"
272 PRINT"in eight predefined directions."
275 PSET(55,55),9
280 DRAW"M100,110 M200,60 M110,170 M20,80"
283 LOCATE 19,1:PRINT"Press <ESC> to end."
285 IF INKEY$=CHR$(27) THEN GOTO 290 ELSE GOTO 285
290 CLS:END
```

● ● ●

Although there are a number of other simple graphics' statements that could have been presented here, it was important to focus on those used most in forthcoming chapters.

Graphics with Circles
LOAD "CIRCLE.BAS"

Ok

RUN

A *circle* is defined as the set of all points on a plane that are a fixed distance, called the radius, from a single point, called the center. We can use the distance formula (itself simply another way of expressing the Pythagorean theorem on the coordinate plane) to find the equation for a circle.

$$a^2 + b^2 = c^2 \quad \text{(Pythagorean theorem)}$$

$$\sqrt{(x_2 - x_1)^2 + (y_2 - y_1)^2} = d \quad \text{(distance formula)}$$

Squaring both sides of the distance formula gives us

$$(x_2 - x_1)^2 + (y_2 - y_1)^2 = d^2$$

We could think of d as the radius r of the circle—since the radius is the distance to all the points (x, y) in the set that happen to have the same distance to the circle's center. Algebraically, then, the equation for a circle is

$$(x - a)^2 + (y - b)^2 = r^2$$

where the radius is r and the coordinates of the center are given by a and b.

Luckily, rather than having to plot points using the equation, GW-BASIC proffers a statement called **CIRCLE** that allows for a wide variety of circle displays. The programs that follow offer you some of **CIRCLE**'s greatest hits.

• • •

CIRCLE1.BAS simply expands and contracts a circle on-screen. Notice that the **STEP** statement needs a negative number to make the circle shrink.

It's with **CIRCLE2.BAS** that things get more interesting. A circle is drawn, piece by piece. Look carefully at the syntax of the **CIRCLE** statement; notice the double commas specifying the ever-changing portion of the circle to show.

CIRCLE3.BAS might put you in a trance if you stare too long. Again, circles grow and shrink, ad infinitum.

A random element is introduced to the proceedings in **CIRCOL.BAS**. Ever-expanding circles of random colors fly at you on the screen.

TUNNEL.BAS permits the user a small degree of flexibility with making circles on-screen, while **CIRMAKER.BAS** allows for a number of circle-customization options.

Although not quite a bouncing ball—that will come in a later chapter—**BOUNCE.BAS** presents you with a bouncing circle. The **CLS** statement helps to give the circle the illusion of movement.

The programs **CIROV.BAS** and **COIN.BAS** leverage another **CIRCLE** statement feature: stretching circles into ellipses with varying eccentricities. An ellipse is similar to a circle, except that instead of each point in the set having a fixed distance from the center, each point in an ellipse has a constant distance from the sum of two foci. (Our solar system's planets have elliptical orbits, with the location of the sun serving as a focus.) The equation for an ellipse, which, like the equation for a circle, is derived by using the distance formula, is given by

$$\frac{x^2}{a^2} + \frac{y^2}{b^2} = 1$$

where the length of the major axis of symmetry (the longer axis) is 2*a*, the length of the minor axis of symmetry (the shorter axis) is 2*b*, and the center of the ellipse is at the origin.

Note the four commas in a row wherever CIRCLE is used in CIROV.BAS. COIN.BAS displays a rotating "coin" on-screen.

Finally, COIN2.BAS is an exercise in abject silliness. Instead of a rotating coin, a visual trick presents a mouth, opening and closing, surrounded by a face made using the DRAW statement.

• • •

CIRCLE1.BAS
```
10 KEY OFF:SCREEN 7:COLOR 2,1:CLS
20 FOR I=10 TO 100 STEP 5
30 CIRCLE(126,98),I
40 CLS:NEXT I
50 CLS:FOR I=100 TO 10 STEP -5
60 CIRCLE(126,98),I
70 CLS:NEXT I
80 CLS:GOTO 20
```

CIRCLE2.BAS
```
10 KEY OFF
20 SCREEN 7:CLS
40 COLOR 3,0,8
50 FOR U=6 TO 0 STEP -.01
60 CIRCLE(126,96),100,,U
67 CLS
70 NEXT U
```

```
80 CLS
90 FOR Y=0 TO 6 STEP .01
100 CIRCLE(126,96),100,,Y
107 CLS
110 NEXT Y
120 GOTO 10
```

CIRCLE3.BAS

```
10 KEY OFF:SCREEN 7:COLOR 2,1:CLS
20 FOR I=10 TO 100 STEP 1.5
30 CIRCLE(126,98),I
40 NEXT I
50 CLS:FOR I=100 TO 10 STEP -1.5
60 CIRCLE(126,98),I
70 NEXT I
80 CLS:GOTO 20
```

CIRCOL.BAS

```
5 SCREEN 7:RANDOMIZE TIMER
10 COLOR 1,15:CLS
15 T=INT(1+15*RND(1)):COLOR T
20 FOR M=1 TO 100 STEP 2
30 CIRCLE(126,96),M
40 NEXT M
50 GOTO 15
```

TUNNEL.BAS

```
0 KEY OFF:SCREEN 7:COLOR 15,1:CLS
1 INPUT"STEPS";D
10 SCREEN 7:COLOR 15,15:COLOR 1:CLS
20 FOR U=1 TO 250 STEP D
30 Y=INT(1+15*RND(1))
40 COLOR Y,1:CIRCLE(139,96),U
50 NEXT U
60 FOR I=1 TO 19000:NEXT:GOTO 1
```

CIRMAKER.BAS

```
1 KEY OFF:CLS
2 SCREEN 9:COLOR 8,2
3 PRINT:PRINT:PRINT:PRINT:PRINT:PRINT:PRINT:PRINT"
  The Circle Maker"
5 COLOR 4,2:PRINT:PRINT"*OK*"
6 COLOR 5,2:LINE INPUT" ";A$
7 IF A$="*OK*" THEN GOTO 10
```

```
8 BEEP:GOTO 6
10 CLS
20 SCREEN 9:COLOR 1,2:CLS
21 INPUT" X POSITION..";G
23 INPUT" Y POSTION..";F:INPUT"TO HOW
   MANY..";X:INPUT" BY HOW MANY STEPS...";C:INPUT"
   FOREGROUND..";S:INPUT"BACKGROUND..";A:INPUT"
   BACKWORDS OR FOREWORDS?";F$:IF F$="FOREWORDS"
   THEN GOTO 130
24 CLS:COLOR S,A
30 FOR U=X TO 1 STEP -C
40 CIRCLE(G,F),U
50 NEXT U
55 IF INKEY$="" THEN GOTO 55
60 CLS:PRINT"     ANOTHER?"
70 PRINT"YES":PRINT"NO"
80 LINE INPUT" ";D$
90 IF D$="YES" THEN GOTO 10
95 IF D$="NO" THEN GOTO 105
100 BEEP:GOTO 80
105 CLS:PRINT:PRINT:PRINT:PRINT:PRINT:PRINT:PRINT"
    Exiting Circle Maker...":BEEP
110 FOR I=1 TO 19999:NEXT
120 CLS:STOP
130 CLS:COLOR S,A:FOR U=1 TO X STEP
    C:CIRCLE(G,F),U:NEXT U:FOR Q=1 TO
    18000:NEXT:GOTO 60
```

BOUNCE.BAS

```
10 CLS:SCREEN 7:COLOR 1,15:CLS
20 FOR H=50 TO 150 STEP 20
30 CIRCLE(126,H-1),50
35 COLOR 1,1:CLS:COLOR 15
40 NEXT H
50 FOR J=150 TO 50 STEP -13
60 CIRCLE(126,J-1),50
70 COLOR 1,1:CLS:COLOR 15
80 NEXT J
90 GOTO 20
```

CIROV.BAS

```
10 SCREEN 7:COLOR 1,15:CLS
20 FOR M=.0001 TO .9 STEP .01
21 I=INT(1+15*RND(1))
```

185

```
22 COLOR I
30 CIRCLE(126,96),50,,,,M
40 NEXT M
50 FOR V=1 TO 10000:NEXT V:GOTO 10
```

COIN.BAS

```
10 KEY OFF:SCREEN 7
20 COLOR 1,15:CLS
30 FOR C=.0001 TO .8 STEP .1
40 COLOR 14:CIRCLE(126,96),30,,,,C
45 FOR TY=1 TO 500:NEXT TY
50 COLOR 1:CIRCLE(126,96),30,,,,C
60 NEXT C
70 FOR X=.8 TO .0001 STEP -.1
80 COLOR 14:CIRCLE(126,96),30,,,,X
85 FOR TY=1 TO 500:NEXT TY
90 COLOR 1:CIRCLE(126,96),30,,,,X
100 NEXT X
110 GOTO 30
```

COIN2.BAS

```
10 KEY OFF:SCREEN 7
20 COLOR 1,14:CLS
21 PSET(70,200):DRAW"M71,154 M51,149 M40,132
   M40,46 M48,39 M146,38 M152,44 M152,128 M140,146
   M118,154 M118,200"
22 PSET(124,52):DRAW"M129,50 M134,49 M140,51
   M141,53 M137,56 M131,57 M126,56 M124,52 BM53,53
   M58,51 M63,50 M66,51 M68,54 M64,56 M55,56 M53,53
   BM95,52"
23 DRAW"M89,63 M86,62 M82,65 M86,69 M91,67 M94,71
   M98,67 M102,70 M105,69 M105,65 M101,63"
24 PAINT(62,53),15,14:PAINT(153,53),15,14
25 PSET(62,53),4:PSET(153,53),4
27 PAINT(100,1),1,14
30 FOR C=.0001 TO .5 STEP .05
40 COLOR 14:CIRCLE(96,96),30,,,,C
50 COLOR 6:CIRCLE(96,96),30,,,,C
60 NEXT C
70 FOR X=.5 TO .0001 STEP -.05
80 COLOR 14:CIRCLE(96,96),30,,,,X
90 COLOR 6:CIRCLE(96,96),30,,,,X
100 NEXT X
110 GOTO 30
```

● ● ●

The programs in this chapter give you a taste of the many options GW-BASIC permits when displaying circles, and thus will (hopefully) whet your appetite to construct your own circle explorations.

Another Pi Approximation

LOAD "PI.BAS"

Ok

RUN_

Recall that the ratio of a circle's circumference to its diameter is given by the Greek letter π, pronounced "pi." Approximations of π began in antiquity.

For example, Eudoxus of Cnidus formalized the method of exhaustion, which, when applied to finding the area of a circle (and, indirectly, π), would inscribe and circumscribe ever-smaller regular polygons into and onto the circle, respectively, resulting in the lower and upper bounds of the approximation.

Perhaps if Eudoxus had lived in the twentieth century, he would have leveraged BASIC to obtain an approximation. Run the program **PI.BAS**, and, after being prompted for a diameter size (in pixel units), you'll see a circle drawn on-screen; shortly after, it will start disappearing, top to bottom. Finally, an approximation of π will be printed.

• • •

The program makes use of the **POINT** function in line **60**, which returns the color of the pixel's coordinates it passes over; each time **POINT** encounters a pixel of color **9** (blue), the program increments the variable **COUNT**. By the time the two **FOR/NEXT** loops are run through, **COUNT** will equal the circumference (in pixels) of the on-screen blue circle.

● ● ●

PI.BAS
```
10 KEY OFF:SCREEN 9:COLOR 9,0:CLS
20 COUNT=0
25 PRINT:PRINT:INPUT"Diameter of the Circle (in
   Pixels): ";D:CLS
30 CIRCLE(300,165),D
40 FOR X=0 TO 639
50 FOR Y=0 TO 349
60 IF POINT(X,Y)=9 THEN COUNT=COUNT+1
65 PSET(X,Y),0
70 NEXT Y,X
80 LOCATE 10,10:PRINT"Circumference in Pixels:
   ";COUNT
90 LOCATE 11,10:PRINT"Diameter in Pixels: ";D*2
100 LOCATE 13,10:PRINT"Cir/Dia = Pi (for computer
    circles) = ";COUNT/(D*2)
```

● ● ●

PI.BAS cheats a bit—by using the **CIRCLE** statement to draw the circle. A more honest approach? Utilize the algebraic equation for a circle, $(x-a)^2 + (y-b)^2 = r^2$, to map the circle on the screen instead; some mathematical transformations will have to be completed first to go from the coordinate plane to graphics on the **SCREEN**, as we'll see in an upcoming chapter.

Screensavers

LOAD "RAND.BAS"

Ok

RUN_

Screensavers, usually images of rapidly changing patterns, arrived decades ago to help prevent computer monitor burn-in, back when computer monitors were constructed using cathode ray tubes (CRTs). *Flying Toasters*, which were winged toasters that flitted around the screen, were probably the most famous of the '90's screensavers. Though no longer necessary to literally save your screen, screensavers can nonetheless still can be fun to watch.

Hence, take a look at the collection of erstwhile screensavers in this chapter.

● ● ●

The simplest images? Stars, and lots of them. **STARS.BAS** randomizes coordinates for a **PSET** statement. **STARS2.BAS** does one better: it randomizes *and* scrolls the stars upward (using **PRINT**), invoking a dizzying feeling of descent.

But **STARS3.BAS** is the sneakiest of the bunch. Instead of showing the stars, real-time, as they're plotted on the screen, the program sets up two screens: a "screen 1" and a "screen 2." Only one of the screens displays at a time; the black, blank screen that's "off-screen" is waylaid with stars, just in time to switch to it as the active, visible screen—and bombard the *other*, now invisible, screen with stars. The extra parameters for the **SCREEN** statement in lines **20** and **80** pull off this neat slideshow-like visual trick, which can be used elsewhere to great effect when smoothing out graphics' animations.

Instead of stars, perhaps you're craving some images of colorful crystals? Then the program **CRYSTAL.BAS** should satisfy you. Using several **FOR/NEXT** loops and the **RND** function, the screen is quickly saturated with color. (If you don't like the colors and would rather just see lots of snowflakes—all of which are unrealistically identical-looking—run **SNOW.BAS** instead.)

LINES.BAS and **LINES2.BAS** stretch randomly colored lines across the screen, horizontally and vertically, respectively. Only **LINES2.BAS**, though, utilizes the **DRAW** statement to construct the lines.

DOTS.BAS is similar to the **LINES.BAS** programs but queries you for line-patterns preferences.

The program **DOTTER.BAS** is more dynamic, leaning on arrays to moves some stars (well, more honestly, dots) around the screen—very slowly. The arrays **ARRAYX** and **ARRAYY** capture all of the random coordinates of the on-screen dots; then, in lines **71** and **75**, a random amount of movement is generated: one pixel left, right, up, or down, or no shift in position at all.

FRACTAL1.BAS is very similar to **DOTTER.BAS**, except that the dots don't disappear after they're drawn and there's only a vague hint of the self-similarity fractals require—hence the program title. A later chapter will delve more deeply into fractal designs.

LINER.BAS uses the **LINE** statement, rather than **PSET** or **DRAW**, to construct lines from the last referenced random coordinate (notice the dash after the **LINE** statement in line **30**). And a circle is slapped on the end of each line segment—making the ever-emerging images look like dystopian worlds made of Tinker Toys.

Anyone wishing for a heart-monitor-like display need look no further than **HEART.BAS**. An rapidly-fluctuating blue line quickly makes its way from the left to the right side of the screen, all made possible with one simple **PSET** and a lot of randomization of movement.

And, finally, **SAVER.BAS** makes use of most of the graphics' statements we've examined so far, including **PSET**, **CIRCLE**, and **DRAW**.

• • •

STARS.BAS
```
10 KEY OFF:CLS:SCREEN 7:COLOR 8,8:CLS:COLOR 15
20 I=INT(1+320*RND(1)):L=INT(1+250*RND(1))
30 PSET(I,L)
40 GOTO 20
```

STARS2.BAS
```
10 RANDOMIZE TIMER:KEY OFF:CLS:SCREEN 7:COLOR
   8,8:CLS:COLOR 15
20 I=INT(1+320*RND(1)):L=INT(1+230*RND(1))
30 PSET(I,L)
31 F=INT(1+320*RND(1)):G=INT(1+230*RND(1))
32 PSET(F,G)
34 LOCATE 25,15:PRINT"S T A R S  2"
35 PRINT
36 I$=INKEY$:IF I$="B" OR I$="b" THEN
   T=INT(14*RND(1)):COLOR ,T
40 GOTO 20
```

STARS3.BAS
```
10 KEY OFF:SCREEN 7:COLOR 15,0:CLS:RANDOMIZE TIMER
20 SCREEN 7,,1,2:CLS
30 FOR T=1 TO 50
40 X=INT(1+320*RND(1)):Y=INT(1+200*RND(1))
50 PSET(X,Y),15
60 NEXT T
70 FOR PAUSE=1 TO 5000:NEXT PAUSE
80 SCREEN 7,,2,1:CLS
90 FOR T=1 TO 50
100 X=INT(1+320*RND(1)):Y=INT(1+200*RND(1))
110 PSET(X,Y),15
120 NEXT T
130 FOR PAUSE=1 TO 5000:NEXT PAUSE
```

```
140 GOTO 20
```

CRYSTAL.BAS

```
10 KEY OFF:SCREEN 7:COLOR 15,0:CLS
20 FOR G=1 TO 700:T=INT(1+320*RND(1)):
   Y=INT(1+200*RND(1))
30 PSET(T,Y):DRAW"C15 NU10 C10 NR10 C2 ND10 C3
   NL10 C12 NG10 C6 NH10 C5 NE10 C14 NF10"
40 NEXT G
50 FOR G=1 TO 700:T=INT(1+320*RND(1)):
   Y=INT(1+200*RND(1))
60 PSET(T,Y),0:DRAW"NU10 NR10 ND10 NL10 NG10 NH10
   NE10 NF10"
70 NEXT G
80 GOTO 20
```

SNOW.BAS

```
10 KEY OFF:SCREEN 9:COLOR 15,1:CLS
20 U=INT(1+649*RND(1)):F=INT(1+349*RND(1))
30 PSET(U,F):DRAW"NR5 NL5 ND5 NU5 NG5 NH5 NE5 NF5"
40 GOTO 20
```

LINES.BAS

```
10 SCREEN 7
20 COLOR 1,1:CLS:COLOR 15
30 F=INT(1+15*RND(1)):IF F=1 THEN GOTO 30
40 COLOR F:FD=INT(1+300*RND(1))
45 FOR G=0 TO 370
50 PSET(G,FD)
55 NEXT G
60 GOTO 30
```

LINES2.BAS

```
10 SCREEN 7:COLOR 7,7:CLS:COLOR 1
20 X=320
30 FOR M=0 TO X STEP 3
50 PSET(M,V),INT(1+15*RND(1)):DRAW"D200
60 NEXT M
80 GOTO 20
```

DOTS.BAS

```
10 KEY OFF:SCREEN 7:COLOR 15,0:CLS
11 INPUT"RANDOM(R) OR SELECTED COLORS(S)";D$
12 IF D$="R" OR D$="r" THEN GOTO 15
```

```
13 IF D$="S" OR D$="s" THEN GOTO 115
15 INPUT"STEP GOING ACROSS";L
16 INPUT"STEP GOING DOWN";M
17 CLS
20 FOR G=1 TO 320 STEP L
30 FOR H=1 TO 190 STEP M
40 Y=INT(1+15*RND(1))
41 I$=INKEY$:IF I$=" " THEN GOTO 90
42 IF I$="B" OR I$="b" THEN AS=AS+1:COLOR ,AS
43 IF AS=>15 THEN AS=0
50 PSET(G,H),Y
60 NEXT H
70 NEXT G
80 FOR J=1 TO 10000:NEXT J
90 FOR NC=1 TO 55:PRINT:NEXT NC:CLS:GOTO 11
115 INPUT"STEP GOING ACROSS";L
116 INPUT"STEP GOING DOWN";M
117 INPUT"COLOR OF LINES(1-15)";X
118 CLS
120 FOR G=1 TO 320 STEP L
130 FOR H=1 TO 190 STEP M
140 Y=X
141 I$=INKEY$:IF I$=" " THEN GOTO 90
142 IF I$="B" OR I$="b" THEN AS=AS+1:COLOR ,AS
143 IF AS=>15 THEN AS=0
150 PSET(G,H),Y
160 NEXT H
170 NEXT G
180 FOR J=1 TO 10000:NEXT J
190 FOR NC=1 TO 55:PRINT:NEXT NC:CLS:GOTO 11
200 END
```

DOTTER.BAS

```
10 RANDOMIZE TIMER:KEY OFF:SCREEN 9:COLOR
   15,0:CLS:DIM ARRAYX(100):DIM ARRAYY(100)
20 FOR TY=1 TO 100
30 X=INT(1+939*RND(1))-100:Y=INT(1+649*RND(1))-100
40 PSET(X,Y),15:ARRAYX(TY)=X:ARRAYY(TY)=Y:FOR
   TIM=1 TO 100:NEXT TIM
50 NEXT TY
70 FOR TY=1 TO 100
71 XA=INT(1+3*RND(1))-2:YA=INT(1+3*RND(1))-2
75 ARRAYX(TY)=ARRAYX(TY)+XA:ARRAYY(TY)=
   ARRAYY(TY)+YA
```

```
80 PSET(ARRAYX(TY),ARRAYY(TY)),15
90 NEXT TY
95 FOR PAUSE=1 TO 100:NEXT PAUSE:CLS
100 GOTO 70
```

FRACTAL1.BAS
```
10 RANDOMIZE TIMER:KEY OFF:SCREEN 9:COLOR
   15,0:CLS:DIM ARRAYX(300):DIM ARRAYY(300)
20 FOR TY=1 TO 300
30 X=INT(1+739*RND(1))-100:Y=INT(1+449*RND(1))-100
40 PSET(X,Y),15:ARRAYX(TY)=X:ARRAYY(TY)=Y
50 NEXT TY
60 XA=INT(1+5*RND(1))-3:YA=INT(1+5*RND(1))-3
70 FOR TY=1 TO 300
75 ARRAYX(TY)=ARRAYX(TY)+XA:ARRAYY(TY)=
   ARRAYY(TY)+YA
80 PSET(ARRAYX(TY),ARRAYY(TY)),15
90 NEXT TY
100 GOTO 60
```

LINER.BAS
```
10 KEY OFF:SCREEN 9:COLOR 15,0:RANDOMIZE TIMER
20 X=INT(1+640*RND(1)):Y=INT(1+350*RND(1)):
   C=INT(1+15*RND(1))
30 LINE -(X,Y),C:FOR ZZ=1 TO 5:CIRCLE(X,Y),ZZ,C:
   NEXT ZZ
35 FOR T=1 TO 10000:NEXT T
40 GOTO 20
```

HEART.BAS
```
10 CLEAR:RANDOMIZE TIMER:KEY OFF:SCREEN 9:COLOR
   15,0:CLS:Y=200
11 I=INT(1+3*RND(1)):I2=INT(1+3*RND(1))
12 U=INT(1+5*RND(1))
13 IF U=1 THEN V=.1
14 IF U=2 THEN V=.2
15 IF U=3 THEN V=.3
16 IF U=4 THEN V=.4
17 IF U=5 THEN V=.5
21 IF I=1 THEN C=1
22 IF I=2 THEN C=0
23 IF I=3 THEN C=-1
25 Y=Y+C:X=X+V:PSET(X,Y),9
26 IF X=<0 THEN X=1
```

```
27 IF X=>640 THEN GOTO 10
30 GOTO 11
```

SAVER.BAS

```
0   RANDOMIZE TIMER:KEY OFF:A=0:COLOR 1,1:CLS:COLOR
    15:PRINT:PRINT:PRINT:INPUT"WHICH SCREEN: 7 to
    9";R
1 SCREEN R:COLOR 1,1:CLS:COLOR 14
2 PRINT:PRINT,,"-THE SCREENSAVER-"
3 FOR Z=1 TO 12000:NEXT Z
4 INPUT"HOW MANY TIMES DO YOU WANT THE SAVER TO
  REPEAT";A
5 FOR Q=1 TO A
10 SCREEN R:COLOR 4,4:CLS:COLOR 1
15 PRINT" NO.";Q:FOR M=1 TO 1000
20 I=INT(1+320*RND(1)):L=INT(1+250*RND(1))
30 PSET(I,L),15:I$=INKEY$:IF I$="E" THEN END
40 NEXT M
50 FOR F=1 TO 55:PRINT:FOR C=1 TO 60:NEXT C:NEXT F
70 FOR K=0 TO 150 STEP 2
80 CIRCLE(K,K),20:FOR F=1 TO 300:NEXT F
90 NEXT K
100 COLOR 15:FOR O=0 TO 150 STEP 1.5
110 CIRCLE(O,150),20:FOR LS=1 TO 100:NEXT LS
120 NEXT O:FOR D=1 TO 9:PRINT:PRINT:PRINT:NEXT D
130 COLOR 1,1:CLS:COLOR 4
140 FOR K=200 TO 1 STEP -1
145 Y=INT(1+15*RND(1)):IF Y=1 THEN GOTO 145
150 CIRCLE(K,K),K,Y
160 NEXT K:FOR BQ=1 TO 2000:NEXT BQ
165 COLOR 1,1:CLS:COLOR 15
170 FOR DA=1 TO 1000:PRINT"$";:NEXT DA
180 FOR N=1 TO 55:PRINT:NEXT N
185 FOR J=1 TO 250 STEP 5
190 PSET(J,150):DRAW"U60 R30 D60 L30":FOR U=1 TO
    400:NEXT U
191 COLOR 1,1:CLS:COLOR 2
195 NEXT J:FOR G=150 TO 50 STEP -
    1.3:PSET(J,G):DRAW"U60 R30 D60 L30
200 NEXT G
210 COLOR 1,1:CLS:COLOR 2
215 FOR S=250 TO 0 STEP -1
220 PSET(0,S),7:DRAW"R400
230 NEXT S
```

```
235 COLOR 1,1:COLOR 7
240 FOR VC=360 TO 0 STEP -2
250 PSET(0,VC),4:DRAW"R400
260 PSET(VC,0),3:DRAW"D400":NEXT VC:FOR BV=1 TO
    55:PRINT:FOR DS=1 TO 100:NEXT DS:NEXT BV
270 NEXT Q
280 PRINT:PRINT:PRINT:PRINT"AGAIN?":PRINT"NO":
    PRINT"YES"
290 LINE INPUT YU$
300 IF YU$="YES" THEN GOTO 0
310 IF YU$="NO" THEN GOTO 320
315 SOUND 1000,1:GOTO 290
320 COLOR 1,1:CLS:COLOR 15:PRINT"BYE!!":SOUND
    500,3:END
```

● ● ●

Refinements could easily be made to any of the programs above. The real entertainment, though, comes in experimenting with patterns of images in GW-BASIC, unwittingly making screensavers of your own.

Altered Fonts
LOAD "WORDS.BAS"

Ok

RUN_

The late Apple Computer cofounder Steve Jobs famously insisted on including a variety of fonts in the first generation Macintosh computers. Jobs' interest in typography stemmed from a calligraphy class he took serendipitously in college.

Although GW-BASIC really only has one font to work with (per **SCREEN**), there are ways to coax different typesets out of the language. Run **WORDS.BAS**, **WORDS2.BAS**, and **SLANTEXT.BAS** to see the results.

• • •

WORDS.BAS uses the **POINT** function to examine, pixel by pixel, the word or words inputted into the string variable **I$**. Then, with those coordinates, in line **35** the statement **PSET** is used to (kind of) magnify the image—according to a multiplier set by the numeric variable **S**.

The downside is that **WORDS.BAS** produces a scaled font that is very light, composed of small dots, rather than more robust, filled-in text. WORDS2.BAS corrects that problem; not a mere repeat of the previous program, WORDS2.BAS utilizes a subroutine—from lines **100** to **120**—to construct a darker, more striking scaled font.

SLANTEXT.BAS takes a slightly different approach. Instead of prompting for the text all at once initially, any letters you type appear on-screen in real time—but they are slanted.

• • •

WORDS.BAS

```
10 KEY OFF:VIEW PRINT:SCREEN 9:COLOR 9,0:CLS:Y=267
15 COLOR 10:PRINT"WORDS TESTER:":PRINT:PRINT:COLOR
   9
16 PRINT"INPUT ANY WORDS, OR SERIES OF WORDS, NO
   LARGER THAT 10-15 CHARACHERS:"
17 INPUT I$:PRINT:INPUT"Size:(1,2,3, or 4 pts)";S:
   CLS:PRINT"WORDS TESTER:"
18 LOCATE 20,2:PRINT"---->"
20 LOCATE 20,10:PRINT I$
30 FOR X=72 TO 200 STEP 1
33 KOLOR=POINT(X,Y)
35 IF KOLOR=9 THEN PSET(X*S,(Y-160)),10
40 NEXT X
50 Y=Y+1
60 IF Y>280 THEN GOTO 80
70 GOTO 30
80 LOCATE 22,25:PRINT"Press Any Key....":
   I$=INKEY$:IF I$="" THEN 80
90 GOTO 10
```

WORDS2.BAS

```
10 KEY OFF:VIEW PRINT:SCREEN 9:COLOR 9,0:CLS:Y=267
15 COLOR 10:PRINT"WORDS2
   TESTER:":PRINT:PRINT:COLOR 9
16 PRINT"INPUT ANY WORDS, OR SERIES OF WORDS, NO
   LARGER THAT 10-15 CHARACHERS:"
17 INPUT I$:PRINT:INPUT"Size:(1,2,3, or 4 pts)";S:
   CLS:PRINT"WORDS2 TESTER:"
18 LOCATE 20,2:PRINT"---->"
20 LOCATE 20,10:PRINT I$
```

```
30 FOR X=72 TO 200 STEP 1
33 KOLOR=POINT(X,Y)
35 IF KOLOR=9 THEN GOSUB 100
40 NEXT X
50 Y=Y+1
60 IF Y>280 THEN GOTO 80
70 GOTO 30
80 LOCATE 22,25:PRINT"Press Any Key....":
   I$=INKEY$:IF I$="" THEN 80
90 GOTO 10
100 PSET((X*S),(Y-160)),10:PSET((X*S)+1,(Y-
    160)),10:PSET((X*S),(Y-
    159)),10:PSET((X*S)+1,(Y-159)),10
120 RETURN
```

SLANTEXT.BAS
```
5 KEY OFF:SCREEN 9:COLOR 15,0
10 CLS:A=0:B=0
20 I$=INKEY$
30 IF I$="" THEN 20
35 LOCATE 1,1:PRINT I$;
40 FOR Y=0 TO 12 STEP 1:FOR X=10 TO 0
STEP -1:PSET(X+A,Y+20+B),POINT(X,Y)
45 NEXT X:A=A+1:NEXT Y
50 IF A>600 THEN B=B+15:A=0
55 FOR G=0 TO 15:FOR T=0 TO 10:PSET(G,T),0:
NEXT T,G
56 IF I$=CHR$(27) THEN END
60 GOTO 20
```

• • •

The first two programs (at least) could easily be merged into one, complete with a font-display option such as "light" or "dark." In addition, more colors and styles could be rigged using **PSET** and the like.

Bouncing Ball
LOAD "BOUNCEB.BAS"
Ok

RUN
■ ■

When you think of Atari's *sui generis* table tennis simulation *Pong*, you visualize a pixelated ball bouncing left and right, deflected only by the edges of the screen and the user-operated paddles.

Let's focus on that deflecting ball. BOUNCEB.BAS is a straightforward simulation of a little white ball that never stops moving, and bouncing, around the four corners of the screen—until you tap the ESCAPE key.

• • •

After constructing and painting a white circle in line 60, four conditional statements (see lines 80 to 100) repeatedly test the location of the electronic ball, ensuring that if it ventures too far up, or down, or left, or right, the sign of the numerical variable—assigned to A for horizontal movement, and B for vertical movement—is switched. Switching the sign reverses the horizontal or vertical (or both) path the ball's traveling on a dime.

• • •

```
BOUNCEB.BAS
5 X=350:Y=150:A=7:B=-7
10 KEY OFF:RANDOMIZE TIMER
20 SCREEN 9
30 COLOR 15,1
```

```
40 CLS
50 WHILE(INKEY$<>CHR$(27))
60 CIRCLE(X,Y),10:PAINT(X,Y),15,15
65 FOR PAUSE=1 TO 800:NEXT PAUSE
70 CLS
80 IF (X<10) THEN A=-(A+INT(1+3*RND(1))-2)
90 IF (X>629) THEN A=-(A+INT(1+3*RND(1))-2)
100 IF (Y<10) THEN B=-(B+INT(1+3*RND(1))-2)
110 IF (Y>339) THEN B=-(B+INT(1+3*RND(1))-2)
120 X=X+A
130 Y=Y+B
140 WEND
150 CLS
160 END
```

• • •

The flicker that results from the recurring **CLS**s is annoying. Toggling between screens 1 and 2, where images are drawn off-screen before they're displayed, would mitigate this problem.

Then, since the ball's physics mostly match *Pong*'s, attempt writing the code for a *Pong*-like game: include player paddles, score tabulations, and the like. (We'll be examining how to leverage **INKEY$** to control moving objects on-screen in later chapters, so you might want to wait until then.)

Slope of Linear Equations
LOAD "SLOPE.BAS"

Ok

RUN_

Perhaps *slope* is not something you've worked with since high school or college, but, if you want to graph or analyze any linear equation (an equation that graphs as a line), you need to have a good handle on what slope means.

You may recall that slope = *rise/run*. In other words, for every *y* units you travel upward (rise), you move *x* units to the left or right (run), depending on whether the slope is a positive or negative quantity. But here's a better definition of slope: for every additional unit *x*, the value of *y* changes numerically by the slope amount.

The form of a linear equation is $y = mx + b$, where *m* is the slope and *b* is the *y*-intercept—the point where the line crosses the *y*-axis. Ancient Greek mathematician and knowledge synthesizer Euclid stated that two unique points make a line, so, if given two unique points, (x_1, y_1) and (x_2, y_2), the slope can be found thusly:

$$m = \frac{rise}{run} = \frac{y_2 - y_1}{x_2 - x_1}$$

Run the program **SLOPE.BAS** and you'll get to experiment with visual representations of slopes. After being asked how many lines to plot on the same coordinate axis—the options are one or two—you're prompted to enter the rise and run of the slope(s). You'll have no means to input a *y*-intercept, though; the *y*-intercept's always set to zero, meaning the lines will always pass through the origin. Thus, the program will only graph what are called *direct variation* linear equations.

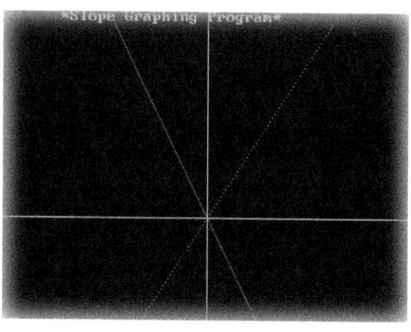

• • •

Depending on your input of a rise (variable **R**) and a run (variable **RR**), **SLOPE.BAS** uses **PSET** commands within **FOR/NEXT** loops to plot the direct variation equation; look at lines **60** to **95** to see how.

• • •

SLOPE.BAS
```
10 KEY OFF:SCREEN 9:COLOR 12,0:CLS:PRINT"
   Slope v1.0"
20 COLOR 15:Y=175:PRINT:PRINT:INPUT"
   GRAPH 1 OR 2 SLOPES AT A TIME";F$
25 IF F$="2" THEN 110
30 PRINT:INPUT"   SLOPE:RISE:";R
40 INPUT"   SLOPE:RUN:";RR
41 CLS
42 LOCATE 10,10:PRINT"   Equation: Y=(";R;"/";RR;
   ")X+";0:FOR GT=1 TO 17000:NEXT GT
50 X=320:CLS:COLOR 14:PRINT TAB(25) "*Slope Gra
   phing Program*"
60 DRAW"C15 NU700 NL700 NR700 ND700"
65 FOR T=1 TO 400
```

```
70 PSET(X,Y),12:Y=Y-RR:X=X+R
80 NEXT T
85 FOR G=1 TO 800
90 PSET(X,Y),12:Y=Y+RR:X=X-R
95 NEXT G
100 INPUT"    Another(Y/N)";A$
102 IF A$="Y" OR A$="y" THEN CLS:GOTO 10
103 IF A$="N" OR A$="n" THEN END
105 GOTO 100
110 INPUT"   SLOPE 1-RISE:";R1
120 INPUT"   SLOPE 1-RUN:";R2
130 PRINT
140 INPUT"   SLOPE 2-RISE:";R3
150 INPUT"   SLOPE 2-RUN:";R4
160 CLS:LOCATE 10,10:PRINT"Eq1-
    Y=(";R1;"/";R2;")X+";0;" Eq2-
    Y=(";R3;"/";R4;")X+";0;"   (intercept at
    0,0)":FOR GY=1 TO 19000:NEXT GY
170 X=320:CLS:COLOR 14:PRINT TAB(25) "*Slope Gra
    phing Program*"
180 DRAW"C15 NU700 NL700 NR700 ND700"
190 FOR T=1 TO 400
200 PSET(X,Y),12:Y=Y-R1:X=X+R2
210 NEXT T
220 FOR D=1 TO 800
230 PSET(X,Y),12:Y=Y+R1:X=X-R2
240 NEXT D
250 FOR S=1 TO 400
260 PSET(X,Y),12:Y=Y-R1:X=X+R2
270 NEXT S
280 FOR GH=1 TO 400
290 PSET(X,Y),10:Y=Y-R3:X=X+R4
300 NEXT GH
310 FOR HG=1 TO 800
320 PSET(X,Y),10:Y=Y+R3:X=X-R4
330 NEXT HG
340 INPUT"    Another(Y/N)";AS$
350 IF AS$="Y" OR AS$="y" THEN GOTO 10
360 IF AS$="N" OR AS$="n" THEN END
370 GOTO 340
```

• • •

Since **SLOPE.BAS** only graphs direct variation equations, any linear equation with a y-intercept other than zero cannot be plotted. In addition, being prompted for two unique points lying on the line, rather than a rise and a run, would make the program more robust.

Graphs of Equations
LOAD "XYGRAPH.BAS"
Ok
RUN

The coordinate plane was not a staple of the mathematics of antiquity; rather, it was not until the Renaissance, that fruitful period of European thought, when the great French mathematician René Descartes developed it. Supposedly, when Descartes was sick in bed as a child, he glanced up at the ceiling of his room only to spot a fly meandering about. And he wondered: How can I track the movements of this fly, so those motions can be reported later? Descartes then realized that if the ceiling is thought of as a plane, the fly's motion can be described using two coordinates: one for the horizontal, and one for the vertical. And the Cartesian Coordinate Plane, along with analytic geometry, was born.

Or something like that. Descartes's contemporary Pierre de Fermat probably came up with the coordinate plane too, not to mention that evidence of the plane's use has been found from centuries earlier. Like so many other "discoveries" in mathematics and science, they are more often than not *re*-discoveries, and are hence ultimately named after the wrong people; this phenomenon, called Stigler's law of eponymy (courtesy of statistics professor Stephen Stigler), states the following: "No scientific discovery is named after its original discoverer." Ironically, Stigler's law *itself* is a member of that set, having not been first identified by Mr. Stigler!

GW-BASIC can do a serviceable job of displaying some functions on a coordinate-type axis; you have to be careful, however, not to "overflow" the inputs—i.e., to bombard the program with domains too large—otherwise GW-BASIC throws up its proverbial hands and terminates the program right on the spot. Trigonometric functions might cause you some problems too, largely because the axes' scales aren't set for radians; you're going to have to experiment a bit and tweak where necessary.

Before running **XYGRAPH.BAS**, make sure you've hard coded your mathematical function into line **36** of the program. Then, it's off to the races: a quick graph is presented to you, with a scale of ten pixels per tick mark. And a quick escape from the graph is provided by pressing the ESCAPE key.

• • •

Note that the constant π in line **7** is stored as a double-precision number using the **#** symbol, so feel free to use the variable name when constructing a function to graph. (Consider coding other mathematical constants, such as e, the Euler number, if the need arises.) Line **36**, which contains the user-inputted function, also is double-precision, to permit the display of as many digits as possible.

• • •

XYGRAPH.BAS
```
5 REM REAL X AND Y COORDINATE GRAPH BASED OF
  SYSTEM OF X BEING IN CENTER
6 'CONSTANTS:
7 PI#=3.1415927#
10 SCREEN 9:KEY OFF:COLOR 12,0:CLS:X=-500
11 LOCATE 8,1:PRINT"X-Y GRAPH"
12 LOCATE 10,1:PRINT"MAKE SURE YOU HAVE ENTERED
   YOUR FUNCTION IN LINE 36"
13 LOCATE 12,1:LINE INPUT"PRESS <ENTER> TO SEE THE
   GRAPH...";L$
17 CLS
20 PSET(320,0):DRAW"D360":PSET(0,174.5):DRAW"R645"
```

```
21 FOR A=330 TO 645 STEP 10
22 PSET(A,164.5),7:DRAW"D20":NEXT A
24 FOR A=310 TO -10 STEP -10
25 PSET(A,164.5),7:DRAW"D20":NEXT A
26 FOR A=184.5 TO 360 STEP 10
27 PSET(310,A),7:DRAW"R20":NEXT A
28 FOR A=164.5 TO -10 STEP -10
29 PSET(310,A),7:DRAW"R20":NEXT A
30 PSET(0,0),0
33 FOR LOOP=1 TO 1500
35 X=X+1 'LINE 36: PUT IN YOUR FUNCTION IN THE ( )
36 Y#=(X+10)
40 LINE-(X+320,-Y#+174.5),15
45 NEXT LOOP
47 COLOR 15
49 PRINT"EACH TICK MARK REPRESENTS TEN UNITS"
50 PRINT"PRESS <ESC> TO EXIT..."
60 I$=INKEY$
70 IF I$=CHR$(27) THEN CLS:END
80 GOTO 60
```

• • •

Being able to adjust the viewing window and the horizontal and vertical scales would make graphical analysis much easier. In addition, instead of having to hard code the function, the program could prompt the user about classes of functions he or she wishes to graph—e.g., Would you like to see a polynomial, trigonometric function, or hyperbolic function? From there, constants—such as linear or quadratic or cubic or quartic terms—could be entered. Although this would reduce the flexibility of **XYGRAPH.BAS**, it would also increase its user-friendliness.

Slope Fields

The slope of a linear equation quantifies its change in y for every unit increase in x. For example, consider this linear function:

$$f(x) = 3x + 1$$

The slope of this function is three—for every three units the graph moves upward (rise), it travels one unit to the right (run).

The *derivative* of a function reveals its slope. So, the derivative of $f(x) = 3x + 1$ is

$$f'(x) = \frac{dy}{dx} = 3$$

confirming that the slope of the function is three.

But let's now focus in on this equation:

$$\frac{dy}{dx} = 3$$

Called a *differential equation*, any function with a slope of three satisfies the equation. So, in addition to $f(x) = 3x + 1$, we might have $f(x) = 3x - 1$, or

$f(x) = 3x + 6$, or $f(x) = 3x + C$, where C is a constant term. And, indeed, the antiderivative of three is given as

$$\int 3dx = 3x + C$$

So any linear function in the form $f(x) = 3x + C$ satisfies the differential equation shown above.

We could graph the differential function $dy/dx = 3$ on the coordinate plane; these sorts of graphs are called *slope fields*, which show the slope of the function at selected coordinates throughout the plane. A slope field of $dy/dx = 3$ would show short line segments, all tilted with a slope equal to three, scattered throughout the plane.

Suppose, instead, that our differential equation had been

$$\frac{dy}{dx} = 3x$$

Now we'd be looking for a function that has a slope of $3x$ at any given set of coordinates. For instance, the slope of the function at the point $(2,4)$ would be $3 \cdot (2) = 6$, and the slope of the function at the point $(-5,2)$ would equal $3 \cdot (-5) = -15$. Using integration, we can find the function (or more accurately, the *family* of functions) that satisfies this criterion:

$$\int 3xdx = \tfrac{3}{2}x^2 + C$$

This family of functions is parabolic. A slope field of $dy/dx = 3x$ would show short line segments of varying steepness spread out in a parabolic manner through the coordinate plane. Note that slope fields can be made of all differential equations, but not all differential equations can be integrated.

The program **DIFF.BAS**, which draws slope fields onscreen, gives you options when entering in your differential equation, although—because you don't have to type the equation directly into the code—there are limitations. However, you can enter in two equations at a time.

When run, you'll be asked to enter your equations in the following form: **(C1*Y1^P1)+(C2*Y2^P2)**, where **C1** and **C2** are the coefficients and **P1** and **P2** are the powers of the two variables.

Once all coefficients and powers for *both* equations have been entered, **DIFF.BAS** maps the slope field. Pressing the ESCAPE key ends the program.

• • •

Note that, like **XYGRAPH.BAS**, the code must convert a graphics screen to the coordinate plane—which has both negative and positive coordinates. Lines **74** and **75** handle the somewhat complex calculations.

• • •

DIFF.BAS
```
10 KEY OFF:SCREEN 9:COLOR 15,0:CLS
20 REM ---TWO DIFF EQUATIONS WILL BE IN THE
   FOLLOWING FORM:
21 REM ---(C1*Y1^P1) + (C2*Y2^P2) FOR Y1 AND Y2
30 PRINT"In the form:(C1*Y1^P1) + (C2*Y2^P2) FOR
   Y1 AND Y2"
40 INPUT
   "C1";C1:INPUT"P1";P1:INPUT"C2";C2:INPUT"P2";P2
45 INPUT
   "C3";C3:INPUT"P3";P3:INPUT"C4";C4:INPUT"P4";P4
50 REM--THE DISPLAYING PART
55 CLS
56 PSET(0,175),4:DRAW"R650":PSET(320,0),4:
   DRAW"D350"
```

```
57 LOCATE 1,46:PRINT"Y1=";C1;"Y1^";P1;" +
   ";C2;"Y2^";P2
58 LOCATE 2,46:PRINT"Y2=";C3;"Y1^";P3;" +
   ";C4;"Y2^";P4
65 FOR R=1 TO 349 STEP 20:Y1L=T:Y2L=R
70 FOR T=1 TO 639 STEP 20:Y1L=T:Y2L=R
71 FOR U=1 TO 10
74 Y2=(C3*-((T-320)/(10+(-T-320)/10*P3))^P3)+(C4*-
   ((R-175)/(10+(-R-175)/10*P4))^P4)+R
75 Y1=(C1*-((T-320)/(10+(-T-320)/10*P1))^P1)+(C2*-
   ((R-175)/(10+(-R-175)/10*P2))^P2)+T
76 LINE(Y1L,Y2L)-(Y1,Y2),14:Y1L=Y1:Y2L=Y2
78 NEXT U
90 NEXT T,R
100 I$=INKEY$
110 IF I$<>CHR$(27) THEN 100
120 CLS
```

• • •

Although it's a good start, **DIFF.BAS** needs more viewing options in order to make it truly useful. The scales for *x* and *y*, as well as the viewing window, shouldn't simply be set to fixed values. And the families of differential equations that the program can graph is extremely limited as well.

User Movement
LOAD "MOVE.BAS"

Ok

RUN_

Watching objects move around the screen, with no control over them, gets tiresome rather quickly.

MOVE.BAS is the first in a series of programs that place movement control firmly in the hands of the user. Although it's very simple, the techniques permitting user control carry through to the more advanced programs presented later on.

Run MOVE.BAS, and you'll be presented with a black box, inside of which is a maroon trapezoid. You can move the trapezoid in eight directions, all set by the numeric keypad (for instance, *9* moves the trapezoid diagonally up and to the right, *4* strictly to the left, and so forth); venture too close to the boarders of the box and you'll be stopped dead in your tracks. Pressing *E* exits the program.

• • •

An INKEY$ variable takes care of the interactivity, while several DRAW statements make sure that when the trapezoid moves, it doesn't leave visible trails behind (see lines 100 and 110).

• • •

MOVE.BAS

```
10 SCREEN 7:COLOR 7,7:CLS:COLOR 8
15 X=120:Y=110
```

```
20 PSET(30,0):DRAW"F40 D120 G40 E40 R180 F40 H40
   U120 E40 G40 L180
30 PSET(X,Y),4:DRAW"E10 R30 F10 L50
40 I$=INKEY$:IF I$="" THEN GOTO 40
50 PSET(X,Y),7:DRAW"E10 R30 F10 L50
60 IF I$="6" THEN X=X+5
70 IF I$="4" THEN X=X-5
80 IF I$="8" THEN Y=Y-5
90 IF I$="2" THEN Y=Y+5
91 IF I$="7" THEN Y=Y-5:X=X-5
92 IF I$="1" THEN X=X-5:Y=Y+5
93 IF I$="9" THEN Y=Y-5:X=X+5
94 IF I$="3" THEN X=X+5:Y=Y+5
95 IF I$="E" THEN END
96 IF I$="e" THEN END
100 PSET(X,Y),4:DRAW"E10 R30 F10 L50
110 PSET(X,Y),7:DRAW"E10 R30 F10 L50
115 IF X>180 THEN X=X-5:SOUND 37,1
116 IF X<85 THEN X=X+5:SOUND 37,1
117 IF Y<65 THEN Y=Y+5:SOUND 37,1
118 IF Y>145 THEN Y=Y-5:SOUND 37,1
190 GOTO 30
```

● ● ●

MOVE.BAS is a simple demo of graphics with user control.
Its code can (and will) serve as a springboard to more
complex programs.

Simple Painting
LOAD "PAINT.BAS"
Ok
RUN

The first electronic painting program was called *Sketchpad*, created by MIT graduate student Ivan Sutherland back in 1963. Using a light pen, simple shapes could be drawn and scaled.

By the time the '80s rolled around, Andy Warhol was excitedly drawing circles with *MacPaint*, and computers haven't released their stranglehold on art to this day.

PAINT.BAS is an exceedingly simple painting program that nonetheless serves as a bare-bones template for more advanced painting-program approaches later on in the book. When run, you'll be asked which SCREEN you wish to paint in, and where, PSET-wise, you wish to begin the sketching. Then, using the numeric keypad, you can move the cursor to your heart's delight, leaving colored trails in its wake. You can also PRESET-style erase what you've drawn one pixel at a time by pressing certain letters—see the code below for the commands—or exit by typing *E*.

• • •

Your canvas is dependent upon the initial prompts. What's constant, though, are the options: eight drawing directions, fifteen colors to cycle through, and erasures pixel-by-pixel or all at once, handled entirely by an INKEY$ statement.

• • •

PAINT.BAS

```
0 KEY OFF:SCREEN 9:COLOR 4,4:CLS:COLOR 15
1 INPUT"SCREEN(7-9)";D:INPUT"BACKGROUND COLOR (1-
  15)";A:INPUT"START AT X POINT";W:INPUT"START AT
  Y POINT";V
2 SCREEN D:COLOR 2,2:CLS:COLOR 15
10 COLOR A,A:CLS:PA=1
20 X=W:Y=V
30 I$=INKEY$:IF I$="" THEN GOTO 30
40 IF I$="8" THEN Y=Y-1
50 IF I$="6" THEN X=X+1
51 IF I$="4" THEN X=X-1
52 IF I$="2" THEN Y=Y+1
53 IF I$="P" THEN PA=PA+1
54 IF I$="C" THEN GOTO 80
55 IF I$="E" THEN GOTO 90
56 IF I$="S" THEN GOTO 0
57 IF I$="A" THEN X=X-1:GOTO 130
58 IF I$="W" THEN Y=Y-1:GOTO 130
59 IF I$="F" THEN X=X+1:GOTO 130
60 IF I$="Z" THEN Y=Y+1:GOTO 130
61 IF I$="7" THEN Y=Y-1:X=X-1
62 IF I$="1" THEN X=X-1:Y=Y+1
63 IF I$="3" THEN Y=Y+1:X=X+1
64 IF I$="9" THEN X=X+1:Y=Y-1
65 IF PA=>16 THEN PA=1
69 PSET(X,Y),PA
70 GOTO 30
80 COLOR A,A:CLS:GOTO 30
90 COLOR 1,1:CLS:COLOR 15
100 SOUND 750,4:SOUND 900,4:PRINT:PRINT:PRINT:
    PRINT:PRINT"EXITING PAINT"
110 FOR N=1 TO 4000:NEXT N:END
130 PRESET(X,Y)
140 GOTO 30
```

• • •

PAINT.BAS is a start—but it's a very limited program. So much more could be done on a GW-BASIC virtual canvas.

Quiz-Per-Play
LOAD "QPP.BAS"

Ok

RUN_

Disney's underrated and now largely forgotten film *The Black Hole* (1979) arrived in theaters at a time when the cinema was awash in *Star Wars* rip-offs. But *The Black Hole* is a cinema original for a number of reasons, not the least being John Barry's hauntingly beautiful score. For instance: in the late '70's on-screen special effects hadn't yet been completed handed over to computers, but *The Black Hole* boasts the longest film sequence (to that time) generated entirely by computer: the vertiginous first-person journey into a warped green chessboard-like spinning black hole.

Several years later, when Tandy Corporation released their line of Color Computer machines, Disney licensed out *The Black Hole* characters and concept for cassette-tape software entitled *Space Probe: Math* (1983). Although ostensibly designed for children to help them reinforce their math skills—"correct answers generate positive, reinforcing responses," as the back of the bright orange-and-black plastic box casing explains—the adventures stories are so compelling, and the production values so high, that you'll win an argument if you claim that the software's narrative is better than the movie's. *Space Probe: Math* was one of the original pieces of personal computer edutainment.

`QPP.BAS` takes `PAINT.BAS` (see the previous chapter) and wraps a question-and-answer structure around it. It's no *Space Probe: Math*, but it's in the same vein. Answer two multiplication questions correctly, and you get a reward: some time to sketch on the screen.

• • •

The math problems are set up in lines **240** and **250**, while line **490** limits your drawing time.

• • •

QPP.BAS

```
10 KEY OFF:SCREEN 7:COLOR 15,0:CLS
20 LOCATE 10,10:PRINT"The Quiz-Per-Play System"
30 FOR V=1 TO 3000
40 IF I$=CHR$(27) THEN CLS:END
50 IF I$="S" OR I$="s" THEN 200
60 NEXT V
70 CLS
80 LOCATE 10,7:PRINT"2 problems, time at the ma
   chine"
90 FOR V=1 TO 3000
91 I$=INKEY$
92 IF I$="S" OR I$="s" THEN 200
93 NEXT V
95 CLS
100 LOCATE 10,5:PRINT"Drawing game when you finish
    Quiz"
110 FOR V=1 TO 3000
120 I$=INKEY$
130 IF I$="S" OR I$="s" THEN 200
140 NEXT V
150 CLS
160 LOCATE 10,7:PRINT"Push 'S' to start when
    ready"
170 FOR V=1 TO 3000
175 I$=INKEY$
180 IF I$="S" OR I$="s" THEN 200
185 NEXT V
190 CLS
195 GOTO 20
200 CLS
210 RANDOMIZE TIMER
220 FOR Z=1 TO 2
230 PRINT:PRINT:PRINT:PRINT"     What is:"
240 C=INT(RND*40):B=INT(RND*9)
```

```
250 V=C*B
260 PRINT:PRINT"          ";C;"Multiplied by:";B;
270 INPUT G
280 IF G=V THEN GOTO 300
290 CLS:GOTO 20
300 PRINT"        Correct.":NEXT Z
310 PRINT:PRINT"       and very nicely
    done.":FOR H=1 TO 9999:NEXT H
320 CLS:PRINT:PRINT:PRINT:PRINT:PRINT"
    Use the numbers 8,4,2,6 to       draw with the
    cursor."
330 PRINT"   Use the + key to scroll through the
    different cursor colors."
340 PRINT:PRINT:PRINT"        PLEASE PRESS <ENTER>
    TO BEGIN.";
350 LINE INPUT E$
360 CLS:T=0
370 X=40:Y=40:C=15
380 I$=INKEY$:T=T+1:IF T=19000 THEN CLS:GOTO 20
390 PSET(X,Y),C
400 IF I$="" THEN 380
410 T=T+1:PSET(X,Y),C
420 IF I$="8" THEN Y=Y-1
430 IF I$="2" THEN Y=Y+1
440 IF I$="6" THEN X=X+1
450 IF I$="4" THEN X=X-1
460 IF C=>16 THEN C=1
470 IF I$=CHR$(27) THEN CLS:END
480 IF I$="+" THEN C=C+1
490 IF T=19000 THEN CLS:GOTO 20
500 GOTO 380
```

• • •

Writing more complex edutainment (or infotainment) programs is not an easy task, but more than feasible with GW-BASIC. If you can, get ahold of *Space Probe: Math* to see the apotheosis of the genre.

Chaos Theory
LOAD "CHAOS.BAS"

Ok

RUN

If you've heard of the butterfly effect—the notion that a butterfly flapping its wings somewhere in the world can somehow have a measurable meteorological effect somewhere else on the Earth—then you have at least a passing familiarity with *chaos theory*. Mathematical systems whose behavior is extremely sensitive to initial conditions can be investigated by using chaos theory.

Mathematician Edward Lorenz, who studied weather prediction, was one of the pioneers of chaos theory. Another was Benoît Mandelbrot, who is probably best known for his Mandelbrot set, which produces the most recognizable fractal in the world. (If you're interested, the Mandelbrot set is an iteration of a polynomial given by $z_{n+1} = z_n^2 + c$, graphed on the complex plane—i.e., you'll have to account for both real and imaginary solutions. Its self-similarity, the key characteristic of fractals, is breathtaking in its complexity.)

CHAOS.BAS puts power to the idea that small changes in initial conditions lead to vastly different outcomes. The program asks the user to both construct a convex polynomial of *n* sides as well as input a *multiplicative factor*. Colorful chaotic patterns result from these variations in user-defined conditions; see the screenshot above for an example.

• • •

After using the keyboard to construct the convex polynomial (see lines **100** to **400**), the formulas resulting in the chaos lie in lines **730** and **740**.

• • •

CHAOS.BAS
```
10 SCREEN 9: COLOR 15,0: CLS: KEY OFF: RANDOMIZE
   TIMER
20 DIM XX(15), YY(15)
25 CLS:X=50: Y=50: SIDES=0: COUNTER=1: FACTOR=0
30 PRINT"THE CHAOS GAME"
40 PRINT:PRINT"You need to draw a convex polygon
   of n sides, where n is greater than 3 and no"
50 PRINT"bigger than 15. Then you need to plot an
   'initial point.'"
55 PRINT"You will also need to give a multiplica
   tive 'factor.' If the factor is 0.5"
56 PRINT"then the point will go half the distance
   to the next point."
60 LOCATE 15,5
70 INPUT"How many sides will your polygon have
   (input 0 to quit)";SIDES
75 IF SIDES=0 THEN CLS:END
80 IF SIDES>15 THEN 70
90 IF SIDES<3 THEN 70
95 INPUT"Which multiplicative 'factor' to use?
   (Hint: 0.5 is standard)";FACTOR
100 CLS
110 I$=INKEY$
115 PSET(X,Y),15
```

```
120 IF I$="" THEN 110
125 PRESET(X,Y)
130 IF I$=CHR$(27) THEN 25
140 IF I$="D" OR I$="d" THEN X=X+4
150 IF I$="A" OR I$="a" THEN X=X-4
160 IF I$="W" OR I$="w" THEN Y=Y-4
170 IF I$="Z" OR I$="z" THEN Y=Y+4
200 IF I$=" " AND COUNTER>SIDES THEN 700
210 IF I$=" " AND COUNTER<=SIDES THEN GOSUB 500
300 PSET(X,Y),15
400 GOTO 110
500 PRESET(X,Y)
510 CIRCLE(X,Y),4,15
515 XX(COUNTER)=X:YY(COUNTER)=Y
520 X=X+8:Y=Y+8
530 COUNTER=COUNTER+1
600 RETURN
700 PSET(X,Y),15
710 WHILE(INKEY$<>CHR$(27))
720 NEX=INT(1+SIDES*RND(1))
730 X=(XX(NEX)+X)*FACTOR
740 Y=(YY(NEX)+Y)*FACTOR
750 PSET(X,Y),NEX
760 WEND
770 GOTO 25
```

● ● ●

More of chaos theory can be explored using GW-BASIC.
Here's a challenge: construct a visual representation of the
Mandelbrot set at various levels of "magnification."

Ok Button

```
LOAD "OK.BAS"
Ok
RUN_
```

Using the **DRAW** statement, without laying out graphics ahead of time, is like drawing blindly.

DRAW offers several options: absolute movement in eight directions from the cursor's current position, absolute movement to a specific coordinate pair, and relative movement in a horizontal and vertical direction from the cursor's current position. (There are even more **DRAW** capabilities, like scaling and rotation, which we will focus on in a later chapter.)

Let's look at the absolute movement in eight directions first: **U10** draws a line ten units up; **D10** draws a line ten units down; **L10** draws a line ten units left; **R10** draws a line ten units right; **E10** draws a line ten units up and right; **H10** draws a line ten units up and left; **F10** draws a line ten units down and right; and **G10** draws a line ten units down and left.

So, for example, if **DRAW"U5 R10 F15** was coded, you'd be telling GW-BASIC to—from the current cursor's position (you can use **PSET** to set that)—move up five units, right ten units, and diagonally downward fifteen, all the while leaving the trails of (instantaneous) movement behind.

Instead of using directional parameters, you might prefer to use **M** instead. For instance, by typing **DRAW"M20,30 M50,90** GW-BASIC will draw lines from the current cursor's position to those two points (use **B** instead of **M** to jump to that location sans line). If you type **DRAW"M-20,+30**, then relative movement would result.

Feel free to copy and use the following graph to plot out **SCREEN 7** images. Note that you'll have to hold the page lengthwise to correspond correctly with the display.

Graphics for the program **OK.BAS**, a blinking "Ok" button, made use of the graph paper above. To stop the button from blinking—and exit out of the program—simply press any key.

• • •

Graphically, **OK.BAS** leans solely on directional movement along with the **PAINT** and **PSET** statements to perform its visual magic.

• • •

```
OK.BAS
10 KEY OFF
20 SCREEN 7:COLOR 15,2:CLS
30 PSET(40,11),8:DRAW"R39 D20 R1 U20 D20 L40 U1
   R40 D1 L40 U20
50 PAINT(60,21),7,8
60 PSET(45,16),8:DRAW"D10 R7 U10 L7
70 PSET(65,16),8:DRAW"D10 U5 E5 G5 F5
75 PSET(45,28),8:DRAW"R7
80 PAINT(60,21),14,8:PAINT(46,18),14,8:T=0
90 I$=INKEY$
100 IF I$<>"" THEN GOTO 180
119 T=T+1:IF T=300 THEN GOTO 140
120 IF I$="" THEN GOTO 90
130 GOTO 90
140 PAINT(60,21),7,8
150 PAINT(46,18),7,8
160 FOR C=1 TO 4000:NEXT C:T=0
170 GOTO 30
180 SOUND 1000,1:PAINT(60,21),4,8
185 PAINT(46,18),4,8
190 END
```

• • •

Making use of graph paper to plot out images has its drawbacks, namely, a lack of precision. Nonetheless, some nice graphical flourishes are easily achieved. Consider this program:

EFFECTS.BAS
```
10 KEY OFF:SCREEN 7:COLOR 8,2:CLS
20 PSET(170,130):DRAW"R20 D20 L20 U20"
30 PAINT(180,140),7,8
40 PSET(190,130),15:DRAW"L20 D20"
50 CIRCLE(126,96),10,4
60 PAINT(126,96),4
70 COLOR 15
80 PSET(123,90):DRAW"R1 L1 D1 L3 D1 R1 L1 D1 L1"
90 PSET(0,10),8:DRAW"R320"
100 PSET(0,20),8:DRAW"R320"
110 PAINT(0,15),7,8
120 PSET(0,10),15:DRAW"R320"
130 PSET(0,180),15:DRAW"R320 U1 L320 U1 R320 U1
    L320"
140 PSET(0,190),8:DRAW"R320 D1 L320 D1 R320 D1
    L320"
150 PSET(126,96):DRAW"R40 D10 L40 U10"
160 PSET(166,96),8:DRAW"D10 L40"
```

Run **EFFECTS.BAS**, and you'll see two thick horizontal bars in bas-relief, classic Windows 3.1-style, along with several pop-up buttons (one transparent, the other opaque) and a glowing red sphere.

Later on we'll explore alternatives to graph paper, but, for now, consider making your own set of high resolution **SCREEN 9** graph paper; it'll need to be 640 pixels wide by 350 pixels high.

The Target Game
LOAD "TARGET.BAS"

Ok

RUN_

After entering the password—it's simply *q*—a giant "T" descends menacingly from the screen, followed quickly by crosshairs which approach from the right. Stopping right in the center of the base of the "T," the crosshairs light up—and the "T" is destroyed.

So begins **TARGET.BAS**, a breathtakingly simple yet maddeningly frustrating game of reflexes. The premise is simple: for three stages, you need to move your crosshairs (using the numeric keypad) to the center of the target, wherever it happens to be on-screen. You have very little time to do so—run out of time, and the game restarts on the first stage.

• • •

Although the code for **TARGET.BAS** is long, it is not particularly complicated. Many lines are devoted to the display of graphics and are thus packed with **PSET**, **DRAW**, and **CIRCLE** statements.

Lines **5** through **8** set the coordinates of the targets for each stage using two arrays: one for *x* and one for *y*. After displaying some graphics on the password-entry screen, the opening animations are shown.

Eventually, you are asked to set your level of play: easy, medium, or hard. The harder the level, the shorter the stages' time limit. See lines **410** to **440** for the details.

Once the timed stages begin, the program needs to constantly check for three things: (1) The direction you're moving the crosshairs; (2) That the crosshairs stay within a tight range on-screen (i.e., error checking); and (3) If, when the trigger was pulled, the crosshairs were right overtop the target (i.e., a successful shot). **INKEY\$**, of course, takes in all of the keyboard data, and conditional statements perform the analyses (read carefully through lines **550** to **750** to see).

The remaining lines of code take care of animations that move the crosshairs off-screen, declare the game over, and award victory to the player.

● ● ●

TARGET.BAS

```
5 DIM TARGETX(3):DIM TARGETY(3)
6 TARGETX(1)=150:TARGETY(1)=100    'STAGE 1
7 TARGETX(2)=170:TARGETY(2)=80     'STAGE 2
8 TARGETX(3)=200:TARGETY(3)=150    'STAGE 3
10 SCREEN 7:COLOR 15,8:CLS
11 PSET(0,185),8:DRAW"R320 D1 L320 D1 R320 D1 L320
   D1 R320 D1 L320 D1 R320 D1 L320 D1 R320 D1 L320
   D1 R320 D1 L320 D1 R320 D1 L320
12 PRINT:PRINT:PRINT"      W H A T   I S   T H E   "
13 PRINT:PRINT:PRINT:PRINT:PRINT:PRINT:PRINT:
   PRINT:PRINT:PRINT:PRINT:PRINT"
   ASSWORD":COLOR 15
20 PSET(50,30):DRAW"R40 F20 D30 G20 D40 L40 U110
30 PSET(65,50):DRAW"R30 D30 L30 U30
40 PAINT(70,100),14,15
50 PSET(160,60):DRAW"E20 R30 F20 D30 G40 D40 L20
   U40 E40 U30 L30 G10 H10
60 PAINT(220,80),11,15
70 CIRCLE(180,185),10:PAINT(180,185),11,15
80 FOR C=1 TO 10000:NEXT C:FOR A=1 TO 15:COLOR
   ,A:NEXT A:COLOR ,8
85 I$=INKEY$:IF I$="q" THEN GOTO 100
90 GOTO 80
```

```
100 COLOR ,4:SOUND 400,3:FOR N=1 TO 1000:NEXT
    N:SOUND 600,5:FOR B=1 TO 10000:NEXT B:COLOR
    3,3:CLS:COLOR 8
110 I$=INKEY$:IF I$="S" THEN GOTO 400:FOR A=1 TO
    5:SOUND 200,1:FOR N=1 TO 1000:NEXT N:SOUND
    100,1:FOR Z=1 TO 1000:NEXT Z:NEXT A
120 FOR A=1 TO 10:SOUND 200,1:FOR C=1 TO 300:NEXT
    C:SOUND 100,1:FOR Z=1 TO 300:NEXT Z:NEXT A
125 FOR Y=0 TO 30 STEP 2
130 PSET(70,Y),15:DRAW"R130 D20 L50 D110 L30 U110
    L50 U20":FOR N=1 TO 2000:NEXT N: SOUND
    100,1:PSET(70,Y),3:DRAW"R130 D20 L50 D110 L30
    U110 L50 U20"
140 NEXT Y
150 PSET(70,30),15:DRAW"R130 D20 L50 D110 L30 U110
    L50 U20"
160 FOR L=230 TO 135 STEP -4
170 PSET(L,90),1:DRAW"U30 D15 R30 L60 R30 D15
175 PSET(70,30),15:DRAW"R130 D20 L50 D110 L30 U110
    L50 U20"
180 FOR N=1 TO 1000:NEXT N
190 PSET(L,90),3:DRAW"U30 D15 R30 L60 R30 D15
200 NEXT L
204 FOR X=1 TO 10
205 FOR K=1 TO 15
210 PSET(135,90),K:DRAW"U30 D15 R30 L60 R30 D15
220 NEXT K
225 NEXT X
230 COLOR 3,3:CLS:COLOR 15
231 PSET(135,90),1:DRAW"U30 D15 R30 L60 R30
    D15":FOR B=1 TO 5000:NEXT B
235 PRINT:PRINT:PRINT:PRINT"
    ";CHR$(34);"BOOM";CHR$(34)
240 FOR Z=1 TO 10000:NEXT Z
250 COLOR 3,3:CLS:COLOR 4
255 T=0
260 FOR X=135 TO 360 STEP 4.5
270 PSET(X,90),1:DRAW"U30 D15 R30 L60 R30 D15"
280 FOR B=1 TO 1000:NEXT B
290 PSET(X,90),3:DRAW"U30 D15 R30 L60 R30 D15
300 NEXT X
305 PRINT:PRINT:PRINT:PRINT:PRINT:PRINT:PRINT:
    PRINT"           ARGET"
```

```
310 PSET(20,30),4:DRAW"R80 D20 L30 D50 L20 U50 L30
    U20
320 PAINT(60,60),15,4
330 FOR N=1 TO 10000:NEXT N
350 PSET(260,60),1:DRAW"U30 D15 R30 L60 R30 D15
360 LOCATE 15,1:PRINT"PRESS 'S' TO START"
380 I$=INKEY$:IF I$="S" THEN GOTO 400
385 IF I$="s" THEN GOTO 400
390 GOTO 380
400 COLOR 1,1:CLS:COLOR 15
410 PRINT"DIFFICULTY?":PRINT:PRINT"PRESS 1 FOR
    EASY"
411 PRINT"PRESS 2 FOR MEDIUM"
412 PRINT"PRESS 3 FOR HARD"
415 PRINT:PRINT:PRINT"INSTRUCTIONS: Use the numer
    ic keypad to move the crosshairs to the cent
    er"
416 PRINT"of the TARGET as quickly as possible.
    When at the center, shoot by pressing"
417 PRINT"the number 5. There are three stages."
418 COUNT=0   'Set stage counter to zero
420 I$=INKEY$
430 IF I$="1" THEN T=150:GOTO 455
435 IF I$="2" THEN T=100:GOTO 455
440 IF I$="3" THEN T=50:GOTO 455
450 GOTO 420
455 FOR LOOP=1 TO 3   'THREE STAGES
457 COUNT=COUNT+1   'Set current stage
460 FOR N=1 TO 15:COLOR ,N:NEXT N
470 COLOR 3,3:CLS:COLOR 1
471 LOCATE 10,1:PRINT"        GET READY FOR STAGE
    ";LOOP;"...."
472 FOR V=1 TO 10000:NEXT V:E=0:XX=90:YY=90
474 COLOR 3,3:CLS:COLOR 1
480 PSET(10,10),8:DRAW"R30 D190 L30 U190
490 PAINT(30,30),2,8:PSET(35,20),15:DRAW"D180
500 PSET(280,10),8:DRAW"R30 D190 L30 U190
510 PAINT(290,40),2,8:PSET(305,20),15:DRAW"D180
520 PSET(50,10),8:DRAW"D10 L10 R10 D10 R220 U10
    R10 L10 U10 L220
530 PAINT(60,20),2,8:PSET(55,15),15:DRAW"R210
540 CIRCLE(TARGETX(LOOP),TARGETY(LOOP)),
    20,1:CIRCLE(TARGETX(LOOP),TARGETY(LOOP)),10,4:
```

```
    CIRCLE(TARGETX(LOOP),TARGETY(LOOP)),5,1:PSET(T
    ARGETX(LOOP),TARGETY(LOOP)),4
550 I$=INKEY$:E=E+1:IF E=T THEN GOTO 850
560 IF I$="5" THEN GOTO 755
570 IF I$="8" THEN YY=YY-2
580 IF I$="2" THEN YY=YY+2
590 IF I$="4" THEN XX=XX-2
600 IF I$="6" THEN XX=XX+2
610 IF I$="3" THEN XX=XX+2:YY=YY+2
620 IF I$="1" THEN XX=XX-2:YY=YY+2
630 IF I$="7" THEN XX=XX-2:YY=YY-2
640 IF I$="9" THEN YY=YY-2:XX=XX+2
650 IF I$="E" THEN END
660 IF I$="e" THEN END
670 IF XX=>240 THEN XX=XX-4
680 IF XX=<80 THEN XX=XX+4
690 IF YY=>180 THEN YY=YY-4
700 IF YY=<50 THEN YY=YY+4
710 PSET(XX,YY),1:DRAW"D40 U20 L30 R60
720 FOR B=1 TO 300:NEXT B
725 PSET(XX,YY),3:DRAW"D40 U20 L30 R60
730 CIRCLE(TARGETX(LOOP),TARGETY(LOOP)),20,1:
    CIRCLE(TARGETX(LOOP),TARGETY(LOOP)),10,4:CIRCL
    E(TARGETX(LOOP),TARGETY(LOOP)),5,1:PSET(TARGET
    X(LOOP),TARGETY(LOOP)),4
750 GOTO 550
755 SOUND 1000,1:IF XX=TARGETX(LOOP) AND
    YY=(TARGETY(LOOP)-20) THEN GOTO 760
756 GOTO 550
760 SOUND 1000,4:SOUND 3000,2:FOR B=1 TO 5
770 FOR V=1 TO 15
780 PSET(XX,YY),V:DRAW"D40 U20 L30 R60
790 NEXT V
800 NEXT B
810 COLOR 3,3:CLS:COLOR 1
820 FOR C=150 TO 370 STEP 6
830 PSET(C,YY),1:DRAW"D40 U20 L30 R60":FOR V=1 TO
    1000:NEXT V:PSET(C,YY),3:DRAW"D40 U20 L30
    R60":NEXT C
840 NEXT LOOP
845 IF COUNT=3 THEN 1100
850 PSET(80,50):DRAW"R20 D20 U20 R20
860 PSET(130,50):DRAW"R15 D20 L15 R30 L15 U20 R15
870 PSET(170,70):DRAW"U20 F15 E15 D20
```

```
880 PSET(240,50):DRAW"L30 D10 R10 L10 D10 R30
890 PSET(100,140):DRAW"R20 D20 L20 U20
900 PSET(130,140):DRAW"F20 E20
910 PSET(210,140):DRAW"L30 D10 R20 L20 D10 R30
920 PSET(250,140):DRAW"D10 L30 U10 R30 L30 D10 R10
    F10 H10 L10 D10
930 SOUND 37,10:FOR B=1 TO 10000:NEXT B:COLOR
    1,1:CLS:COLOR 3:DS=DS+1:IF DS=3 THEN GOTO 1000
950 COLOR 1,1:CLS:COLOR 15
1000 PRINT:PRINT:PRINT:PRINT:PRINT:PRINT:PRINT:
     PRINT:PRINT:PRINT:PRINT:PRINT:PRINT"
     AME OVER":FOR Z=0 TO 70 STEP 10
1010 ED=INT(1+15*RND(1))
1020 PSET(70,Z),ED:DRAW"R60 D10 L50 D30 R40 U10
     L20 U10 R30 D30 L60 U50
1025 PSET(70,Z),1:DRAW"R60 D10 L50 D30 R40 U10 L20
     U10 R30 D30 L60 U50
1030 NEXT Z
1035 FOR F=1 TO 4
1036 FOR V=1 TO 15
1040 PSET(70,70),V:DRAW"R60 D10 L50 D30 R40 U10
     L20 U10 R30 D30 L60 U50
1045 NEXT V
1046 NEXT F:SOUND 37,10
1047 FOR B=1 TO 25000:NEXT B:COLOR 3,3:CLS:COLOR
     4:FOR X=1 TO 10000:NEXT X:GOTO 305
1100 CLS
1110 LOCATE 10,1:PRINT"     YOU WON!"
1115 IF T=150 THEN PRINT"But you did it on the
     EASY level."
1120 IF T=100 THEN PRINT"Good, you did it on the
     MEDIUM level."
1125 IF T=50 THEN PRINT"Great, you did it on the
     HARD level!"
1130 PRINT:PRINT"Press <ESCAPE> to end the game."
1135 I$=INKEY$:IF I$<>CHR$(27) THEN 1135
1140 CLS:END
```

● ● ●

TARGET.BAS could be made a much more frustrating and nail-biting experience if the targets themselves either were randomly located on-screen or moved independently while the player raced to line up the crosshairs. Get to work!

Com-Sport

LOAD "COMSPORT.BAS"

Ok

RUN

COMSPORT.BAS is a two-player game that is to fencing what *Pong* is to table tennis. Two combatants face off to lightly "poke" the other with his (or her) single-tipped electronic "foil" first.

• • •

COMSPORT.BAS is coded very similarly to the TARGET.BAS game. The block of code from lines **590** to **740** handles the moving graphics and the very simple two-player user inputs.

• • •

COMSPORT.BAS
```
100 KEY OFF:SCREEN 7:COLOR 15,3:RANDOMIZE TIMER
140 CLS
145 PSET(0,191),15:DRAW"R320"
150 PSET(0,161),15:DRAW"R320"
160 PSET(0,170),8:DRAW"R320"
170 PSET(0,171),15:DRAW"R320"
180 PSET(0,180),8:DRAW"R320"
190 PSET(0,181),15:DRAW"R320"
200 PSET(0,190),8:DRAW"R320"
210 COLOR 15:PSET(60,30):DRAW"L60 D50 R60 U10 L50
    U30 R50 U10"
220 PSET(60,30),8:DRAW"D10 L50 D30"
230 PSET(60,70),8:DRAW"D10 L60"
240 PSET(130,30):DRAW"L60 D50 R60 U50"
```

```
250 PSET(120,40):DRAW"L40 D30 R40 U30"
260 PSET(70,30),8:DRAW"R60 D50"
270 PSET(80,40),8:DRAW"D30 R40"
280 PSET(140,80):DRAW"U50 R20 F20 E20 R20 D50 L10
    U40 L10 G20 H20 L10 D40 L10"
290 PSET(150,40),8:DRAW"D40"
300 PSET(160,30),8:DRAW"F20"
310 PSET(200,40),8:DRAW"G20"
320 PSET(220,30),8:DRAW"D50"
330 PSET(230,50):DRAW"R30 D10 L30 U10"
340 PSET(230,50),8:DRAW"D10 R30"
350 FOR GDS=1 TO 9000:NEXT GDS
360 COLOR 15
370 PSET(60,100):DRAW"L40 D10 R40 D10 L40"
371 PSET(60,100),8:DRAW"L40"
372 PSET(60,110),8:DRAW"L40"
373 PSET(60,120),8:DRAW"L40"
374 FOR GH=1 TO 4000:NEXT GH
380 PSET(70,120):DRAW"U20 R40 D10 L40"
381 PSET(110,100),8:DRAW"L40"
382 PSET(110,110),8:DRAW"L40"
383 FOR GH=1 TO 4000:NEXT GH
390 PSET(160,100):DRAW"L40 D20 R40 U20"
391 PSET(160,100),8:DRAW"L40"
392 PSET(160,120),8:DRAW"L40"
393 FOR GH=1 TO 4000:NEXT GH
400 PSET(210,100):DRAW"L40 D10 R40 U10 D10 L40 D10
    U10 F10"
401 PSET(210,100),8:DRAW"L40"
402 PSET(210,110),8:DRAW"L40"
403 PSET(180,120),8:DRAW"H10"
404 FOR GH=1 TO 4000:NEXT GH
410 PSET(260,100):DRAW"L40 R20 D20"
411 PSET(260,100),8:DRAW"L40"
412 FOR GH=1 TO 4000:NEXT GH
420 FOR FD=20 TO 260
421 PSET(FD,124),15
422 PSET(FD,125),8
423 FOR GT=1 TO 50:NEXT GT
424 NEXT FD
430 FOR TG=9 TO 3 STEP -1:COLOR ,TG:NEXT TG
440 FOR YR=1 TO 16000:NEXT YR
500 CLS:COLOR 14,3
```

```
510 LOCATE 10,2:PRINT" Hit opponent with foil on
    weak spot."
520 LOCATE 12,2:PRINT" Weak spot will be in blue."
530 PSET(0,10),15:DRAW"R320 D1 L320"
540 PSET(0,20),8:DRAW"R320 D1 L320"
550 PSET(0,160),15:DRAW"R320 D1 L320 D1 R320"
560 PSET(0,190),8:DRAW"R320 D1 L320 D1 R320"
570 X=160:Y=140:A=110:B=130:FOR YT=1 TO 18000:NEXT
    YT
580 CLS:COLOR 14,0:PRINT:PRINT:PRINT:PRINT:PRINT:
    PRINT:PRINT"              S T A R T ! !":SOUND
    4000,1:FOR GH=1 TO 3000:NEXT GH:SOUND
    4000,1:FOR GH=1 TO 3000:NEXT GH:SOUND
    4000,1:FOR GH=1 TO 3000:NEXT GH:CLS:COLOR 15
585 LOCATE 1,1:PRINT"To control Yellow: Use 2,8,4,
    and 6."
587 LOCATE 2,1:PRINT"To control Blue: Use T,V,F,
    and H."
590 I$=INKEY$
600 PSET(X,Y),14:DRAW"C14 U20 L9 C1 L1 C14 L10 U20
    R20 D20
605 FOR T=1 TO 200:NEXT T
610 PSET(X,Y),0:DRAW"U20 L20 U20 R20 D20"
620 PSET(A,B),11:DRAW"C11 D20 L9 C1 L1 C11 L10 D20
    R20 U20"
625 FOR T=1 TO 200:NEXT T
630 PSET(A,B),0:DRAW"D20 L20 D20 R20 U20"
640 IF I$="2" THEN Y=Y+1
650 IF I$="8" THEN Y=Y-1
660 IF I$="4" THEN X=X-1
670 IF I$="6" THEN X=X+1
680 IF I$="T" THEN B=B-1
690 IF I$="V" THEN B=B+1
700 IF I$="F" THEN A=A-1
710 IF I$="H" THEN A=A+1
720 IF X=A-9 AND Y=B+20 THEN GOTO 750
730 IF B=Y-20 AND A=X-9 THEN GOTO 765
740 GOTO 590
750 FOR HG=15 TO 0 STEP -1:COLOR ,HG:NEXT HG
760 CLS:SOUND 4000,5:PRINT:PRINT:PRINT:PRINT:
    PRINT:PRINT"   Here is your winner:
    YELLOW!!":GOTO 780
765 FOR HG=15 TO 0 STEP -1:COLOR ,HG:NEXT HG
```

237

```
770 COLOR 11:CLS:SOUND 4000,5:PRINT:PRINT:PRINT:
    PRINT:PRINT:PRINT"    Here is your winner:
    BLUE!!"
780 FOR PAUSE=1 TO 10000:NEXT PAUSE
790 GOTO 100
```

● ● ●

More graphical flourishes, along with some options like different colors for the characters and the background, a time limit, and a designated scoring system would help to make COMSPORT.BAS a richer, more rewarding game.

Rotation Using Trigonometry
LOAD "ROTATION.BAS"

Ok

RUN_

Rotating graphics around the screen is a bit trickier than simply moving images, unchanged, left or right or up or down. In the next chapter, we'll take a look at a simple, GW-BASIC-built-in way to rotate images, but in this chapter, we'll delve a bit into the mathematics of rotation.

Imagine a unit circle—that is, a circle with a radius of one unit (the units could be anything: inches, meters, miles, light years, it makes no difference). Also imagine that this unit circle's center is located at the origin of the coordinate plane. Every coordinate pair on the circle can not only be represented by an (x, y); each coordinate pair can also be given as a $(\cos\theta, \sin\theta)$, where the Greek letter θ (pronounced "theta") represents the angle of rotation in radians (you may recall that 2π is equivalent to 360 degrees, or one full rotation counterclockwise on the coordinate plane). To see why requires a bit of trigonometry.

Suppose, from the base of the positive x-axis, we draw a line at a 45-degree angle that passes right through the unit circle. Consider the line segment that runs from the origin to the point of intersection (x, y) on the unit circle to be the hypotenuse of a right triangle. From (x, y), drop a line downward and perpendicular to the positive x-axis—this will give us a right triangle lying within the unit circle. Specifically, a special right triangle: a 45-45-90, meaning the inside angles are 45, 45, and 90 degrees. We already know the length of the hypotenuse of this special triangle: it's one unit, since the hypotenuse also serves as a radius for the unit circle. With that in mind, let's use the Pythagorean theorem to find the other two sides (which, of course, have the same length, since they're opposite angles with the same measurement):

$$c^2 = a^2 + b^2$$
$$1^2 = x^2 + x^2$$
$$1 = 2x^2$$
$$\tfrac{1}{2} = x^2$$
$$\sqrt{\tfrac{1}{2}} = x$$
$$x = \tfrac{\sqrt{2}}{2} \approx 0.707$$

Since both (non-hypotenuse) sides of the special right triangle have size lengths of around 0.707, we can say that the point (x, y)—which, recall, is the point on the unit circle that the line drawn at a 45-degree angle passes through—is actually at

$$\left(\tfrac{\sqrt{2}}{2}, \tfrac{\sqrt{2}}{2}\right) \approx \left(0.707, 0.707\right)$$

Likewise, we could find the coordinates of angles of any multiple of 45 degrees. And, because there's also a 30-60-90 special triangle that's inscribable, angles of multiples of 30 degrees are easy to come by, too. (Those details, and the trigonometry behind finding the coordinates of messier angles, are left to the intrepid reader.)

But, although we just found the coordinates of a single point, this still doesn't connect the two trigonometric ratios sine and cosine to the point (x, y), which is what we were initially attempting to do.

Remember the definitions of sine and cosine from grade school? If not, here they are:

$$\sin\theta = \frac{opposite}{hypotenuse} \qquad \cos\theta = \frac{adjacent}{hypotenuse}$$

The terms "opposite" and "adjacent" refer to the side opposite and the side adjacent (i.e., next to) the angle of interest, respectively, on a right triangle. With the unit circle, however, the hypotenuse is a radius—and thus has a value of one. Therefore, we can re-express the two ratios as

$$\sin\theta = opposite \qquad \cos\theta = adjacent$$

Reconsidering the 45-degree angle coordinates above, which were calculated off of a triangle within the unit circle, this means that

$$\sin\theta = opposite = \tfrac{\sqrt{2}}{2} \quad \cos\theta = adjacent = \tfrac{\sqrt{2}}{2}$$

With a little further experimentation (with finding coordinates of angles outside of the first quadrant), we realize that at any point (x, y) on the unit circle,

$$(x, y) = (\cos\theta, \sin\theta)$$

which neatly connects all coordinate pairs to trigonometric ratios.

Although the **SCREEN 7** graphics mode is not set up like a coordinate axis—for example, as you travel downward on your computer monitor, the y values increase rather than decrease—we can lean on trigonometry to rotate a point around a circle at the center of the screen, leaving multi-colored trails of pixels in its wake. After a quick pause, the screen clears—and you'll see a white line rotating around the screen. Run **UNITCIR.BAS** and **SINCOS.BAS** to see the colorful, circular shows.

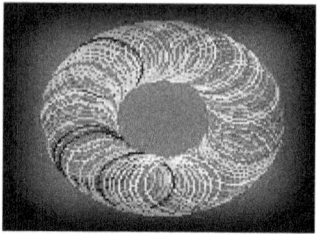

A *rotation matrix* can also permit rotations of coordinates on a plane (or in space) with respect to an angle θ. Consider this rotation matrix:

$$\begin{bmatrix} \cos\theta & -\sin\theta \\ \sin\theta & \cos\theta \end{bmatrix}$$

For instance, if we wished to rotate the point $(5,5)$ at an angle of 45 degrees about the origin, the following matrix-multiplication operation results in the new coordinates.

$$\begin{bmatrix} \cos 45° & -\sin 45° \\ \sin 45° & \cos 45° \end{bmatrix} \cdot \begin{bmatrix} 5 \\ 5 \end{bmatrix} = \begin{bmatrix} 5\cos 45° - 5\sin 45° \\ 5\sin 45° + 5\cos 45° \end{bmatrix} = \begin{bmatrix} 0 \\ 7 \end{bmatrix}$$

Thus, the coordinates $(5,5)$ rotated at a 45-degree angle with respect to the origin ends up at $(0,7)$. In general, then, we can say that any rotation at angle θ about the origin is given by

$$(x \cdot \cos\theta - y \cdot \sin\theta, x \cdot \sin\theta + y\cos\theta)$$

The program **ROTATION.BAS** demonstrates the utility of the rotation matrix.

• • •

Note that both **UNITCIR.BAS** and **SINCOS.BAS** use the **SIN** and **COS** functions, which take radians (rather than degrees) as input. Also note that, in both programs, the **STEP** is small; make the factor a little bigger, and the circle won't be continuous.

The **ROTATION.BAS** program, while similar to its in-chapter brethren, makes use of the rotation matrix and the **LINE** statement to plot some colorful patterns.

• • •

UNITCIR.BAS
```
5 PI=3.14159
10 KEY OFF:SCREEN 7:COLOR 15,0:CLS
20 FOR T=0 TO 2*PI STEP .01
30 PSET(150+COS(T)*30,100+SIN(T)*30),
   INT(1+15*RND(1))
40 NEXT T
50 FOR PAUSE=1 TO 10000:NEXT PAUSE
60 CLS
70 FOR T=0 TO 2*PI STEP .01
80 LINE (150,100)-(150+COS(T)*30,100+SIN(T)*30),15
85 FOR PAUSE=1 TO 100:NEXT PAUSE
86 CLS
90 NEXT T
100 FOR PAUSE=1 TO 10000:NEXT PAUSE
110 CLS:END
```

SINCOS.BAS
```
5 SCREEN 9: COLOR 15,0: KEY OFF
10 CLS
20 PRINT"PRESS <ESC> TO SEE THE NEXT CIRCLE DEMO
   ...."
30 CIRCLE(COS(R)*45+340,SIN(R)*35+140),20,
   INT(1+15*RND(1))
40 R=R-3.14159/50
45 FOR PAUSE=1 TO 100:NEXT PAUSE
46 IF INKEY$=CHR$(27) THEN 60
50 GOTO 30
```

```
60 CLS
62 FOR STEPPER=.1 TO .001 STEP -.01
65 FOR SPIRAL=1 TO 400 STEP STEPPER
70 PSET(COS(R)*SPIRAL+340,SIN(R)*SPIRAL+140),
   INT(1+15*RND(1))
80 R=R-3.14159/50
90 FOR PAUSE=1 TO 100:NEXT PAUSE
100 NEXT SPIRAL
110 NEXT STEPPER
```

ROTATION.BAS
```
10 KEY OFF:SCREEN 9:COLOR 15,0:CLS
20 X=300:Y=200
30 PSET(X,Y),15
35 FOR ANGLE=1 TO 2.32*3.14159 STEP .001
40 X1=(COS(ANGLE)*(X)+(-SIN(ANGLE)*(Y)))
50 Y1=((-SIN(ANGLE))*(X)+(COS(ANGLE)*(Y)))
60 LINE(X,Y)-(X1+200,Y1+200),INT(1+2*RND(1))
70 NEXT ANGLE
```

● ● ●

Although rotating a line is easy, rotating a more complex shape can be tedious using a purely trigonometric method.

Rotation and Scaling Using DRAW
LOAD "SPIN.BAS"

Ok
RUN

Although brute-force trigonometric calculations can help you rotate images on-screen as well as scale them (using rotation matrices), GW-BASIC offers some simple DRAW statement commands to rotate (use TA, or turn at an angle; for instance, TA45 turns the image 45 degrees) and scale (use S, or set scaling factor; for example, S10 sets a scaling factor of 10. The scaling factor can be between 1 and 255). Let's take a look at some programs.

• • •

The first program below, called SPIN.BAS, makes use of the TA command in order to spin a yellow line around the center of the screen. There is a significant drawback with the program, though: since the DRAW command is a string (captured in quotations), and TA must reside inside the string, there seems to be no way to hook a FOR/NEXT loop and a variable around the rotation command, automatizing it. Do you really have to type out a new DRAW statement for every single rotation—and, by extension, every change in the scaling factor?

Luckily, you don't. But you'll need to make use of the VARPTR$ function. Pore over the code of the programs SE1.BAS and SE2.BAS carefully. SE1.BAS is a demo of rotation only; an SE BOOKS (this book's publisher) logo is spun around and centered on-screen. SE2.BAS fiddles with both rotation and scaling, as the letters *S* and *E* fall away from you, only to quickly pop up again.

AIRPLANE.BAS is just that: a third-person view of the back of an airplane. By pressing *4* or *6* on the numeric keypad, you "turn" the plane (the horizon rotates, making it sort of look like the plane's banking).

Finally, run **SROB.BAS** to see a program that puts both scaling and rotation to good use. A rotating box flies from one end of the screen to the other, increasing in size just a bit each time it bounces off the left and right sides of the screen.

● ● ●

SPIN.BAS

```
10 KEY OFF:SCREEN 7
20 COLOR 14:CLS
30 DRAW"TA10 R40"
31 FOR H=1 TO 400:NEXT:CLS
40 DRAW"TA20 R40"
41 FOR H=1 TO 400:NEXT:CLS
50 DRAW"TA30 R40"
51 FOR H=1 TO 400:NEXT:CLS
60 DRAW"TA50 R40"
61 FOR H=1 TO 400:NEXT:CLS
70 DRAW"TA60 R40"
71 FOR H=1 TO 400:NEXT:CLS
80 DRAW"TA70 R40"
81 FOR H=1 TO 400:NEXT:CLS
90 DRAW"TA90 R40":FOR V=1 TO 400:NEXT:CLS
91 DRAW"TA110 R40":FOR V=1 TO 400:NEXT:CLS
92 DRAW"TA140 R40":FOR V=1 TO 400:NEXT:CLS
93 DRAW"TA160 R40":FOR V=1 TO 400:NEXT:CLS
100 DRAW"TA180 R40"
105 FOR K=1 TO 400:NEXT:CLS
110 DRAW"TA200 R40"
115 FOR K=1 TO 400:NEXT:CLS
120 DRAW"TA210 R40"
125 FOR K=1 TO 400:NEXT:CLS
130 DRAW"TA230 R40"
135 FOR K=1 TO 400:NEXT:CLS
```

```
140 DRAW"TA250 R40"
145 FOR K=1 TO 400:NEXT:CLS
150 DRAW"TA280 R40"
155 FOR K=1 TO 400:NEXT:CLS
160 DRAW"TA310 R40"
165 FOR K=1 TO 400:NEXT:CLS
170 DRAW"TA330 R40"
175 FOR K=1 TO 400:NEXT:CLS
180 DRAW"TA350 R40"
185 FOR K=1 TO 400:NEXT:CLS
190 DRAW"TA360 R40"
195 FOR K=1 TO 400:NEXT:CLS
200 GOTO 20
```

SE1.BAS

```
10 KEY OFF:SCREEN 7:COLOR 15,1:CLS:FOR V=1 TO
   14000:NEXT
20 PSET(150,96)
30 FOR HI=0 TO 350 STEP 10
40 DRAW"TA="+VARPTR$(HI)
41 DRAW"S02"
50 DRAW"L30 G10 R30 E10 G10 L30 D20 E10 U10 D10
   R30 G10 L30 E10 R30 D20 G10 U20 E10 D20"
51 DRAW"G10 L30 E10 R20 D10"
52 FOR V=1 TO 400:NEXT V:CLS
53 NEXT HI
54 DRAW"TA360 S02 L30 G10 R30 E10 G10 L30 D20 E10
   U10 D10 R30 G10 L30 E10 R30 D20 G10 U20 E10 D20"
55 DRAW"G10 L30 E10 R20 D10"
56 FOR H=1 TO 19000:NEXT H
61 FOR X=95 TO 45 STEP -1.5
62 PSET(160,X+5)
70 DRAW"TA360 S02 L30 G10 R30 E10 G10 L30 D20 E10
   U10 D10 R30 G10 L30 E10 R30 D20 G10 U20 E10 D20"
80 DRAW"G10 L30 E10 R20 D10"
81 FOR J=1 TO 400:NEXT J:CLS
85 NEXT X
90 PSET(160,X+5):DRAW"TA360 S02 L30 G10 R30 E10
   G10 L30 D20 E10 U10 D10 R30 G10 L30 E10 R30 D20
   G10 U20 E10 D20"
95 DRAW"G10 L30 E10 R20 D10"
100 FOR B=1 TO 10000:NEXT B
110 FOR YI=2 TO 9 STEP 1
120 DRAW"S="+VARPTR$(YI)
```

```
130 PSET(160,X+5)
140 DRAW"TA360 L30 G10 R30 E10 G10 L30 D20 E10 U10
    D10 R30 G10 L30 E10 R30 D20 G10 U20 E10 D20"
150 DRAW"G10 L30 E10 R20 D10"
160 FOR H=1 TO 1000:NEXT H:CLS:NEXT YI
165 PSET(160,X+5)
170 DRAW"S10 TA360 L30 G10 R30 E10 G10 L30 D20 E10
    U10 D10 R30 G10 L30 E10 R30 D20 G10 U20 E10
    D20"
180 DRAW"G10 L30 E10 R20 D10"
190 FOR B=1 TO 10000:NEXT B
200 PSET(170,76):DRAW"R10 L10 D5 R5 L5 D5 R10
210 FOR H=9 TO 1 STEP -1:COLOR ,H:NEXT H
250 FOR A=1 TO 23000:NEXT A:CLS
```

SE2.BAS

```
10 T=0:KEY OFF:SCREEN 7:COLOR 15,4:CLS:FOR L=1 TO
   16000:NEXT
15 FOR GI=60 TO 1 STEP -1:T=T+4
16 DRAW"S="+VARPTR$(GI)
17 DRAW"TA="+VARPTR$(T)
20 DRAW"U10 R10 L10 D10 R10 D10 L10
25 FOR H=1 TO 200:NEXT H:CLS
30 NEXT GI:T=0:FOR Y=1 TO 5000:NEXT Y
40 FOR UI=60 TO 1 STEP -1:T=T+4
50 DRAW"S="+VARPTR$(UI)
60 DRAW"TA="+VARPTR$(T)
70 DRAW"U10 R10 L10 D10 R5 L5 D10 R10
80 FOR H=1 TO 200:NEXT H:CLS
90 NEXT UI:FOR H=1 TO 5000:NEXT H
100 FOR FI=1 TO 60 STEP 4
110 DRAW"S="+VARPTR$(FI)
120 DRAW"U10 R10 L10 D10 R10 D10 L10
130 FOR H=1 TO 200:NEXT H:CLS
140 NEXT FI
150 CLS:FOR H=1 TO 5000:NEXT H
160 FOR DI=1 TO 60 STEP 4
170 DRAW"S="+VARPTR$(DI)
180 DRAW"U10 R10 L10 D10 R5 L5 D10 R10
190 FOR H=1 TO 200:NEXT H:CLS
200 NEXT DI
240 FOR X=1 TO 16000:NEXT X:CLS
```

AIRPLANE.BAS

```
10 KEY OFF:SCREEN 7:COLOR 2,2:CLS:COLOR 14
11 INPUT"Airplane Color:";COL
12 INPUT"Stripe Color:";STCOL:COLOR 1,1:CLS:COLOR
   14
13 INPUT"Size of plane(1-10)";SI:CLS
14 DRAW"S="+VARPTR$(SI)
20 CIRCLE(150,100),3.5,COL
30 PAINT(150,100),7,COL
40 PSET(150,97),COL:DRAW"U15
50 PSET(149,96),STCOL:DRAW"U10
60 PSET(151,96),STCOL:DRAW"U10
70 PSET(154,102),COL:DRAW"R20 D1
80 PSET(152,103),7:DRAW"R21
90 PSET(146,102),COL:DRAW"L20 D1
100 PSET(148,103),7:DRAW"L21
110 PSET(154,99),COL:DRAW"R30 D1
120 PSET(155,100),7:DRAW"R28
130 PSET(146,99),COL:DRAW"L30 D1
140 PSET(145,100),7:DRAW"L28
170 COLOR 3:CIRCLE(80,30),30,,,,.2
180 PAINT(80,30),15,3
190 CIRCLE(160,40),20,,,,.2:PAINT(160,40),15,3
200 CIRCLE(250,30),40,,,,.1:PAINT(250,30),15,3:X=0
210 I$=INKEY$
220 PSET(150,150),2:DRAW"TA="+VARPTR$(X):DRAW"S3
    R320 L640
236 IF I$="" THEN 210
237 PSET(150,150),2:DRAW"S3 R320 L640
238 PSET(150,150),1:DRAW"S3 R320 L640
240 IF I$="4" THEN X=X+4
250 IF I$="6" THEN X=X-4
260 IF X>25 THEN X=X-4
261 IF ASC(I$)=27 THEN END
270 IF X<-25 THEN X=X+4
280 GOTO 210
```

SROB.BAS

```
10 T=1:SCREEN 7:KEY OFF:COLOR 15,1
20 CLS
30 T=T+1:FOR GI=290 TO 0 STEP -5
35 PSET(GI,100)
40 DRAW"TA="+VARPTR$(GI)
45 DRAW"S="+VARPTR$(T)
```

```
50 DRAW"U10 R10 D10 L10
60 FOR L=1 TO 400:NEXT L:CLS
70 NEXT GI:SOUND 100,1:T=T+1
80 FOR CI=0 TO 290 STEP 5
90 PSET(CI,100)
100 DRAW"TA="+VARPTR$(CI)
105 DRAW"S="+VARPTR$(T)
110 DRAW"U10 R10 D10 L10
120 FOR K=1 TO 400:NEXT K:CLS
130 NEXT CI:SOUND 100,1:T=T+1
140 GOTO 20
```

• • •

The **TA** and **S** commands, coupled with **VARPTR$**, bring simplicity and convenience to the rotation and scaling of images. But images are mighty tough to construct in GW-BASIC to begin with; mapping out graphics on graph paper is tedious at best, torturous at worst. Perhaps you've already thought of a better way; if not, stay tuned.

Electronic Art
LOAD "ART1.BAS"
Ok
RUN_

What follows is a small collection of art- or drawing-type programs that make use of scaling, rotation, or both.

● ● ●

ART1.BAS shows connected lines shooting all over the screen; their length is dynamically controlled by you: pressing the + key increases their size, and the − key decreases them.

DRWRND.BAS is almost the same program as ART1.BAS, except instead of lines you control the size of a rapidly moving, flashing box.

ETCH.BAS lets you have a little fun: you can draw patterns of circles and squares, all of varying sizes and colors. Study the code around the INKEY$ statements to see the plethora of options.

COLMAK.BAS lets you see a short DRAW statement pattern mapped all over the screen. If you're unsatisfied with the limited color palette, with a little creativity this program offers you a (rather slight) workaround to an expanded color base. (Another workaround, which we'll encounter later: using the PALETTE statement.)

If you're in a rotten mood, run DMOLTION.BAS—it'll allow you to destroy whatever's on the screen by moving a little block around.

And **TEST.BAS** allows you to, well, test the scaling and rotation of an image. You input the **DRAW** statement as an string from an **INPUT** during the run; then, you can move the image around the screen using the numeric keypad, increase its size using the + key, decrease its size using the − key, and rotate it clockwise and counterclockwise using the *Y* and *T* keys, respectively. The **PCOPY** command on line **260**, which copies from one active screen page to another, reduces some of the flicker when moving the object.

● ● ●

ART1.BAS

```
0 KEY OFF:VIEW PRINT:SCREEN 9:COLOR
   15,0:CLS:PRINT:PRINT:PRINT::AS=4
2 PRINT"ADJUST SIZE OF LINES BY PRESSING + OR -"
3 PRINT"CHANGE BACKGROUND COLOR BY PRESSING B"
4 PRINT"CLEAR SCREEN BY PRESSING C"
5 FOR PAUSE=1 TO 15000:NEXT PAUSE
6 X=INT(1+640*RND(1))
7 Y=INT(1+350*RND(1))
10 KEY OFF:SCREEN 9:COLOR 15,0:CLS
15 RANDOMIZE TIMER
30 T=INT(1+AS*RND(1))
35 V=INT(1+AS*RND(1))
40 C=INT(1+AS*RND(1))
41 B=INT(1+2*RND(1))
42 N=INT(1+2*RND(1))
43 IF B=2 THEN V=-(V)
44 IF N=2 THEN C=-(C)
45 R=15
100 FOR A=1 TO T
101 I$=INKEY$:DRAW"S="+VARPTR$(AS)
102 IF I$="+" THEN AS=AS+1
103 IF AS=>250 THEN AS=250
104 IF I$="-" THEN AS=AS-1
105 IF AS=<1 THEN AS=1
106 IF I$="C" OR I$="c" THEN GOTO 150
107 IF I$="B" OR I$="b" THEN FG=FG+1
108 IF FG=16 THEN FG=1
109 COLOR ,FG
```

```
120 LINE -(X,Y),R
125 X=X+V:Y=Y+C
126 IF X=>650 THEN X=650
127 IF X=<-2 THEN X=-2
128 IF Y=<-2 THEN Y=-2
129 IF Y=>350 THEN Y=350
130 NEXT A
140 GOTO 30
150 FOR AD=1 TO 55:PRINT:NEXT AD
155 GOTO 6
```

DRWRND.BAS

```
0 KEY OFF:SCREEN 9:COLOR 15,0:CLS:RANDOMIZE
  TIMER:AS=4
1 PRINT:PRINT
2 PRINT"ADJUST SIZE OF BOX BY PRESSING + OR -"
3 PRINT"CHANGE BACKGROUND COLOR BY PRESSING B"
4 PRINT"CLEAR SCREEN BY PRESSING C"
5 FOR PAUSE=1 TO 15000:NEXT PAUSE
6 X=INT(1+640*RND(1))
7 Y=INT(1+350*RND(1))
10 KEY OFF:SCREEN 9:COLOR 15,0:CLS
15 RANDOMIZE TIMER
30 T=INT(1+5*RND(1))
35 V=INT(1+5*RND(1))
40 C=INT(1+5*RND(1))
41 B=INT(1+2*RND(1))
42 N=INT(1+2*RND(1))
43 IF B=2 THEN V=-(V)
44 IF N=2 THEN C=-(C)
45 R=INT(1+15*RND(1))
100 FOR A=1 TO T
101 I$=INKEY$:DRAW"S="+VARPTR$(AS)
102 IF I$="+" THEN AS=AS+4
103 IF AS=>250 THEN AS=250
104 IF I$="-" THEN AS=AS-4
105 IF AS=<4 THEN AS=4
106 IF I$="C" OR I$="c" THEN GOTO 150
107 IF I$="B" OR I$="b" THEN FG=FG+1
108 IF FG=16 THEN FG=1
109 COLOR ,FG
120 PSET(X,Y),R:DRAW"R1 D1 L1 U1":PAINT(X+1,Y+1),R
125 X=X+V:Y=Y+C
126 IF X=>650 THEN X=650
```

```
127 IF X=<-2 THEN X=-2
128 IF Y=<-2 THEN Y=-2
129 IF Y=>349 THEN Y=349
130 NEXT A
140 GOTO 30
150 FOR AD=1 TO 55:PRINT:NEXT AD
155 GOTO 6
```

ETCH.BAS

```
10 CLS:INPUT"SCREEN(7-9)";SC:TR=0:BB=0:T=1:
   X=150:Y=96:RANDOMIZE TIMER:KEY OFF:CLS:SCREEN
   SC:COLOR ,BB
15 GOTO 310
20 I$=INKEY$:DRAW"TA="+VARPTR$(TR)
21 IF I$="C" OR I$="c" THEN GOTO 140
22 IF I$="E" OR I$="e" THEN END
23 IF I$="R" OR I$="r" THEN GOTO 150
30 IF I$="4" THEN X=X-1
40 IF I$="6" THEN X=X+1
50 IF I$="8" THEN Y=Y-1
51 IF I$="T" OR I$="t" THEN
   TR=TR+1:DRAW"TA="+VARPTR$(TR)
52 IF TR=>360 THEN TR=0
53 IF I$="N" OR I$="n" THEN
   TR=0:DRAW"TA="+VARPTR$(TR)
54 IF I$="Y" OR I$="y" THEN TR=TR-
   1:DRAW"TA="+VARPTR$(TR)
55 IF I$="B" OR I$="b" THEN BB=BB+1:COLOR ,BB
56 IF BB=15 THEN BB=0:COLOR ,BB
57 IF I$="V" OR I$="v" THEN GOTO 425
60 IF I$="2" THEN Y=Y+1
70 IF I$="1" THEN X=X-1:Y=Y+1
80 IF I$="3" THEN Y=Y+1:X=X+1
81 IF TR=<-360 THEN TR=0:DRAW"TA="+VARPTR$(TR)
90 IF I$="9" THEN Y=Y-1:X=X+1
91 IF I$="+" THEN T=T+4
92 IF I$="-" THEN T=T-4
93 IF T=>250 THEN T=250
94 IF T=<1 THEN T=1
95 IF I$="S" OR I$="s" THEN GOTO 230
100 IF I$="7" THEN X=X-1:Y=Y-1
105 IF I$="D" OR I$="d" THEN GOTO 305
110 R=INT(RND*15)
111 IF R=BB THEN GOTO 110
```

```
120 PSET(X,Y),R:DRAW"S="+VARPTR$(T):DRAW"R1 D1 L1
    U1"
130 GOTO 20
140 FOR H=1 TO 65:PRINT:FOR G=1 TO 200:NEXT G:NEXT
    H:CLS:GOTO 20
150 D=INT(RND*999)
160 S=INT(RND*999)
170 A=INT(RND*15):IF A=BB THEN GOTO 170
190 PSET(D,S),A
200 I$=INKEY$
210 IF I$="R" OR I$="r" THEN GOTO 20
220 GOTO 150
230 D=INT(RND*999)
240 S=INT(RND*999)
250 A=INT(RND*15):IF A=BB THEN GOTO 250
255 IF A=8 THEN GOTO 250
260 W=INT(RND*20)
270 CIRCLE(D,S),W,A
280 I$=INKEY$
290 IF I$="S" OR I$="s" THEN GOTO 130
300 GOTO 230
305 T=1
310 I$=INKEY$:DRAW"S="+VARPTR$(T):DRAW"TA0"
330 IF I$="8" THEN Y=Y-1
335 IF I$="V" OR I$="v" THEN GOTO 425
340 IF I$="2" THEN Y=Y+1
350 IF I$="4" THEN X=X-1
360 IF I$="6" THEN X=X+1
370 IF I$="7" THEN Y=Y-1:X=X-1
380 IF I$="1" THEN X=X-1:Y=Y+1
390 IF I$="3" THEN Y=Y+1:X=X+1
400 IF I$="9" THEN Y=Y-1:X=X+1
401 IF I$="+" THEN T=T+4:DRAW"S="+VARPTR$(T)
402 IF T=>250 THEN T=250
403 IF I$="-" THEN T=T-2
404 IF T=<2 THEN T=2
405 IF I$="E" OR I$="e" THEN GOTO 20
410 PSET(X,Y),15:DRAW"R1 D1 L1
    U1":PRESET(X,Y):DRAW"R1 D1 L1 U1"
420 GOTO 310
425 G=1
430 I$=INKEY$
440 IF I$="8" THEN Y=Y-1
445 IF I$="E" OR I$="e" THEN GOTO 20
```

```
450 IF I$="2" THEN Y=Y+1
460 IF I$="4" THEN X=X-1
470 IF I$="6" THEN X=X+1
480 IF I$="7" THEN Y=Y-.5:X=X-.5
490 IF I$="1" THEN X=X-.5:Y=Y+.5
500 IF I$="3" THEN Y=Y+.5:X=X+.5
510 IF I$="9" THEN Y=Y-.5:X=X+.5
520 IF I$="+" THEN G=G+1
530 IF G=>60 THEN G=60
540 IF I$="-" THEN G=G-1
550 IF G=<1 THEN G=1
560 C=INT(RND*15):IF C=BB THEN GOTO 560
570 CIRCLE(X,Y),G,C
580 GOTO 430
```

COLMAK.BAS

```
10 KEY OFF:CLS:INPUT"SCREEN(7-9)";S:SCREEN S:COLOR
   ,0:CLS
20 G$="C15 R1 C14 R1 C15 D1 C14 L1"
30 FOR GH=0 TO 640 STEP 2
40 FOR GF=0 TO 200 STEP 2
50 PSET(GH,GF):DRAW G$
60 NEXT GF:NEXT GH
```

DMOLTION.BAS

```
0 X=100:Y=110:KEY OFF
10 COLOR 15
20 PSET (X,Y)
30 DRAW"U10 R1 D10 R1 U10 R1 D10 R1 U10 R1 D10 R1
   U10
35 D$ = INKEY$: IF D$ = "" THEN 35
40 FOR T = 1 TO 50: NEXT T
45 COLOR 4
50 PSET (X,Y),0
60 DRAW"U10 R1 D10 R1 U10 R1 D10 R1 U10 R1 D10 R1
   U10
65 COLOR 1
70 IF D$="6" THEN X = X + 3
71 IF D$="4" THEN X=X-3
72 IF D$="2" THEN Y=Y+3
73 IF D$="8" THEN Y=Y-3
74 IF D$="7" THEN Y=Y-1.5:X=X-1.5
75 IF D$="1" THEN Y=Y+1.5:X=X-1.5
```

```
76 IF D$="9" THEN Y=Y-1.5:X=X+1.5
77 IF D$="3" THEN Y=Y+1.5:X=X+1.5
79 IF D$=CHR$(27) THEN END
80 GOTO 10
```

TEST.BAS

```
10 G=0:T=4:X=150:Y=96:KEY OFF:SCREEN 7:COLOR
   15,1:CLS
20 LOCATE 2,5:PRINT" *TEST*":LOCATE 10,1:COLOR
   14:LINE INPUT"Drawing directions-->";D$
30 CLS:LOCATE 10,1:INPUT"Are you sure(Y/N)";F$
40 IF F$="N" OR F$="n" THEN GOTO 10
50 IF F$="Y" OR F$="y" THEN GOTO 70
60 GOTO 30
70 CLS:COLOR ,0
80 I$=INKEY$:PSET(X,Y),15:DRAW D$
90 IF I$="" THEN GOTO 80
100 PSET(X,Y),0:DRAW D$
110 IF I$="8" THEN Y=Y-6
120 IF I$="2" THEN Y=Y+6
130 IF I$="4" THEN X=X-6
140 IF I$="6" THEN X=X+6
150 IF I$="+" THEN T=T+1
160 IF T=2 THEN T=2
170 IF T>100 THEN T=100
180 IF I$="-" THEN T=T-1
190 IF I$="T" OR I$="t" THEN G=G+5
191 IF I$="N" OR I$="n" THEN G=0
195 IF I$="Y" OR I$="y" THEN G=G-5
200 IF G=>360 THEN G=0
210 IF G=<-360 THEN G=0
220 IF I$="R" OR I$="r" THEN GOTO 10
230 IF I$="E" OR I$="e" THEN END
240 DRAW"S="+VARPTR$(T)
250 DRAW"TA="+VARPTR$(G)
260 PCOPY 0,1:PSET(X,Y),15:DRAW D$
270 GOTO 80
```

• • •

Though possessing little real usefulness, many more of these art- or drawing-type programs could be easily created. You are limited only by your imagination.

The Box Game
LOAD "BOXGAME.BAS"
Ok
RUN_

Purely a test of reflexes, The Box Game presents you with
an unsteady, floating box that you have to steer from the
left side of the screen to the right side—without hitting the
top, bottom, or left sides of the screen. Each time you
manage to complete your mission, you restart, albeit with
less time to spare. Good luck.

• • •

Lots of randomization—random movement left and right,
random movement up and down—best characterizes the
code of **BOXGAME.BAS**. Note that the numeric variable
GA sets the time limit of each "level."

• • •

BOXGAME.BAS
```
0 GA=500
1 RANDOMIZE TIMER
6 X=INT(1+40*RND(1))+40
7 Y=INT(1+300*RND(1))+40
10 KEY OFF:SCREEN 9:COLOR 15,1:CLS:PRINT"THE
   BOXGAME":PRINT"Use the numeric keypad to move
   the box to the right side of the screen":
   PRINT"Box cannot touch any other side of
   screen.":PRINT"PRESS <ENTER> READY...";:LINE
   INPUT V$:CLS
15 RANDOMIZE TIMER
30 T=INT(1+5*RND(1))
```

```
31 I$=INKEY$:IF I$="6" THEN X=X+20
32 IF I$="4" THEN X=X-20
33 IF I$="2" THEN Y=Y+20
34 IF I$="8" THEN Y=Y-20
35 V=INT(1+6*RND(1))-6
40 C=INT(1+6*RND(1))
41 B=INT(1+6*RND(1))
42 N=INT(1+6*RND(1))
43 IF B=2 THEN V=-(V)
44 IF N=2 THEN C=-(C)
45 FD=INT(1+GA*RND(1))
100 FOR A=1 TO T
110 PSET(X,Y),12:DRAW"R20 D20 L20 U20"
115 FOR DF=1 TO FD:NEXT DF
120 PSET(X,Y),0:DRAW"R20 D20 L20 U20"
125 X=X+V:Y=Y+C
126 IF X=>629 THEN X=629:GOTO 170
127 IF X=<0 THEN X=0:GOTO 150
128 IF Y=<0 THEN Y=0:GOTO 150
129 IF Y=>329 THEN Y=329:GOTO 150
130 NEXT A
140 GOTO 30
150 CLS:PRINT:PRINT:PRINT:PRINT"YOUR GAME IS OVER.
    PRESS ENTER TO TRY AGAIN:":LINE INPUT M$
160 GOTO 0
170 CLS:PRINT:PRINT:PRINT:PRINT"  CONGRATS. YOU
    WON.":GA=GA-50
180 IF GA<0 THEN PRINT" ...THE WHOLE GAME":END
190 FOR GC=1 TO 10000:NEXT GC:GOTO 1
```

• • •

Imagine if you not only had to avoid the left, top, and bottom of the screen, but also obstacles as well. Imagine if those obstacles were moving, too. Imagine…or, instead of imagining, get to work coding!

Throw Out the Graph Paper
LOAD "POSITION.BAS"

Ok

RUN

A truly useful GW-BASIC image-creation program—one in which you could throw out the graph paper—would have to do the following: Allow you to (1) draw in low- and high-resolution screens; (2) draw both dots and lines; (3) paint at specified locations; (4) note absolute movement versus relative movement; and (5) be able to save your work, either in text format or some sort of image-file format.

POSITION.BAS satisfies all five criteria. Run POSITION.BAS, and you'll be asked two questions: What SCREEN do you wish to draw in? and What would you like to call your file? (Note that the file extension must be *.bas*, and here's why: POSITION.BAS produces a nearly ready-to-run GW-BASIC program containing your just-sketched masterpiece.)

• • •

There several coding techniques presented in this program that we haven't encountered thus far. Most notably, examine line **10**, containing the GET statement. GET captures an image on-screen and stores it as an array, in this case called DEG. The image captured here is of a white-colored dot, which gets used as the drawing cursor.

Line **35** takes the image acquired by GET and utilizes the PUT statement to affix it to the screen. The XOR parameter permits the white dot to move around the screen while leaving the background unmolested; so, if the dot passes over some lines drawn earlier, those lines stay there, unchanged.

Multiple **PRINT #1** statements organize the output *.bas* file—accounting for things like line numbers (assigned to the variable **L**)—and both absolute and relative movement are on-the-fly options, easily toggled by a key press. (Relative movement, however, is a bit harder to output to the file since any shift in the positive direction in either *x* or *y* needs a plus sign in front of the movement's magnitude; hence, the necessity of the **SIGNX$** and **SIGNY$** string variables.)

Although **POSITION.BAS** accounts for the **PAINT** statement, it will not actually **PAINT** on the screen, merely showing a bright dot as a placeholder for the fill location. There are two reasons for this. First, if a shape to be filled isn't completely enclosed, the paint will "spill out" and leave a mess on the entire screen. Second, even if the shape is enclosed, its perimeter must be *entirely* of one color. For this reason, when a **PAINT** statement is inserted into the *.bas* file **POSITION.BAS** builds, the user must manually hard code the correct border color parameter.

• • •

POSITION.BAS
```
5 GOTO 250  'Run Start Up Screen
10 T=0:DIM DEG(20):KEY
   OFF:X=10:Y=10:PSET(1,1),15:GET(1,1)-
   (1,1),DEG:PSET(1,1),0
20 C=1:RMX=0:RMY=0   'Color starts at blue; rela
   tive movement for x,y set to 0
22 SIGNX$="":SIGNY$=""       'Signs (positive or
   negative) of relative movement set to NULL
25 RM$="OFF"   'Set relative movement to OFF
30 I$=INKEY$
31 IF Y>MAXY THEN Y=MAXY
32 IF Y<0 THEN Y=0
```

```
33 IF X<0 THEN X=0
34 IF X>MAXX THEN X=MAXX
35 PUT(X,Y),DEG,XOR:FOR G=1 TO 100:NEXT
   G:PUT(X,Y),DEG,XOR
36 IF I$="" THEN GOTO 30
38 IF I$=CHR$(27) THEN GOTO 330
40 IF I$="6" THEN X=X+1:RMX=RMX+1
41 IF I$="A" THEN X=X-10:RMX=RMX-10
42 IF I$="S" THEN X=X+10:RMX=RMX+10
43 IF I$="W" THEN Y=Y-10:RMY=RMY-10
44 IF I$="Z" THEN Y=Y+10:RMY=RMY+10
50 IF I$="4" THEN X=X-1:RMX=RMX-1
60 IF I$="8" THEN Y=Y-1:RMY=RMY-1
70 IF I$="2" THEN Y=Y+1:RMY=RMY+1
75 IF I$="R" OR I$="r" THEN RM$="ON "
76 IF I$="O" OR I$="o" THEN RM$="OFF"
85 IF I$="N" OR I$="n" THEN GOSUB 170
86 IF I$="B" OR I$="b" THEN GOSUB 220
95 IF I$="P" OR I$="p" THEN GOSUB 200
105 IF I$="+" THEN C=C+1
106 IF I$="-" THEN C=C-1
107 IF C<0 THEN C=15
108 IF C>15 THEN C=0
109 LOCATE 23,12:PRINT"C=";C
110 LOCATE 23,25:PRINT"Rel. Mov = ";RM$
111 IF RMX>-1 THEN SIGNX$="+" ELSE SIGNX$=""
    'Because relative movement needs a positive or
    negative sign in front of coordinates
112 IF RMY>-1 THEN SIGNY$="+" ELSE SIGNY$=""
    'Because relative movement needs a positive or
    negative sign in front of coordinates
120 IF I$=" " THEN GOSUB 135
125 IF RM$="OFF" THEN LOCATE 23,1:PRINT X;",";Y
126 IF RM$<>"OFF" THEN LOCATE 23,1:PRINT
    RMX;",";RMY
130 GOTO 30
135 'ABSOLUTE/RELATIVE MOVEMENT SUBROUTINE
137 LINE (R,S)-(X,Y),C
140 PSET(X,Y),12
145 IF (RM$="OFF" AND COUNT=0) THEN L=L+5:PRINT
    #1,L;"DRAW";CHR$(34);"C";C;" M";X;",";Y;"";
146 IF (RM$<>"OFF" AND COUNT=0) THEN L=L+5:PRINT
    #1,L;"DRAW";CHR$(34);"C";C;"
    M";SIGNX$;"";RMX;",";SIGNY$;"";RMY;"";
```

262

```
147 IF (RM$="OFF" AND COUNT <>0 AND COUNT<10) THEN
    PRINT #1,"C";C;" M";X;",";Y;"";
148 IF (RM$<>"OFF" AND COUNT<>0 AND COUNT<10) THEN
    PRINT #1,"C";C;"
    M";SIGNX$;"";RMX;",";SIGNY$;"";RMY;"";
149 IF (RM$="OFF" AND COUNT=>10) THEN PRINT
    #1,"C";C;" M";X;",";Y;"";CHR$(34)
150 IF (RM$<>"OFF" AND COUNT=>10) THEN PRINT
    #1,"C";C;"
    M";SIGNX$;"";RMX;",";SIGNY$;"";RMY;"";CHR$(34)
156 R=X:S=Y:X=X+1:Y=Y+1:RMX=1:RMY=1
158 IF COUNT=>10 THEN COUNT=0 ELSE COUNT=COUNT+1
160 RETURN
170 'PSET SUBROUTINE
171 PSET(X,Y),9:R=X:S=Y
172 IF COUNT>0 THEN PRINT #1,CHR$(34)
173 L=L+5
174 COUNT=0    'Resets COUNT for next DRAW command
175 PRINT #1,L;"PSET(";X;",";Y;"),";C
180 X=X+1:Y=Y+1    'Move the cursor one down, one
    over
185 RMX=1:RMY=1
190 RETURN
200 'PAINT SUBROUTINE
202 PSET(X,Y),10
203 IF COUNT>0 THEN PRINT #1,CHR$(34)
204 L=L+5
205 PRINT #1,L;"PAINT(";X;",";Y;"),";C;",INSERT
    CORRECT BACKGROUND COLOR HERE!"
208 COUNT=0    'Resets COUNT for next DRAW command
210 X=X+1:Y=Y+1    'Move the cursor one down, one
    over
212 RMX=1:RMY=1
215 RETURN
220 'BLANK MOVEMENT--BOTH ABSOLUTE AND RELATIVE--
    SUBROUTINE
222 PSET(X,Y),11:R=X:S=Y:L=L+5
223 IF (RM$="OFF" AND COUNT=0) THEN L=L+5:PRINT
    #1,L;"DRAW";CHR$(34);"BM";X;",";Y;"";
224 IF (RM$<>"OFF" AND COUNT=0) THEN L=L+5:PRINT
    #1,L;"DRAW";CHR$(34);"BM";SIGNX$;"";RMX;",";SI
    GNY$;"";RMY;"";
225 IF (RM$="OFF" AND COUNT <>0 AND COUNT<10) THEN
    PRINT #1,"BM";X;",";Y;"";
```

```
226 IF (RM$<>"OFF" AND COUNT<>0 AND COUNT<10) THEN
    PRINT
    #1,"BM";SIGNX$;"";RMX;",";SIGNY$;"";RMY;"";
227 IF (RM$="OFF" AND COUNT=>10) THEN PRINT
    #1,"BM";X;",";Y;"";CHR$(34)
228 IF (RM$<>"OFF" AND COUNT=>10) THEN PRINT
    #1,"BM";SIGNX$;"";RMX;",";SIGNY$;"";RMY;"";CHR
    $(34)
230 X=X+1:Y=Y+1:RMX=1:RMY=1
235 IF COUNT=>10 THEN COUNT=0 ELSE COUNT=COUNT+1
240 RETURN
250 'START UP SCREEN
252 SCREEN 9:CLS:KEY OFF
255 PRINT"Program 'POSITION'"
257 PRINT:INPUT"What SCREEN do you wish to draw in
    (7 or 9)";SC
258 PRINT:INPUT"What would you like to call your
    .BAS file (place a .BAS extension)";NAM$
260 OPEN "O",#1,NAM$
261 L=10    'Keeps track of current line number in
    NAM$ program
262 COUNT=0  'Keeps track of how many DRAW com
    mands on each line
263 PRINT #1,L;"REM ";NAM$:L=L+5
264 PRINT #1,L;"SCREEN ";SC;":CLS"
265 PRINT:PRINT"INSTRUCTIONS:":PRINT"Use the num
    eric keypad to move the cursor"
266 PRINT"Press A,W,S,Z to move the cursor even
    quicker in four directions on-screen"
270 PRINT"Press 'N' to represent a new PSET"
280 PRINT"Press <SPACE> to connect a line from the
    old location to the new one"
290 PRINT"Press 'P' to PAINT at that location,
    though the program won't actually PAINT"
296 PRINT"Press 'B' for Blank Movement to the cur
    sor's location"
297 PRINT"Press + or - to cycle through the avail
    able colors"
298 PRINT"Press 'R' to turn relative movement on,
    'O' to turn it off"
300 PRINT"Press <ESCAPE> to save your image's co
    ordinates"
305 PRINT:PRINT"PRESS <ENTER> TO BEGIN
    DRAWING....";
```

```
306 LINE INPUT STAR$
310 SCREEN SC:COLOR 15,0:CLS
314 IF SC=7 THEN MAXX=319:MAXY=199
315 IF SC=9 THEN MAXX=639:MAXY=349
320 GOTO 10
330 CLS:PRINT"Closing your file called ";NAM$
340 CLOSE #1
350 FOR PAUSE=1 TO 2000:NEXT PAUSE
360 PRINT"You can open this text file up and in
    sert the drawing specs into a new program"
370 PRINT:PRINT"Press <ENTER> to exit....";
380 LINE INPUT STA$
390 CLS:END
```

I used **POSITION.BAS** to draw a palm tree and called the saved file **PALM.BAS**. When I completed the quick sketch, here's what the (unaltered) output code of **PALM.BAS** looked like:

PALM.BAS

```
10 REM PALM.BAS
15 SCREEN  9 :CLS
20 PSET( 277 , 222 ), 8
25 DRAW"C 8  M 265 , 178 C 8  M 261 , 150 C 8  M
   261 , 135 C 8  M 267 , 134 C 8  M 274 , 164 C 8
   M 285 , 199 C 8  M 297 , 222 C 8  M 298 , 223 C
   8  M 289 , 220 C 8  M 282 , 220 C 8  M 277 , 222
   "
30 PAINT( 278 , 205 ), 8 ,8
35 PSET( 277 , 222 ), 8
40 DRAW"C 8  M 266 , 224 C 8  M 274 , 227 C 8  M
   282 , 227 C 8  M 312 , 228 C 8  M 298 , 223 "
45 PAINT( 289 , 225 ), 8 ,INSERT CORRECT
   BACKGROUND COLOR HERE!
50 PSET( 261 , 135 ), 2
55 DRAW"C 2  M 247 , 132 C 2  M 234 , 152 C 2  M
   240 , 130 C 2  M 246 , 123 C 2  M 215 , 178 C 2
   M 208 , 175 C 2  M 227 , 120 C 2  M 206 , 127 C
   2  M 221 , 107 C 2  M 204 , 105 C 2  M 230 , 99
   "
60 DRAW"C 2  M 228 , 89 C 2  M 232 , 89 C 2  M 235
   , 80 C 2  M 242 , 89 C 2  M 250 , 73 C 2  M 255
```

```
   , 85 C 2  M 267 , 74 C 2  M 296 , 67 C 2  M 273
   , 81 C 2  M 273 , 88 C 2  M 315 , 77 "
65 DRAW"C 2  M 328 , 92 C 2  M 282 , 93 C 2  M 319
   , 127 C 2  M 280 , 108 C 2  M 303 , 142 C 2  M
   305 , 157 C 2  M 275 , 121 C 2  M 267 , 135 C 2
   M 261 , 135 "
70 PAINT( 263 , 126 ), 2 ,INSERT CORRECT
   BACKGROUND COLOR HERE!
```

Despite the extra spacing between coordinates, GW-BASIC reads the code just fine. However, note that the border color for the **PAINT** command is not present—inserting the correct color in the code manually is required (for line **45**, the **COLOR** is **8**, and for line **70**, the **COLOR** is **2**). Run **PALM.BAS** with these minor alterations and this is what you'll see:

The tree's almost swaying in the breeze. I can feel myself relaxing already.

● ● ●

POSITION.BAS, though very useful, is decidedly not a user-friendly program. Also, many may object to its output of the image: as a wholly coded GW-BASIC program, rather than some sort of image file. (Look at the code of any of the output programs, like **PALM.BAS** above, and you'll notice a bit too much spacing between drawing commands, among other stylistic oddities; although GW-BASIC will happily ignore the spaces, you may be bothered aesthetically by the presentation. To shift the numbers, letters, and commas closer together, consider turning the output into a single string, concatenated using functions like **STR$**, which converts a number into a string; also, instead of **SIGNX$** and **SIGNY$**, consider using a **PRINT USING "+###"** statement to format relative movement coordinates with leading plus and minus signs.) In addition, there is no way to load previously made drawings for modification, and—perhaps most frustratingly of all—once a particular drawing command is executed, and thus written to the output program, the command cannot be undone. Successfully addressing any of these challenges will take a significant amount of work—but the rewards will speak for themselves, even though I hasten to point out that several of the challenges will be solved in programs later on.

Two Openings
LOAD "OPENING.BAS"

Ok

RUN_

■■

POSITION.BAS can do more than just make a static palm tree; it also can greatly reduce the time needed to make some complicated opening animations. Two programs below, OPENING.BAS, which puts you in a darkened movie theater at the start of a picture, and FEATHER.BAS, a "cut scene" of a feather falling, prove the point.

• • •

After composing the images with POSITION.BAS, the lines of code were cleaned up to remove spaces and other unnecessary characters (like COLOR assignments).

• • •

OPENING.BAS
```
10 VIEW PRINT: RANDOMIZE TIMER:KEY OFF:SCREEN 7:
   SCREEN 9:COLOR 15, 0:CLS
20 FOR AX=-10 TO 640 STEP 75:PSET(AX, 349),8:
   DRAW"U40 E1 R65 F1 D40":NEXT AX
30 PSET(0, 35),7:DRAW"R640":PSET(0, 255),7:
   DRAW"R640"
```

```
40 FOR GH=10 TO 639 STEP 75:PAINT(GH, 340),8,8:
   NEXT GH
50 VIEW PRINT 4 TO 18:VIEW SCREEN (0, 36)-(638,
   254)
60 LOCATE 10, 23: COLOR 15:PRINT"SE PICTURES
   PRESENTS"
70 DIM N(500):GET(172, 125)-(441, 138),N
80 CLS:FOR TY=1 TO 20000:NEXT TY:PAINT(100, 100),1
   ,15:FOR GT=230 TO 125 STEP -1:PUT(172, GT), N,
   XOR:FOR TY = 1 TO 500: NEXT TY:PUT(172, GT), N,
   XOR:NEXT GT:PUT(171, GT),N,XOR
90 FOR GH=1 TO 20:FG=INT(1+629*RND(1))+1:GF=INT(1+
   215*RND(1))+37:PSET(FG,GF),15:DRAW"R3":FOR TV=1
   TO 200:NEXT TV:PSET(FG,GF),1:DRAW"R3":FOR CD=1
   TO 200:NEXT CD:NEXT GH
95 CLS
```

FEATHER.BAS

```
10 KEY OFF:SCREEN 9:COLOR 15,0:CLS
15 FOR GH=1 TO 3000:NEXT GH
16 PSET(260,100),15:DRAW"M262,94 M281,66 M296,50
   M306,43 M302,58 M307,52 M304,62 M297,73 M305,67
   M293,81 M275,97 M260,100 BM279,81 M250,108"
17 PAINT(290,62),12,15
20 PSET(571,298),10:DRAW"M606,298 M606,336
   M570,336
   M570,298":PAINT(600,333),2,10:PSET(582,303),8:DR
   AW"M598,303 M598,315 M594,315 M594,323 M591,324
   M592,327 M591,329 M591,331 M589,333 M585,331
   M585,315 M580,315 M580,303 M582,303"
25 PSET(588,305),8:DRAW"M585,307 M589,310 M592,307
   M588,305":PAINT(595,311),14,8
30 FOR IK=1 TO 50:NEXT IK
35 FOR U=338 TO 297 STEP -1
40 PSET(564,U),0:DRAW"R45":FOR GH=1 TO 500:NEXT GH
45 NEXT U:DIM M(1000):GET(235,38)-(307,110),M
50 PUT(235,38),M,XOR
60 FOR UI=38 TO 250 STEP 10
70 PUT(235,UI),M,XOR:FOR TY=1 TO 200:NEXT TY
75 PUT(235,UI),M,XOR
80 NEXT UI:PUT(235,UI),M,XOR
90 FOR Y=1 TO 6:FOR GH=10 TO 0 STEP -1:COLOR
   ,GH:NEXT GH:NEXT Y:CLS
```

• • •

If you really want to stretch GW-BASIC to the interpreter-hobbled limit, try coding the opening shots to some classic movies or television shows—a serviceable cinema-like presentation can be produced. For example, though they're not included in this book for obvious lack-of-permission reasons, I've managed to use **POSITION.BAS** to conjure up GW-BASIC cinema scenes from the opening of *Star Wars*,* the Maurice Binder-designed gun barrel shot from the James Bond movies, and the snickering of the cartoon leads in *Beavis and Butt-head*. Although other iconic openings could be coded, it's surely a better use of your time to code your own fresh and original program openings.

---

* Made for a rather extensive interactive fiction game—kind of an electronic version of *Dungeons & Dragons* in the *Star Wars* universe, replete with character creation, skills' building, and text-based fighting—which, alas, my editor has informed me that I am forbidden from including here. *[Sorry—Ed.]*

An Interactive Presentation
LOAD "TOWEL.BAS"

Ok

RUN_
■ ■

More than just recreating iconic openings of the big and small screen, **POSITION.BAS** also can assist in making interactive presentations, à la PowerPoint, albeit you'll have to code them.

Take **TOWEL.BAS**, for instance. If you've ever wondered which of several brands of paper towel is the best absorber of water, wonder no further—through an interactive presentation of a science experiment, **TOWEL.BAS** leads you to the *quickest* picker-upper.

• • •

There's a lot of code here, obviously; nonetheless, **TOWEL.BAS** handles each component of the towels' presentation in chunks and thus isn't too difficult to parse (notwithstanding all of the graphics code, that is). There's nothing in **TOWEL.BAS** that we haven't already encountered in prior programs.

• • •

```
TOWEL.BAS
0 X=47:Y=25
10 LI=7:HEA=0:IN=1:OT=9:KEY OFF:SCREEN 9:COLOR
   8,0:CLS
20 FOR GH=1 TO 10000:NEXT GH
30 COLOR 8,7:CLS
40 PSET(280,67),8:DRAW"M356,120 M280,197 M214,121
   M280,67":PAINT(281,69),12,8
52 PSET(278,77),15:DRAW"M224,121 M274,188"
53 PSET(279,77),15:DRAW"M225,121 M275,188"
54 PSET(280,77),15:DRAW"M226,121 M276,188"
55 PSET(281,77),15:DRAW"M227,121 M277,188"
56 PSET(282,77),15:DRAW"M228,121 M278,188"
57 PSET(283,77),15:DRAW"M229,121 M279,188"
60 PSET(291,93),15:DRAW"M324,121 M291,152 M291,93"
61 PSET(290,93),15:DRAW"M323,121 M290,152 M290,93"
62 PSET(289,93),15:DRAW"M322,121 M289,152 M289,93"
63 PSET(288,93),15:DRAW"M321,121 M288,152 M288,93"
64 PSET(287,93),15:DRAW"M320,121 M287,152 M287,93"
65 PSET(286,93),15:DRAW"M319,121 M286,152 M286,93"
70 PSET(656,199),5:DRAW"M402,355":
   PAINT(603,305),5,5:PSET(334,0),5:DRAW"M0,184":PA
   INT(1,159),5:PCOPY 0,1:SCREEN 9
90 FOR GH=700 TO 200 STEP -5
95 FOR DF=1 TO 200:NEXT DF
96 I$=INKEY$:IF I$<>"" THEN GOTO 240
100 PSET(GH,250),4:DRAW"D30":NEXT GH
110 FOR DF=1 TO 10000:NEXT DF
120 COLOR 8,4:CLS
130 PSET(0,70),12:DRAW"R800":PAINT(10,200),12,12
140 PSET(20,10),15:DRAW"M613,10 M613,311 M20,311
    M20,10"
141 PSET(21,10),15:DRAW"M614,10 M614,311 M21,311
    M21,10"
142 PSET(19,10),15:DRAW"M612,10 M612,311 M19,311
    M19,10"
143 PSET(20,11),15:DRAW"M613,11 M613,312 M20,312
    M20,11"
144 PSET(20,9),15:DRAW"M613,09 M613,310 M20,310
    M20,09"
```

```
150 PSET(83,35):DRAW"M122,32 M171,38 M182,48
    M183,86 M174,92 M134,95 M122,98 M122,146
    M100,146 M96,76
    M83,35":PSET(124,51):DRAW"M149,51 M155,53
    M159,76 M157,79 M129,82
    M124,51":PAINT(117,49),14,8
155 PSET(212,148):DRAW"M213,92 M249,38 M277,91
    M275,148 M251,146 M252,99 M232,100 M233,139
    M212,148":PSET(235,86):DRAW"M254,85 M246,56
    M235,86":PAINT(219,134),14,8
160 PSET(298,35):DRAW"M304,80 M300,149 M324,149
    M329,102 M355,97 M368,86 M369,52 M359,43
    M329,36 M298,35":PSET(319,52):DRAW"M342,53
    M346,58 M347,75 M343,79 M325,80
    M319,52":PAINT(308,45),14,8
165 PSET(393,37):DRAW"M397,82 M385,150 M444,147
    M445,117 M415,127 M416,99 M444,100 M445,80
    M420,81 M421,57 M443,62 M444,33
    M393,37":PAINT(399,42),14,8
170 PSET(465,34):DRAW"M461,81 M471,147 M503,144
    M494,102 M533,145 M555,142 M521,96 M530,85
    M536,72 M539,56 M532,42 M505,36 M465,34"
175 PSET(490,51):DRAW"M509,52 M513,54 M514,73
    M508,80 M497,81
    M490,51":PAINT(504,45),14,8:PSET(80,167):DRAW"
    M186,171 M175,199 M138,197 M144,266 M109,266
    M115,197 M84,201 M80,167":PAINT(86,172),14,8
180 PSET(208,172):DRAW"M270,171 M269,264 M201,264
    M208,172":PSET(221,188):DRAW"M248,185 M249,241
    M226,241 M221,188":PAINT(225,179),14,8
185 PSET(291,171):DRAW"M292,210 M303,265 M325,220
    M333,217 M349,241 M362,264 M377,173 M353,210
    M335,202 M319,212 M308,223
    M291,171":PAINT(304,226),14,8
190 PSET(387,173):DRAW"M383,206 M386,264 M431,261
    M431,236 M404,246 M405,219 M427,220 M428,203
    M407,204 M408,187 M427,191 M425,172
    M387,173":PAINT(393,176),14,8
195 PSET(441,173):DRAW"M442,208 M449,264 M492,259
    M493,235 M463,242 M466,170
    M441,173":PAINT(449,178),14,8
200 PSET(578,169):DRAW"M510,170 M515,205 M571,207
    M572,251 M517,254 M518,274 M591,271 M592,194
```

```
    M536,195 M537,185 M575,186
    M578,169":PAINT(568,173),14,8
210 FOR GH=1 TO 5000:NEXT GH
211 COLOR 14,7
220 I$=INKEY$:IF I$<>"" THEN GOTO 240
221 HEA=HEA+1:IF HEA=10000 THEN GOTO 10
222 COLOR 10:LOCATE 2,27:PRINT">P R E S S   A N Y
    K E Y<"
223 FOR GH=1 TO 1000:NEXT GH
224 COLOR 7:LOCATE 2,27:PRINT">P R E S S   A N Y   K
    E Y<"
225 FOR GH=1 TO 1000:NEXT GH
230 GOTO 220
240 COLOR ,7:CLS
250 PSET(0,30),15:DRAW"R700":PSET(0,50),8:
    DRAW"R700"
260 PSET(0,300),15:DRAW"R700":PSET(0,320),8:
    DRAW"R700"
270 LOCATE 1,15:COLOR 10:PRINT"Press 'S' to move
    cursor, <SPACE> to select"
280 COLOR 12:LOCATE 7,15:PRINT"Problem"
290 LOCATE 8,15:PRINT"Procedure"
300 LOCATE 9,15:PRINT"Experimental and Controlled
    Variables"
310 LOCATE 10,15:PRINT"Individual Data"
320 LOCATE 11,15:PRINT"Data Chart"
330 LOCATE 12,15:PRINT"Materials"
350 LOCATE 13,15:PRINT"Create Towel"
355 LOCATE 14,15:PRINT"Help"
356 LOCATE 15,15:PRINT"Exit"
360 I$=INKEY$
370 COLOR 14:LOCATE LI,10:PRINT"--->"
371 IF I$="" THEN GOTO 360
375 COLOR 7:LOCATE LI,10:PRINT"--->"
380 IF I$="S" OR I$="s" THEN LI=LI+1
390 IF LI=>16 THEN LI=7
400 IF I$=" " THEN GOTO 420
410 GOTO 360
420 IF LI=7 THEN GOTO 480
430 IF LI=8 THEN GOTO 900
440 IF LI=9 THEN GOTO 570
450 IF LI=10 THEN GOTO 1440
455 IF LI=11 THEN GOTO 710
460 IF LI=12 THEN GOTO 815
```

```
470 IF LI=13 THEN GOTO 1820
471 IF LI=14 THEN GOTO 1765
475 IF LI=15 THEN SYSTEM
480 COLOR ,1:CLS:RO=1
490 PSET(43,18),8:DRAW"M150,24 M452,13 M583,4
    M544,90 M565,150 M546,251 M587,313 M486,304
    M263,316 M104,307 M16,328 M47,244 M18,144
    M49,73 M43,18"
495 PAINT(1,1),7,8
500 COLOR 14:LOCATE 10,15:PRINT"Problem:":COLOR 10
510 LOCATE 12,15:PRINT"Which of five paper towels"
520 LOCATE 13,15:PRINT"absorbs the most water?"
530 I$=INKEY$
540 IF I$<>"" THEN GOTO 240
545 DRAW"TA="+VARPTR$(RO)
546 RO=RO+10:IF RO=>360 THEN RO=1
550 PSET(400,107),14:DRAW"M+4,-8 M+11,-4 M+17,+1
    M+9,+7 M-2,+9 M-6,+6 M-10,+1 M+0,+14 M-11,+0
    M+0,-18 M+11,-2 M+6,-4 M-3,-5 M-10,+0 M+0,+3
    M-16,+0 BM+12,+36 M+12,+0 M+0,+9 M-12,+0 M+0,-
    9"
552 PSET(400,107),0:DRAW"M+4,-8 M+11,-4 M+17,+1
    M+9,+7 M-2,+9 M-6,+6 M-10,+1 M+0,+14 M-11,+0
    M+0,-18 M+11,-2 M+6,-4 M-3,-5 M-10,+0 M+0,+3
    M-16,+0 BM+12,+36 M+12,+0 M+0,+9 M-12,+0 M+0,-
    9"
560 GOTO 530
570 COLOR 12,7:CLS
575 PSET(160,119),8:DRAW"M160,230 M295,230
    M295,119":PSET(160,164),8:DRAW"M165,162
    M200,163 M208,165 M246,166 M259,165 M278,167
    M288,167 M295,167":PAINT(282,187),1,8
580 PSET(160,119),8:DRAW"M160,230 M295,230
    M295,119"
581 PSET(161,119),8:DRAW"M161,230 M296,230
    M296,119"
582 PSET(159,119),8:DRAW"M159,230 M294,230
    M294,119"
583 PSET(160,120),8:DRAW"M160,231 M295,231
    M295,120"
584 PSET(160,118),8:DRAW"M160,229 M295,229
    M295,118"
590 LOCATE 2,15:PRINT"Experimental Variable"
```

```
595 COLOR 10:LOCATE 4,13:PRINT"The amount of water
    absorbed"
600 I$=INKEY$:IF I$<>"" THEN GOTO 620
610 GOTO 600
620 CLS
630 PSET(60,112),9:DRAW"M66,110 M118,110 M122,112
    M118,114 M66,114 M60,112 M60,175 M63,177
    M114,177 M122,174 M122,112 M122,129 M117,131
    M110,132 BM80,130 M84,130 M84,132 M80,132
    M80,134 M84,134 BM94,130 M89,130 M89,132
    M94,132 M94,134 M89,134"
635 COLOR 9:DRAW"BM98,130 M103,130 M103,134
    M98,134 M98,130":PSET(60,130),9:DRAW"M66,132
    M73,133":PSET(143,200),8:DRAW"M167,193
    M197,188 M221,179 M232,208 M214,217 M182,225
    M159,229 M143,200":PAINT(155,202),15,8
640 PSET(264,124),8:DRAW"M271,121 M299,121
    M304,124 M299,127 M271,127 M264,124 M268,134
    M298,134 M304,124":PAINT(294,125),8,8:
    PAINT(294,131),6,8
650 PSET(377,118),8:DRAW"M377,190 M397,190
    M397,118":PSET(385,134),8:DRAW"M390,134
    BM390,146 M385,146 BM385,159 M390,159
    BM390,171
    M384,171":PSET(416,141),15:DRAW"M440,141
    M441,135 M454,147 M442,157 M440,152 M416,152
    M416,141":PAINT(420,147),12,15
655 PSET(470,135),8:DRAW"M504,135 M504,161
    M470,161 M470,135":PAINT(478,141),8,8
660 PSET(476,140),15:DRAW"M482,140 M482,154
    M476,154 M476,140":PAINT(479,143),15,15
665 PSET(487,140),15:DRAW"M487,154 M498,154
    M498,140
    M487,140":PSET(492,145),15:DRAW"M492,149
    M495,149 M495,145
    M492,145":PAINT(493,143),15,15
670 PSET(313,272),15:DRAW"M314,261 M329,253
    M507,253 M507,270 M504,272
    M313,272":PAINT(320,266),6,15:PSET(341,253),15
    :DRAW"M341,246 M483,246
    M483,253":PAINT(478,249),15,15
675 PSET(341,246),15:DRAW"M325,246 M325,237
    M328,237 M329,242 M507,242 M507,234 M513,234
    M513,245 M483,246":PAINT(510,239),8,15
```

```
680 LOCATE 2,15:COLOR 14:PRINT"Controlled Varia-
    bles":COLOR 12:LOCATE 4,13:PRINT"Same size
    beaker, same balance,":LOCATE 5,13:PRINT"same
    evaporation dish,":LOCATE 6,13:PRINT"same size
    towel, same amount of":LOCATE 7,13:PRINT"water
    to test(10mL)"
690 I$=INKEY$
695 IF I$<>"" THEN GOTO 240
700 GOTO 690
710 COLOR ,7:CLS
720 COLOR 14:PRINT
730 PRINT"Tests        Scot      Shop-Rite
    Mardi Gras    Brawny     School"
733 COLOR 5
735 PRINT"1            10.53    11.56
    10.96         10.11    7.36"
740 PRINT"2            8.97     8.64
    9.71          13.93    8.08"
745 PRINT"3            7.77     8.64
    9.73          11.87    3.39"
750 PRINT"4            8.16     10.10
    8.14          11.84    5.54"
755 PRINT"5            9.65     6.26
    9.80          12.25    6.5"
760 PRINT"6            11.72    7.03
    10.60         10.98    5.52"
770 PRINT"7            9.93     5.91
    9.25          11.26    8.5"
775 PRINT"8            9.95     5.79
    7.40          10.66    7.98"
780 PRINT"9            8.85     7.59
    8.66          10.15    6.69"
785 PRINT"10           8.74     4.78
    10.45         11.58    8.84"
787 PRINT"11           9.48     4.70
    9.43          12.43    7.89"
788 PRINT"12           10.06    6.25
    8.01          11.93    7.83"
789 PRINT"13           11.16    4.04
    9.93          11.20    6.25"
790 PRINT"14           7.80     5.54
    11.20         10.43    7.26"
792 PRINT"15           9.67     5.24
    10.69         9.97     4.27"
```

```
793 PRINT"16              11.20    7.2
    10.45        10.40      6.77"
794 PRINT"17              9.5      6.30
    8.71         10.74      9.01"
795 PRINT"18              7.76     5.76
    11.13        10.27      6.35"
796 PRINT"19              6.47     8.94
    10.78        13.15      5.13"
797 PRINT"20             10.70     5.97
    9.51         10.11      5.36"
800 I$=INKEY$:IF I$<>"" THEN GOTO 240
810 GOTO 800
815 COLOR ,7:CLS
820 PSET(48,107),8:DRAW"M57,103 M87,103 M92,106
    M87,110 M57,111 M48,107 M56,118 M88,118
    M92,106":PAINT(83,113),6,8:PAINT(79,107),8,8
825 PSET(143,145),8:DRAW"M181,179 M170,183
    M154,191 M145,201 M135,209 M115,220 M95,235
    M61,195 M76,185 M93,177 M113,162 M133,154
    M143,145":PAINT(141,161),15,8
830 PSET(219,205),3:DRAW"M215,212 M206,224
    M200,238 M199,254 M202,260 M210,263 M236,263
    M244,259 M245,250 M241,234 M234,218 M227,201
    M223,193 M219,205":PAINT(219,230),1,3
835 PSET(227,232),15:DRAW"M229,236 M231,244
    M230,252 M232,254 M236,249 M235,238 M232,231
    M227,232":PAINT(231,234),15,15
840 PSET(312,165),8:DRAW"M318,165 M318,279
    M344,279 M344,166 M352,166"
850 PSET(326,188),8:DRAW"R10 BD10 L10 BD10 R10
    BD10 L10 BD10 R10 BD10 L10 BD10 R10 BD10 L10
    BD10 R10"
855 PSET(409,208),8:DRAW"M426,208 M426,259
    M494,259 M494,209
    M510,209":PSET(433,220),8:DRAW"M449,220
    BM454,217 M458,217 M458,219 M454,219 M454,221
    M458,221 BM469,217 M462,217 M462,219 M469,219
    M469,221 M462,221"
860 DRAW"BM473,217 M480,217 M480,221 M473,221
    M473,217 BM491,219 M485,219 BM402,181 M402,175
    M410,169 M504,169 M504,181
    M402,181":PAINT(419,174),6,8
865 PSET(421,169),8:DRAW"M421,164 M484,164
    M484,169":PAINT(479,167),8,8:PSET(421,164),15:
```

278

```
    DRAW"M409,164 M409,160 BM492,160 M492,164
    M485,164 M421,164"
870 LOCATE 1,15:COLOR 14:PRINT"Materials"
875 LOCATE 3,13:COLOR 12:PRINT"Evaporation Dish,
    10mL of water,"
880 LOCATE 4,13:COLOR 12:PRINT"paper towels, bal
    ance, beaker,"
890 LOCATE 5,13:PRINT"and a graduated cylinder"
895 I$=INKEY$:IF I$<>"" THEN GOTO 240
898 GOTO 895
900 COLOR ,7:CLS
910 PSET(130,221),15:DRAW"M130,80 M492,80 C8
    M492,221 M131,221"
915 PSET(216,122),8:DRAW"M224,122 M224,207
    M254,207 M254,123 M263,123"
920 FOR GH=1 TO 5000:NEXT GH
925 FOR TG=206 TO 143 STEP -1
930 PSET(225,TG),1:DRAW"R28"
935 FOR TH=1 TO 400:NEXT TH
940 NEXT TG
945 PSET(229,143),15:DRAW"M233,143 BM236,140
    M236,146 BM241,146 M245,146 M245,140 M241,140
    M241,146 BM249,143 M252,143"
950 LOCATE 1,18:COLOR 12:PRINT"1. Fill graduated
    cylinder up"
955 LOCATE 2,18:PRINT"with 10mL of water"
960 I$=INKEY$:IF I$<>"" THEN GOTO 970
965 GOTO 960
970 CLS
975 PSET(130,221),15:DRAW"M130,80 M492,80 C8
    M492,221 M131,221"
980 PSET(188,167),8:DRAW"M194,163 M200,162
    M261,162 M266,164 M269,168 M265,173 M258,175
    M198,175 M190,173 M186,169
    M188,167":PSET(186,169),8:DRAW"M193,185
    M203,187 M253,187 M261,184 M269,168"
985 PAINT(258,180),6,8:PAINT(253,170),8,8
990 GD$="M+5,+0 M+0,+59 M+17,+0 M+0,-59 M+4,+0"
995 PSET(346,143),8:DRAW GD$
1000 FOR JK=1 TO 5000:NEXT JK
1010 FOR TY=0 TO 90 STEP 2
1015 DRAW"TA="+VARPTR$(TY)
1020 PSET(346,143),8:DRAW GD$
1021 FOR YU=1 TO 200:NEXT YU
```

```
1025 PSET(346,143),0:DRAW GD$
1030 NEXT TY
1040 PSET(346,143),8:DRAW GD$
1045 FOR FR=346 TO 248 STEP -2
1050 PSET(FR,143),8:DRAW GD$
1055 FOR YU=1 TO 200:NEXT YU
1060 PSET(FR,143),0:DRAW GD$
1065 NEXT FR
1070 PSET(FR,143),8:DRAW GD$
1075 FOR IJ=90 TO 135 STEP 2
1080 DRAW"TA="+VARPTR$(IJ)
1085 PSET(FR,143),8:DRAW GD$
1090 FOR YU=1 TO 200:NEXT YU
1095 PSET(FR,143),0:DRAW GD$
1100 NEXT IJ
1110 PSET(FR,143),8:DRAW GD$
1120 LOCATE 1,18:COLOR 12:PRINT"2. Pour water into
     "
1125 LOCATE 2,18:PRINT"evaporation dish"
1130 I$=INKEY$:IF I$<>"" THEN GOTO 1140
1135 GOTO 1130
1140 CLS
1145 PSET(130,221),15:DRAW"M130,80 M492,80 C8
     M492,221 M131,221"
1150 PSET(336,109),8:DRAW"M361,159 M347,165
     M338,173 M315,185 M296,200 M275,210 M253,161
     M269,152 M288,144 M301,134 M315,127 M327,121
     M336,109":PAINT(329,131),15,8
1155 LOCATE 1,18:COLOR 12:PRINT"3. Take paper tow-
     el..."
1160 I$=INKEY$:IF I$<>"" THEN GOTO 1170
1165 GOTO 1160
1170 CLS
1175 LOCATE 1,18:COLOR 12:PRINT"3. Take paper tow-
     el..."
1180 PSET(130,221),15:DRAW"M130,80 M492,80 C8
     M492,221 M131,221"
1185 PSET(226,127),8:DRAW"M232,126 M238,131
     M243,129 M249,134 M248,138 M253,143 M252,148
     M256,152 M255,157 M250,156 M248,160 M242,159
     M239,164 M233,162 M226,165 M219,161 M213,163
     M213,159 M216,156 M210,154 M209,149 M213,148
     M211,145 M213,141 M217,141"
```

```
1190 DRAW"M218,135 M221,136 M222,133 M224,130
     M226,131 M226,127":PAINT(231,135),15,8
1195 PSET(225,141),8:DRAW"M224,145 M227,151
     M226,155":PSET(236,145),8:DRAW"M238,147
     M244,149
     M244,153":PSET(233,150),8:DRAW"M236,155
     M235,159":PSET(231,137),8:DRAW"M235,137
     M241,140 M246,142 M247,145"
1200 LOCATE 2,18:COLOR 12:PRINT"crumple it up..."
1210 I$=INKEY$:IF I$<>"" THEN GOTO 1235
1215 GOTO 1210
1235 PSET(278,133),12:DRAW"M301,133 M301,127
     M312,133 M301,139
     M301,133":PAINT(305,134),12,12
1240 LOCATE 3,18:COLOR 12:PRINT"and place into
     evaporation dish"
1245 PSET(396,147),8:DRAW"M402,144 M406,143
     M427,143 M431,145 M434,147 M431,149 M427,150
     M406,150 M400,150 M397,147 M401,154 M428,154
     M434,147":PAINT(422,153),6,8:PAINT(418,147),8
     ,8
1250 I$=INKEY$:IF I$<>"" THEN GOTO 1260
1255 GOTO 1250
1260 CLS
1265 PSET(130,221),15:DRAW"M130,80 M492,80 C8
     M492,221 M131,221"
1270 PSET(270,178),8:DRAW"M277,175 M314,175
     M318,178 M314,181 M277,181 M271,177 M275,188
     M316,188 M318,178":PAINT(310,184),6,8:
     PAINT(306,179),8,8
1275 PSET(285,96),8:DRAW"M281,100 M282,103
     M276,106 M278,109 M271,115 M273,121 M279,120
     M282,123 M284,121 M287,123 M290,124 M294,122
     M297,125 M302,125 M305,123 M308,126 M312,128
     M314,125 M312,119 M308,116 M309,114 M307,110
     M302,106 M299,106"
1280 DRAW"M295,103 M296,100 M290,98
     M285,96":PAINT(286,106),15,8
1285 PSET(283,110),8:DRAW"M283,114 M286,117
     BM292,107 M296,110 M299,115 M303,118
     BM290,111 M293,114 M292,117 M296,119"
1290 LOCATE 1,18:COLOR 12:PRINT"4. Take out of
     evaporation dish..."
1295 I$=INKEY$:IF I$<>"" THEN GOTO 1300
```

```
1296 GOTO 1295
1300 CLS
1310 PSET(130,221),15:DRAW"M130,80 M492,80 C8
     M492,221 M131,221"
1320 PSET(285,96),8:DRAW"M281,100 M282,103
     M276,106 M278,109 M271,115 M273,121 M279,120
     M282,123 M284,121 M287,123 M290,124 M294,122
     M297,125 M302,125 M305,123 M308,126 M312,128
     M314,125 M312,119 M308,116 M309,114 M307,110
     M302,106 M299,106"
1325 DRAW"M295,103 M296,100 M290,98
     M285,96":PAINT(286,106),15,8
1330 PSET(283,110),8:DRAW"M283,114 M286,117
     BM292,107 M296,110 M299,115 M303,118
     BM290,111 M293,114 M292,117 M296,119"
1335 PSET(180,212),8:DRAW"M180,206 M189,199
     M353,199 M353,210 M351,212
     M180,212":PAINT(207,207),6,8:PSET(202,199),8:
     DRAW"M202,194 M334,194
     M334,199":PAINT(330,197),8,8
1340 PSET(202,194),8:DRAW"M185,194 M184,188
     M187,188 M187,191 M346,191 M346,188 M349,188
     M349,194 M334,194":PAINT(348,190),15,8
1345 PSET(322,190),9:DRAW"M322,152 M332,152
     BM266,153 M257,153 M266,153 M266,190
     M322,190":PSET(275,165),8:DRAW"M283,165
     BM287,162 M292,162 M292,165 M287,165 M287,167
     M292,167 BM304,162 M297,162"
1350 DRAW"M297,165 M304,165 M304,167 M297,167
     BM308,162 M308,167 M313,167 M313,162 M308,162
     BM316,165 M319,165"
1355 LOCATE 1,18:COLOR 12:PRINT"4. Take out of
     evaporation dish..."
1360 LOCATE 2,18:COLOR 12:PRINT"and place wet tow
     el into "
1365 LOCATE 3,18:COLOR 12:PRINT"beaker on balance"
1370 I$=INKEY$:IF I$<>"" THEN GOTO 1380
1375 GOTO 1370
1380 CLS
1385 PSET(130,221),15:DRAW"M130,80 M492,80 C8
     M492,221 M131,221"
1390 PSET(300,121),8:DRAW"M338,128 M308,168
     M271,162
     M300,121":PAINT(303,131),15,8:PSET(300,133),8
```

```
     :DRAW"M316,136 BM312,142 M297,139 BM291,147
     M306,151"
1400 PSET(191,114),8:DRAW"M213,135 M221,131
     M200,110
     M191,114":PAINT(200,117),14,8:PSET(213,135),8
     :DRAW"M222,138 M221,131":PAINT(220,135),8,8
1405 PSET(191,114),4:DRAW"M187,109 M194,106
     M200,110 M191,114":PAINT(194,110),4,4
1410 LOCATE 1,18:COLOR 12:PRINT"5. Record and re
     peat 20 more"
1420 LOCATE 2,18:COLOR 12:PRINT"times for each of
     the 5 towels"
1425 I$=INKEY$:IF I$<>"" THEN GOTO 240
1430 GOTO 1425
1440 COLOR ,7:CLS
1445 PSET(0,10),15:DRAW"R700":PSET(0,20),8:
     DRAW"R700":PSET(0,21),15:DRAW"R700":PSET(0,30
     ),8:DRAW"R700":PSET(0,31),15:DRAW"R700":PSET(
     0,40),8:DRAW"R700"
1446 PSET(0,41),15:DRAW"R700":PSET(0,50),8:
     DRAW"R700":PSET(0,51),15:DRAW"R700":PSET(0,60
     ),8:DRAW"R700"
1447 PSET(0,100),15:DRAW"R700"
1448 PSET(0,300),8:DRAW"R700"
1449 PSET(0,330),15:DRAW"R700":PSET(0,340),8:
     DRAW"R700":PSET(0,341),15:DRAW"R700"
1450 LOCATE 11,25:COLOR 9:PRINT"Mardi Gras"
1455 LOCATE 12,25:PRINT"Scot Towels"
1460 LOCATE 13,25:PRINT"Brawny"
1465 LOCATE 14,25:PRINT"Shop-Rite"
1470 LOCATE 15,25:PRINT"School Brand":GH=11
1471 LOCATE 16,25:PRINT"Exit Screen"
1475 I$=INKEY$
1476 LOCATE GH,20:COLOR 14:PRINT"-->"
1477 IF I$="" THEN GOTO 1475
1478 LOCATE GH,20:COLOR 7:PRINT"-->"
1480 IF I$="S" OR I$="s" THEN GH=GH+1
1485 IF I$=" " THEN GOTO 1500
1490 IF GH=>17 THEN GH=11
1496 GOTO 1475
1500 IF GH=11 THEN GOTO 1680
1510 IF GH=12 THEN GOTO 1630
1515 IF GH=13 THEN GOTO 1720
1520 IF GH=14 THEN GOTO 1580
```

```
1525 IF GH=15 THEN GOTO 1540
1530 IF GH=16 THEN GOTO 240
1540 CLS
1545 PSET(130,18),8:DRAW"M138,15 M144,15 M148,17
     M149,21 M148,27 M145,37 M141,39 M132,39
     M129,36 M130,18 BM138,23 M140,23 M142,25
     M142,30 M140,32 M136,32 M135,29 M136,26
     M138,23":PAINT(144,19),15,8
1550 PSET(144,15),8:DRAW"M200,16 M202,18 M202,31
     M200,34
     M141,39":PAINT(154,31),15,8:PAINT(138,28),8,8
1551 PSET(0,50),15:DRAW"R700":PSET(0,60),8:
     DRAW"R700"
1552 PSET(0,200),15:DRAW"R700":PSET(0,210),8:
     DRAW"R700"
1553 PSET(0,340),15:DRAW"R700":PSET(0,350),8:
     DRAW"R700"
1555 COLOR 14:LOCATE 2,29:PRINT"Results:School
     Brand"
1560 COLOR 12:LOCATE 10,18:PRINT"Average of num
     bers:6.27"
1565 COLOR 12:LOCATE 20,18:PRINT"Ranking(1-5):#5"
1570 I$=INKEY$:IF I$<>"" THEN GOTO 1440
1575 GOTO 1570
1580 CLS
1585 PSET(130,18),8:DRAW"M138,15 M144,15 M148,17
     M149,21 M148,27 M145,37 M141,39 M132,39
     M129,36 M130,18 BM138,23 M140,23 M142,25
     M142,30 M140,32 M136,32 M135,29 M136,26
     M138,23":PAINT(144,19),15,8
1590 PSET(144,15),8:DRAW"M200,16 M202,18 M202,31
     M200,34
     M141,39":PAINT(154,31),15,8:PAINT(138,28),8,8
1591 PSET(0,50),15:DRAW"R700":PSET(0,60),8:
     DRAW"R700"
1592 PSET(0,200),15:DRAW"R700":PSET(0,210),8:
     DRAW"R700"
1593 PSET(0,340),15:DRAW"R700":PSET(0,350),8:
     DRAW"R700"
1595 COLOR 14:LOCATE 2,29:PRINT"Results:Shop-Rite"
1600 COLOR 12:LOCATE 10,18:PRINT"Average of num
     bers:7.07"
1610 COLOR 12:LOCATE 20,18:PRINT"Ranking(1-5):#4"
1615 I$=INKEY$:IF I$<>"" THEN GOTO 1440
```

```
1620 GOTO 1615
1630 CLS
1635 PSET(130,18),8:DRAW"M138,15 M144,15 M148,17
     M149,21 M148,27 M145,37 M141,39 M132,39
     M129,36 M130,18 BM138,23 M140,23 M142,25
     M142,30 M140,32 M136,32 M135,29 M136,26
     M138,23":PAINT(144,19),15,8
1640 PSET(144,15),8:DRAW"M200,16 M202,18 M202,31
     M200,34 M141,39":PAINT(154,31),15,8:
     PAINT(138,28),8,8
1641 PSET(0,50),15:DRAW"R700":PSET(0,60),8:
     DRAW"R700"
1642 PSET(0,200),15:DRAW"R700":PSET(0,210),8:
     DRAW"R700"
1643 PSET(0,340),15:DRAW"R700":PSET(0,350),8:
     DRAW"R700"
1645 COLOR 14:LOCATE 2,29:PRINT"Results:Scot Tow
     els"
1650 COLOR 12:LOCATE 10,18:PRINT"Average of num
     bers:8.02"
1660 COLOR 12:LOCATE 20,18:PRINT"Ranking(1-5):#3"
1665 I$=INKEY$:IF I$<>"" THEN GOTO 1440
1670 GOTO 1665
1680 CLS
1685 PSET(130,18),8:DRAW"M138,15 M144,15 M148,17
     M149,21 M148,27 M145,37 M141,39 M132,39
     M129,36 M130,18 BM138,23 M140,23 M142,25
     M142,30 M140,32 M136,32 M135,29 M136,26
     M138,23":PAINT(144,19),15,8
1690 PSET(144,15),8:DRAW"M200,16 M202,18 M202,31
     M200,34 M141,39":PAINT(154,31),15,8:
     PAINT(138,28),8,8
1691 PSET(0,50),15:DRAW"R700":PSET(0,60),8:
     DRAW"R700"
1692 PSET(0,200),15:DRAW"R700":PSET(0,210),8:
     DRAW"R700"
1693 PSET(0,340),15:DRAW"R700":PSET(0,350),8:
     DRAW"R700"
1695 COLOR 14:LOCATE 2,29:PRINT"Results:Mardi
     Gras"
1700 COLOR 12:LOCATE 10,18:PRINT"Average of num
     bers:8.67"
1710 COLOR 12:LOCATE 20,18:PRINT"Ranking(1-5):#2"
1715 I$=INKEY$:IF I$<>"" THEN GOTO 1440
```

```
1716 GOTO 1715
1720 CLS
1725 PSET(130,18),8:DRAW"M138,15 M144,15 M148,17
     M149,21 M148,27 M145,37 M141,39 M132,39
     M129,36 M130,18 BM138,23 M140,23 M142,25
     M142,30 M140,32 M136,32 M135,29 M136,26
     M138,23":PAINT(144,19),15,8
1730 PSET(144,15),8:DRAW"M200,16 M202,18 M202,31
     M200,34
     M141,39":PAINT(154,31),15,8:PAINT(138,28),8,8
1731 PSET(0,50),15:DRAW"R700":PSET(0,60),8:
     DRAW"R700"
1732 PSET(0,200),15:DRAW"R700":PSET(0,210),8:
     DRAW"R700"
1733 PSET(0,340),15:DRAW"R700":PSET(0,350),8:
     DRAW"R700"
1735 COLOR 14:LOCATE 2,29:PRINT"Results:Brawny"
1740 COLOR 12:LOCATE 10,18:PRINT"Average of num
     bers:11.58"
1750 COLOR 12:LOCATE 20,18:PRINT"Ranking(1-
     5):";:COLOR 10:PRINT;"#1"
1755 I$=INKEY$:IF I$<>"" THEN GOTO 1440
1760 GOTO 1755
1765 COLOR ,7:CLS
1770 PSET(0,10),15:DRAW"R700":PSET(0,20),8:
     DRAW"R700"
1775 PSET(0,330),15:DRAW"R700":PSET(0,340),8:
     DRAW"R700"
1776 LOCATE 8,12:COLOR 10:PRINT"        H E L P"
1780 COLOR 12:LOCATE 10,13:PRINT"On a selection
     screen, to"
1785 LOCATE 11,13:PRINT"move the cursor down,"
1790 LOCATE 12,13:PRINT"press 'S'. To select the "
1795 LOCATE 13,13:PRINT"highlighted file, press
     <SPACE>."
1800 LOCATE 14,13:PRINT"To move through any other"
1805 LOCATE 15,13:PRINT"screens, press any key."
1806 LOCATE 16,13:PRINT"All of this applies to"
1807 LOCATE 17,13:PRINT"everything except Create
     Towel."
1810 I$=INKEY$:IF I$<>"" THEN GOTO 240
1815 GOTO 1810
1820 COLOR ,7:CLS
```

```
1825 PSET(40,10),8:DRAW"M232,21 M228,32 M226,48
     M227,70 M228,100 M225,134 M228,173 M229,205
     M37,196 M43,171 M40,132 M44,100 M43,73 M41,45
     M43,25 M40,10":PAINT(55,23),15,8
1830 COLOR 12:LOCATE 1,23:PRINT"Create Towel v1.0"
1835 COLOR 10:LOCATE 4,38:PRINT"Change inside col
     or"
1840 COLOR 10:LOCATE 5,38:PRINT"Change outline
     color"
1855 COLOR 10:LOCATE 6,38:PRINT"Random dots"
1860 COLOR 10:LOCATE 7,38:PRINT"Draw":COLOR
     14:ML=4
1861 COLOR 10:LOCATE 8,38:PRINT"Help"
1862 COLOR 10:LOCATE 9,38:PRINT"Exit Screen"
1865 PSET(0,250),15:DRAW"R700":PSET(0,300),8:
     DRAW"R700":IN=15:OT=8
1870 I$=INKEY$
1875 COLOR 14:LOCATE ML,36:PRINT">"
1880 IF I$="" THEN GOTO 1870
1885 COLOR 7:LOCATE ML,36:PRINT">"
1895 IF I$="S" OR I$="s" THEN ML=ML+1
1896 IF ML=>10 THEN ML=4
1900 IF I$=" " THEN GOTO 1910
1905 GOTO 1870
1910 IF ML=4 THEN GOTO 1936
1915 IF ML=5 THEN GOTO 1950
1920 IF ML=6 THEN GOTO 1970
1925 IF ML=7 THEN GOTO 2030
1926 IF ML=8 THEN GOTO 2100
1930 IF ML=9 THEN GOTO 240
1936 IN=IN+1:IF IN=OT THEN IN=IN+1
1937 IF IN=>16 THEN IN=1
1940 PAINT(55,23),IN,OT
1945 GOTO 1870
1950 OT=OT+1:IF OT=IN THEN OT=OT+1
1951 IF OT=>16 THEN OT=1
1955 PSET(40,10),OT:DRAW"M232,21 M228,32 M226,48
     M227,70 M228,100 M225,134 M228,173 M229,205
     M37,196 M43,171 M40,132 M44,100 M43,73 M41,45
     M43,25 M40,10"
1960 GOTO 1870
1970 U=INT(1+224*RND(1)):V=INT(1+194*RND(1))
1980 IF U=<46 THEN GOTO 1970
1985 IF V=<25 THEN GOTO 1970
```

```
1990 C=INT(1+15*RND(1))
1995 I$=INKEY$
2000 PSET(U,V),C
2010 IF I$=" " THEN GOTO 1870
2020 GOTO 1970
2030 I$=INKEY$
2035 IF I$=" " THEN GOTO 1870
2040 IF I$="6" THEN X=X+1
2050 IF I$="4" THEN X=X-1
2060 IF I$="8" THEN Y=Y-1
2070 IF I$="2" THEN Y=Y+1
2075 IF I$="9" THEN X=X+1:Y=Y-1
2076 IF I$="3" THEN X=X+1:Y=Y+1
2077 IF I$="7" THEN X=X-1:Y=Y-1
2078 IF I$="1" THEN X=X-1:Y=Y+1
2080 IF X=>224 THEN X=224
2085 IF X=<47 THEN X=47
2090 IF Y=>194 THEN Y=194
2095 IF Y=<25 THEN Y=25
2096 D=INT(1+15*RND(1))
2097 PSET(X,Y),D
2098 GOTO 2030
2100 COLOR ,7:CLS
2110 PSET(0,10),15:DRAW"R700":PSET(0,30),8:
     DRAW"R700"
2120 PSET(0,320),15:DRAW"R700":PSET(0,340),8:
     DRAW"R700"
2130 COLOR 10:LOCATE 5,10:PRINT"H E L P  F O R  C
     R E A T E  T O W E L"
2135 COLOR 12:LOCATE 7,10:PRINT"Use 'S' to move
     cursor down, and use "
2140 COLOR 12:LOCATE 8,10:PRINT"<SPACE> to select
     an option. When in random"
2145 COLOR 12:LOCATE 9,10:PRINT"dots, use space to
     exit out of them. When in"
2150 COLOR 12:LOCATE 10,10:PRINT"draw, have NUM
     LOCK on and use the numeric"
2155 COLOR 12:LOCATE 11,10:PRINT"keypad to draw in
     8 directions. Use the space"
2160 COLOR 12:LOCATE 12,10:PRINT"bar to exit out
     of draw."
2170 I$=INKEY$:IF I$<>"" THEN GOTO 1820
2175 GOTO 2170
2180 END
```

● ● ●

Rather than typing in **TOWEL.BAS** and running it outright, pore through the code, looking for segments that can help you construct your own interactive presentation-themed projects.

Space Wars

The militant Questar Empire is on a rampage, and they're taking no prisoners. They even turned the SSQ Space Station—home to over one million people—into a pile of rubble. Such aggression by the Questars cannot be allowed to stand.

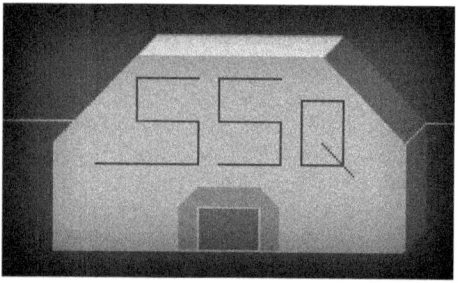

First, you'll have to shoot down eight Questar cargo ships, which are carrying vital troops and materiel. Then it's up to you to destroy the Questar Battle Ship, but you'll have to do it in one shot. Run **SW.BAS** to begin your mission.

• • •

Many lines of code are dedicated to the graphics; note how the **DRAW** statement sometimes utilizes absolute movement, whereas other times—like with the moving objects—relative movement is leveraged. Some of the graphics for SW.BAS were designed using POSITION.BAS.

• • •

SW.BAS
```
0 CX=2:CZ=4:GB=1:LE=1
1 RANDOMIZE TIMER:KA=0
10 T=0:KEY OFF:SCREEN 7:COLOR 14,0:CLS
220 LOCATE 10,5:PRINT"M J L  E N T E R P R I S E
    S":FOR G=1 TO 5000:I$=INKEY$:IF I$<>"" THEN
    GOTO 1010
225 NEXT G:COLOR 15
230 FOR G=4 TO 0 STEP -1:COLOR ,G:NEXT G
240 FOR X=1 TO 16000:NEXT X
250 COLOR 15
260 FOR D=1 TO 120
270 U=INT(1+320*RND(1)):GH=INT(1+15*RND(1)):PRINT
275 PSET(U,190),GH
280 NEXT D
290 FOR A=1 TO 12000:NEXT A
300 FOR D=1 TO 9999:NEXT D
310 COLOR 15
320 PSET(90,20):DRAW"L60 D40 R50 D30 L50 D10 R60
    U50 L50 U20 R50 U10"
330 PAINT(85,25),7,15:PSET(40,30),8:DRAW"R50":
    PSET(30,60),8:DRAW"R50":PSET(30,100),8:DRAW"R6
    0"
340 COLOR 15
350 PSET(110,130):DRAW"U60 R30 D30 L30"
360 PSET(160,100):DRAW"U15 R30 D15 U30 L30 D30"
370 PSET(240,70):DRAW"L30 D30 R30"
380 PSET(290,70):DRAW"L30 D15 R20 L20 D15 R30"
390 FOR I=1 TO 9999:NEXT I:COLOR 14
400 PSET(40,120):DRAW"D70 R50 E30 F30 R50 U70 D40
    BR5 D30 U30 R30 D15 L30 R60 L30 D15 U15 R30
    L20 F15 H15 R20 U15 L60"
410 PSET(285,160):DRAW"L20 D15 R20 D15 L20"
420 FOR F=1 TO 5000:NEXT F
425 PLAY"MB O1 C1"
430 FOR H=1 TO 10:FOR G=6 TO 0 STEP -1:COLOR
    ,G:NEXT G:NEXT H
```

```
440 FOR S=1 TO 15000:NEXT S
450 CLS
460 LOCATE 10,9:PRINT"    Copyright 2015 MJL En-
    terprises(R)"
470 FOR D=1 TO 9999:NEXT D:CLS:COLOR ,7
480 PSET(0,20),15:DRAW"R320"
490 PSET(0,30),15:DRAW"R320"
500 PAINT(10,25),4,15:PSET(0,30),8:DRAW"R320"
510 PSET(0,170),15:DRAW"R320"
520 PSET(0,180),15:DRAW"R320"
530 PAINT(10,175),4,15:PSET(0,180),8:DRAW"R320"
540 PSET(220,40),15:DRAW"L50 D40 R40 D20 L40 D10
    R50 U40 L40 U20 R40 U10"
550 PAINT(200,45),3,15
560 PSET(180,50),8:DRAW"R40"
570 PSET(170,80),8:DRAW"R40"
580 PSET(170,110),8:DRAW"R50"
590 COLOR 9:LOCATE 10,4:PRINT"           PRESS"
600 D$=INKEY$:IF D$="S" OR D$="s" THEN GOTO 620
610 GOTO 600
620 FOR V=0 TO 200 STEP 1
630 CIRCLE(150,96),V,0
640 NEXT V:FOR V=1 TO 9999:NEXT V
650 CLS
660 COLOR ,5
670 COLOR 7
680 PSET(120,50):DRAW"R90 F40 G10 H40 L90 E10 G50
    D50 R170 U50 E10 D50 G10 U50 H40 E10"
690 PSET(130,150):DRAW"U20 E10 R30 F10 D20 L10 U20
    L30 D20"
700 PAINT(170,80),7,7:PAINT(150,125),3,7:
    PAINT(150,140),8,7
710 PAINT(140,55),15,7:PAINT(220,70),8,7:
    PAINT(245,110),8,7
720 PSET(210,50),8:DRAW"F40 D50 G10"
730 PAINT(150,140),8,7
740 COLOR 4
750 PSET(140,70):DRAW"L30 D20 R30 D20 L50"
760 PSET(180,70):DRAW"L30 D20 R30 D20 L30"
770 PSET(210,80):DRAW"L20 D30 R20 U30 D30 H10 F15"
780 COLOR 9:PRINT:PRINT"           THE SSQ Space
    Station...."
790 PRINT"...home to more than 1,000,000 peo-
    ple..."
```

```
800 PSET(0,90),7:DRAW"r80"
810 PSET(250,90),7:DRAW"R70"
820 PSET(0,190),7:DRAW"R320"
830 FOR V=1 TO 19000:NEXT V:CLS
840 PSET(0,90),7:DRAW"R320"
850 PSET(0,190),7:DRAW"R320"
860 PSET(70,140),8:DRAW"R20 E10 F10 R10 E10 R10
    D10 R10 E10 F10 U10 R10 D10 E10 D10 R20 D7 R10
    U7 E10 R10 D20 L190 U10 R20"
870 PAINT(80,145),7,8
880 PRINT:PRINT"..and was reduced to a pile of
    rubble..."
890 PRINT"        by the Questar Empire. You...."
900 PRINT"       ...can make the Questars pay...."
910 PRINT"          ...for what they did!!!!!!!!"
920 FOR I=1 TO 10:COLOR 7
930 PSET(110,125):DRAW"H10 E10 H9"
940 PSET(190,125):DRAW"E10 H10 E9"
950 FOR B=1 TO 2500:NEXT B
960 PSET(110,125),0:DRAW"H10 E10 H9"
970 PSET(190,125),0:DRAW"E10 H10 E9"
980 PSET(190,125):DRAW"H10 E10 H9"
990 PSET(110,125):DRAW"E10 H10 E9":FOR G=1 TO
    2500:NEXT G
991 PSET(190,125),0:DRAW"H10 E10 H9"
992 PSET(110,125),0:DRAW"E10 H10 E9"
994 NEXT I
1000 FOR U=1 TO 20000:NEXT U
1010 CLS:COLOR 11,3
1020 PRINT:PRINT:PRINT:PRINT:PRINT:PRINT:PRINT:
     PRINT:PRINT:PRINT:PRINT:PRINT"      Now you
     must shoot down 8"
1030 PRINT"    cargo ships of the Questar Em-
     pire."
1040 PSET(0,20):DRAW"R320"
1050 PSET(0,30):DRAW"R320"
1060 PAINT(10,25),1,11:PSET(0,30),8:DRAW"R320"
1070 PSET(0,170):DRAW"R320"
1080 PSET(0,180):DRAW"R320"
1090 PAINT(10,175),1,11:PSET(0,180),8:DRAW"R320"
1100 FOR S=1 TO 19000:NEXT S:COLOR ,0:CLS
1110 COLOR 3,0:X=150:Y=70
1120 PSET(0,152),7:DRAW"M40,131 M60,144 BM53,140
     M114,120 M156,150 BM148,145 M187,134 M229,148
```

```
     BM223,146 M256,123 M292,157 BM282,148
     M320,127"
1130 PAINT(268,164),14,7
1140 T=320:R=40:F=0:E=320:C=20
1150 I$=INKEY$
1180 PSET(X,Y),15:DRAW"NU05 ND05 NL05 NR05"
1181 PSET(X,Y),14:DRAW"NR05 NU05 NL05 ND05"
1185 PSET(X,Y),0:DRAW"NU05 ND05 NL05 NR105"
1190 IF I$="4" THEN X=X-1
1200 IF I$="6" THEN X=X+1
1210 IF I$="2" THEN Y=Y+1
1220 IF I$="8" THEN Y=Y-1
1230 IF Y=>112 THEN Y=112
1231 IF I$="5" THEN GOTO 1270
1235 T=T-CX:PSET(T,R),10:DRAW"M+2,-2 M+3,-2 M+4,-1
     M+36,+0 M+0,+13 M-36,+0 M-4,-1 M-4,-2 M-4,-3
     M+3,-2 C15 BM+0,+0 M+45,+0"
1236 PSET(T,R),0:DRAW"C0 M+2,-2 M+3,-2 M+4,-1
     M+36,+0 M+0,+13 M-36,+0 M-4,-1 M-4,-2 M-4,-3
     M+3,-2 BM+0,+0 M+45,+0"
1240 IF T=-40 THEN T=320:R=INT(1+100*RND(1))
1241 E=E-CZ:PSET(E,C),11:DRAW"M+2,-2 M+3,-2 M+4,-1
     M+36,+0 M+0,+13 M-36,+0 M-4,-1 M-4,-2 M-4,-3
     M+3,-2 C15 BM+0,+0 M+45,+0"
1242 PSET(E,C),0:DRAW"C0 M+2,-2 M+3,-2 M+4,-1
     M+36,+0 M+0,+13 M-36,+0 M-4,-1 M-4,-2 M-4,-3
     M+3,-2 BM+0,+0 M+45,+0"
1243 IF E=-40 THEN E=320:C=INT(1+100*RND(1))
1260 FOR TA=1 TO 40:NEXT TA:GOTO 1150
1270 FOR G=5 TO 0 STEP -1:COLOR ,G:NEXT G
1280 IF Y=R THEN F=F+1:GOTO 1310
1285 IF Y=C THEN F=F+1:GOTO 1330
1290 IF F=8 THEN GOTO 1341
1300 FOR XI=1 TO 900:NEXT XI:GOTO 1150
1310 REM PSET(T,R),0:DRAW"E10 R20 D20 L20 H10 R30"
1320 R=INT(1+100*RND(1)):T=320:GOTO 1290
1330 REM PSET(E,C),0:DRAW"E10 R20 D20 L20 H10 R30"
1340 C=INT(1+100*RND(1)):E=320:GOTO 1290
1341 COLOR 11:PRINT:PRINT:PRINT"
     Spectacular!":FOR CD=1 TO 10000:NEXT CD:GOTO
     1350
1350 COLOR 11,1:CLS:PRINT:PRINT:PRINT:PRINT:
     PRINT:PRINT:PRINT:PRINT:PRINT:PRINT"
     Your next goal is to destroy":PRINT"    the
```

Questar Battle Ship. It will take 1 shot on
its weak point."
```
1360 PSET(0,20),3:DRAW"R320"
1370 PSET(0,30),3:DRAW"R320"
1380 PAINT(10,25),7,3:PSET(0,30),8:DRAW"R320"
1390 PSET(0,170),3:DRAW"R320"
1400 PSET(0,180),3:DRAW"R320"
1410 PAINT(10,175),7,3:PSET(0,180),8:DRAW"R320"
1420 FOR HXC=1 TO 25000:NEXT:CLS:COLOR 15,0
1430 CIRCLE(150,350),250,1
1440 PAINT(150,180),9,1
1441 PSET(80,155),10:DRAW"M73,158 M59,165 M56,169
     M54,176 M58,181 M68,185 M80,188 M121,189
     M127,185 M133,179 M137,187 M142,180 M140,164
     M135,160 M148,161 M152,167 M157,172 M162,177
     M166,177 M168,171 M172,162 M176,159 M172,154
     M150,147 M113,148 M80,155"
1442 PAINT(81,160),10,10
1444 PSET(187,154),10:DRAW"M189,157 M190,165
     M188,172 M179,184 M168,185 M169,188 M175,193
     M216,194 M257,195 M281,198 M296,197 M296,194
     M284,186 M281,178 M264,178 M257,185 M246,171
     M231,158 M208,154
     M187,154":PAINT(193,158),10,10
1450 ZX=INT(1+100*RND(1)):ZC=INT(1+100*RND(1)):
     X=ZX:Y=ZC:T=400:F=0:R=75:COLOR 15
1460 I$=INKEY$:IF T=60 THEN R=R+3
1500 IF I$="6" THEN X=X+1
1510 IF I$="4" THEN X=X-1
1520 IF I$="2" THEN Y=Y+1
1530 IF I$="8" THEN Y=Y-1
1540 IF I$="5" THEN GOTO 1620
1541 IF T=<-100 THEN GOTO 1610
1545 IF Y=>130 THEN Y=130
1550 T=T-GB:PSET(T,R),15:DRAW"BM-3,+16 M-45,-2 M-
     21,-11 M+6,-9 M+9,-3 M+31,-3 M+7,-3 M+52,+0
     M+5,+4 M+50,+1 M+15,-8 M+1,+15 M+2,+19 M-4,+3
     M-39,-2 M-69,-1"
1560 PSET(T,R),0:DRAW"BM-3,+16 M-45,-2 M-21,-11
     M+6,-9 M+9,-3 M+31,-3 M+7,-3 M+52,+0 M+5,+4
     M+50,+1 M+15,-8 M+1,+15 M+2,+19 M-4,+3 M-39,-
     2 M-69,-1"
1580 PSET(X,Y),15:DRAW"NL05 NR05 ND05 NU05"
1581 PSET(X,Y),14:DRAW"NL05 NR05 ND05 NU05"
```

```
1590 PSET(X,Y),0:DRAW"NL05 NR05 ND05 NU05"
1600 GOTO 1460
1610 PRINT:PRINT:PRINT:PRINT"        Sorry!!!":FOR
     GH=1 TO 10000:NEXT GH:GOTO 1010
1620 FOR YH=10 TO 0 STEP -1:COLOR ,YH:NEXT YH
1630 IF Y=R THEN GOTO 1650
1631 KA=KA+1:IF KA=2 THEN GOTO 1641
1640 GOTO 1460
1641 PRINT:PRINT:PRINT"   Out of bullets!!":FOR
     TY=1 TO 10000:NEXT TY:GOTO 1010
1650 FOR I=1 TO 4
1655 FOR HJ=9 TO 0 STEP -1:COLOR ,HJ:NEXT HJ
1660 NEXT I
1670 PRINT:PRINT:PRINT:PRINT:PRINT"           i
     n n e r ! !":PSET(13,11),15:DRAW"M36,11
     M42,39 M52,26 M62,39 M77,11 M98,11 M80,51
     M28,51 M13,11":PAINT(23,23),7,15
1680 FOR YH=1 TO 10000:NEXT YH
1690 PRINT:PRINT:PRINT:PRINT"  You win on level
     ";LE:PRINT:PRINT"   Presented by MJL Enter
     prises":
1695 FOR YU=1 TO 20000:NEXT
     YU:GB=GB+1:CX=CX+1:CZ=CZ+1:LE=LE+1
1697 GOTO 1
1700 END
```

● ● ●

SW.BAS would be well served to use **PUT** and **GET** for graphics movement rather than simple **DRAW** commands—the **PUT** and **GET** statements would cut down on the annoying flickering. And more levels, more variation in play—for example, why must you shoot down *eight* cargo ships? Why is there no distinction between shooting down the faster and the slower ships? And why don't you ever run out of bullets, or out of time?—among other improvements would turn "Space Wars," currently a rather middling game, into something memorable.

The Kentucky Derby
LOAD "DERBY.BAS"

Ok

RUN

The Kentucky Derby, inaugurated in 1875, is run every May in Louisville, Kentucky. The course is 1.25 miles long, but the Thoroughbreds cover it at a rapid clip.

When you run **DERBY.BAS**, you'll have an opportunity to place your bets on a Thoroughbred in the Derby: Ace, Lucky, Spade, or Clover. Bet wisely, or you may lose it all.

• • •

Extensive use of the **PUT** and **GET** statements best characterize **DERBY.BAS**. Not only the horses—which were conjured up using the **POSITION.BAS** program—but also the title-screen words are captured into a graphics array for the almost flicker-free movement.

The first line of code contains the **PALETTE** statement. Although only sixteen colors are available at once, other colors, besides the default sixteen, are for the taking. **PALETTE 6,20**, for instance, replaces the default **COLOR**

6 with **COLOR 20**. The **PALETTE** changes are necessary because **DERBY.BAS** requires several shades of brown for horses' coloring. To view all sixty-three different colors, run **COLORS.BAS**, listed right after **DERBY.BAS** below. Observe that the **PALETTE** statement, coded without any arguments, reverts the colors to their default values.

• • •

DERBY.BAS

```
10 CLEAR:DIM WQ(5000):DIM A1(1000):DIM
   A2(1000):DIM A3(1000):DIM A4(1000):VIEW
   PRINT:RANDOMIZE TIMER:KEY OFF:SCREEN 9:COLOR
   15,0:CLS:PALETTE 8,32:PALETTE 6,20
11 A1$="Ace":A2$="Lucky":A3$="Spade":A4$="Clover"
20 PRINT"              K E N T U C K Y   D E R B
   Y   V E R S I O N   1 . 0"
30 GET(125,0)-(513,11),WQ
40 PUT(125,0),WQ,XOR
50 FOR GH=1 TO 150 STEP 2:PUT(125,GH),WQ,XOR:FOR
   VA=1 TO 100:NEXT VA:PUT(125,GH),WQ,XOR:NEXT GH
60 PUT(125,155),WQ,XOR
70 PSET(72,144),6:DRAW"M73,146 M77,149 M77,150
   M80,154 M78,156 M75,156 M71,152 M68,152 M66,152
   M64,163 M67,171 M63,177 M63,179 M59,179 M61,175
   M63,173 M60,165 M56,163 M47,165 M33,165 M28,163
   M20,180 M18,181 M16,178 M18,175 M18,167 M22,161"
75 DRAW"M19,159 M19,153 M22,151 M17,150 M20,148
   M24,149 M29,150 M60,150 M61,148 M60,147 M64,145
   M68,144 M70,142 M72,144":PAINT(46,159),6,6
76 COLOR 7:LOCATE 16,26:PRINT"---p r e s s   a n y
   k e y---":COLOR 15
80 I$=INKEY$:IF I$="" THEN GOTO 80
81 GET(9,141)-(80,182),A1
82 GET(9,141)-(80,182),A2
83 GET(9,141)-(80,182),A3
84 GET(9,141)-(80,182),A4
90 CLS:FOR TY=1 TO 7000:NEXT TY:LOCATE
   13,15:INPUT"Your bank has(1-1000)$";BANK
91 IF BANK=12345 THEN BANK=999999!:GOTO 100
95 IF BANK>1000 THEN GOTO 90
96 IF BANK=<0 THEN BANK=1000
```

```
100 COLOR ,7:CLS:PSET(18,11),15:DRAW"M620,11 C08
    M620,211 M18,211 C15 M18,11"
110 PUT(30,20),A1,XOR:PUT(30,60),A2,XOR:
    PUT(30,100),A3,XOR:PUT(30,140),A4,XOR
115 LOCATE 3,20:PRINT"1.";A1$:LOCATE
    6,20:PRINT"2.";A2$:LOCATE
    9,20:PRINT"3.";A3$:LOCATE 12,20:PRINT"4.";A4$
120 LOCATE 17,25:PRINT"Your bank has
    $";BANK:PSET(187,222),15:DRAW"M427,222 C08
    M427,237 M187,237 C15 M187,222"
130 LOCATE 20,20:INPUT"Number of horse to bet
    on(1-4)";HOR
135 IF HOR=<0 OR HOR>4 THEN HOR=1
140 LOCATE 21,20:INPUT"Amount of $ to bet";MON
145 IF MON<0 OR MON>BANK THEN MON=0
150 RANDOMIZE
    TIMER:A=INT(1+5*RND(1))+5:L=INT(1+5*RND(1))+5:
    S=INT(1+5*RND(1))+5:C=INT(1+5*RND(1))+5:X1=30:
    X2=30:X3=30:X4=30
160 PUT(30,20),A1,XOR:PUT(30,60),A2,XOR:
    PUT(30,100),A3,XOR:PUT(30,140),A4,XOR
165 COLOR 7:LOCATE 3,20:PRINT"1.";A1$:LOCATE
    6,20:PRINT"2.";A2$:LOCATE
    9,20:PRINT"3.";A3$:LOCATE
    12,20:PRINT"4.";A4$:COLOR 15
166 IF X1=>540 THEN F=1:GOTO 200
167 IF X2=>540 THEN F=2:GOTO 200
168 IF X3=>540 THEN F=3:GOTO 200
169 IF X4=>540 THEN F=4:GOTO 200
170 Z1=INT(1+15*RND(1)):Z2=INT(1+15*RND(1)):
    Z3=INT(1+15*RND(1)):Z4=INT(1+15*RND(1)):X1=X1+
    A+Z1:X2=X2+L+Z2:X3=X3+S+Z3:X4=X4+C+Z4
171 IF X1=>540 THEN F=1:GOTO 200
172 IF X2=>540 THEN F=2:GOTO 200
173 IF X3=>540 THEN F=3:GOTO 200
174 IF X4=>540 THEN F=4:GOTO 200
175 PUT(X1,20),A1,XOR:PUT(X2,60),A2,XOR:
    PUT(X3,100),A3,XOR:PUT(X4,140),A4,XOR
176 FOR GH=1 TO 50:NEXT GH
180 PUT(X1,20),A1,XOR:PUT(X2,60),A2,XOR:
    PUT(X3,100),A3,XOR:PUT(X4,140),A4,XOR
190 GOTO 166
200 PUT(X1,20),A1,XOR:PUT(X2,60),A2,XOR:
    PUT(X3,100),A3,XOR:PUT(X4,140),A4,XOR
```

```
205 LOCATE 8,15:PRINT"Press any key to contin-
    ue....."
210 I$=INKEY$:IF I$="" THEN GOTO 210
220 COLOR ,0:CLS:LOCATE 5,25
225 IF F=1 THEN PRINT A1$;" Wins!!"
230 IF F=2 THEN PRINT A2$;" Wins!!"
235 IF F=3 THEN PRINT A3$;" Wins!!"
240 IF F=4 THEN PRINT A4$;" Wins!!"
250 IF F=HOR THEN GOTO 270
260 PRINT:PRINT"          You have lost the bet
    and lost $";MON".":BANK=BANK-MON
261 IF BANK=<0 THEN GOTO 267
262 PRINT:PRINT"          Press any key to
    continue....... "
263 I$=INKEY$:IF I$="" THEN GOTO 263
264 GOTO 100
267 PRINT:PRINT"          Press any key to
    start over again....."
268 I$=INKEY$:IF I$="" THEN GOTO 268
269 GOTO 10
270 PRINT:PRINT"          You have won the bet
    and won $";MON".":BANK=BANK+MON
275 GOTO 262
```

COLORS.BAS

```
10 KEY OFF:SCREEN 9:COLOR 15,0:CLS
15 X=1:PALETTE
17 I$=INKEY$
20 PSET(10,10),1
30 DRAW"r40 d40 l40 u40"
40 PAINT(11,11),1,1
50 LOCATE 7,1:PRINT"COLOR = ";X
60 LOCATE 9,1:PRINT"Press + or - to increase or
   decrease color selection"
65 LOCATE 10,1:PRINT"Press <ESCAPE> to exit"
70 IF I$="" THEN 17
80 IF I$="+" THEN X=X+1
90 IF I$="-" THEN X=X-1
95 IF I$=CHR$(27) THEN PALETTE:END
100 IF X<1 THEN X=63
110 IF X>63 THEN X=1
120 PALETTE 1,X
130 GOTO 17
```

• • •

Although for what it is **DERBY.BAS** is well presented, it commits a cardinal sin: it's boring. Once you've seen a couple of races, and bet your savings, what more is there? There's no overarching purpose to the game— **DERBY.BAS** suffers from a lack of narrative. It has the opposite problem of **SW.BAS**, which has plenty of story but mediocrely executed play. It's up to you to wrap a tight narrative around **DERBY.BAS**, (hopefully) making it fun.

Swimming with the Fishes
LOAD "FISH.BAS"

Ok

RUN_

Run **ARTIF.BAS**, and watch a small fish bob around the screen. The stakes are a bit higher in **FISH.BAS**: a bigger, better-looking fish requires some attention—and food.

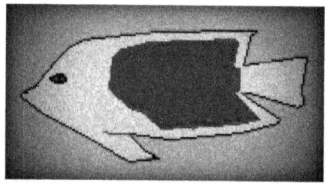

• • •

ARTIF.BAS makes use of the **DRAW** statement's relative movement feature to display the fish, while **FISH.BAS** relies on **PUT/GET** statements to bring the fish to life.

• • •

```
ARTIF.BAS
0 RANDOMIZE TIMER
6 X=INT(1+320*RND(1))
7 Y=INT(1+200*RND(1))
10 KEY OFF:SCREEN 7:COLOR 15,1:CLS:INPUT"Fish Col
   or(1-15)";H:INPUT"Outline of Fish Color(1-15)";
   JD:CLS
15 RANDOMIZE TIMER
30 T=INT(1+5*RND(1))
35 V=INT(1+5*RND(1))
```

```
40 C=INT(1+5*RND(1))
41 B=INT(1+2*RND(1))
42 N=INT(1+2*RND(1))
43 IF B=2 THEN V=-(V)
44 IF N=2 THEN C=-(C)
45 FD=INT(1+500*RND(1))
100 FOR A=1 TO T
110 PSET(X,Y),JD:DRAW"M+2,-3 M+3,-3 M+4,-3 M+5,-1
    M+5,+2 M+6,-3 M-4,+7 M+5,+4 M-8,-1 M-2,+3 M-
    5,+1 M-6,+0 M-5,-3 BM+5,-2 M+3,-1 M-1,+2 M-2,-
    1":PAINT(X+2,Y-1),H,JD
115 FOR DF=1 TO FD:NEXT DF
120 PSET(X,Y),0:DRAW"M+2,-3 M+3,-3 M+4,-3 M+5,-1
    M+5,+2 M+6,-3 M-4,+7 M+5,+4 M-8,-1 M-2,+3 M-
    5,+1 M-6,+0 M-5,-3 BM+5,-2 M+3,-1 M-1,+2 M-2,-
    1":PAINT(X+2,Y-1),1,JD
125 X=X+V:Y=Y+C
126 IF X=>320 THEN X=320:SOUND 100,1
127 IF X=<0 THEN X=0:SOUND 100,1
128 IF Y=<20 THEN Y=20:SOUND 100,1
129 IF Y=>200 THEN Y=200:SOUND 100,1
130 NEXT A
140 GOTO 30
```

FISH.BAS

```
10 CLEAR:RANDOMIZE TIMER:VIEW PRINT:CLEAR:KEY
   OFF:SCREEN 7:SCREEN 9,,0,1:PALETTE 8,32:PALETTE
   14,38:PALETTE 6,20:COLOR
   8,0:CLS:X=INT(1+200*RND(1)):Y=INT(1+200*RND(1))
11 FOR GH=1 TO 10000:NEXT GH:COLOR ,3:CLS
20 PSET(104,108),8:DRAW"M+3,-3 M+10,-12 M+8,-8
   M+8,-4 M+45,-5 M+51,-1 M+8,+0 M-4,+3 M+0,+2 M-
   4,+15 M+33,-5 M+5,+0 M-3,+19 M+1,+8 M-3,+2 M-
   29,-8 M-5,+0 M+23,+15 M-1,+2 M-22,+6 M-42,+4 M-
   25,-3 M+9,+9 M+7,+4 M-5,+1 M+7,+0 M-18,+2 M-25,-
   14 M-27,-13"
30 DRAW"M-13,-10 M+1,-2 M+3,+0 M-2,-1 M+5,-2 M+3,-
   1"
40 PSET(504,108),8:DRAW"M-3,-3 M-10,-12 M-8,-8 M-
   8,-4 M-45,-5 M-51,-1 M-8,+0 M+4,+3 M+0,+2
   M+4,+15 M-33,-5 M-5,+0 M+3,+19 M-1,+8 M+3,+2
   M+29,-8 M+5,+0 M-23,+15 M+1,+2 M+22,+6 M+42,+4
   M+25,-3 M-9,+9 M-7,+4 M+5,+1 M-7,+0 M+18,+2
   M+25,-14 M+27,-13"
```

```
50 DRAW"M+13,-10 M-1,-2 M-3,+0 M+2,-1 M-5,-2 M-3,-
   1"
60 PAINT(134,85),14,8:PSET(113,103),1:DRAW"M118,
   101 M121,101 M123,103 M123,105 M120,106 M116,106
   M113,104":PAINT(118,104),8,1:PSET(161,135),8:DRA
   W"M151,135 M146,134":PAINT(495,107),14,8
65 PSET(495,107),1:DRAW"M492,105 M489,105 M486,106
   M486,108 M489,109 M493,109
   M495,107":PAINT(491,107),8,1:PSET(447,135),8:DRA
   W"M459,133 M467,131":PSET(151,91),8:DRAW"M156,86
   M162,85 M172,82 M224,80 M226,82 M223,96 M227,97
   M227,109 M224,111"
70 DRAW"M239,126 M225,129 M180,132 M170,123
   M161,120 M149,109
   M151,91":PAINT(159,95),8,8:PSET(383,80),8:DRAW"M
   385,94 M384,97 M379,98 M379,108 M383,109
   M384,111 M369,126 M374,129 M398,132 M434,133
   M445,131 M453,130 M456,119 M453,101 M445,96"
75 DRAW"M443,90 M432,82 M403,79
   M383,80":PAINT(397,86),8,8
80 DIM A(1999):DIM B(1999):GET(90,70)-
   (271,152),A:GET(335,72)-(515,152),B
90 PCOPY 0,1:SCREEN 9:RANDOMIZE TIMER:CLS:COLOR ,3
100 R=INT(1+5*RND(1)):V=INT(1+30*RND(1)):N=INT(
    1+20*RND(1)):FAX=INT(1+2*RND(1)):C=INT(1+2*RND
    (1)):Q=INT(1+1000*RND(1))
113 FE=FE+1
114 IF FE=>250 THEN GOTO 200
115 KAR=KAR+1:YT=INT(1+20*RND(1))+10
116 IF KAR=>YT THEN GOTO 300
117 I$=INKEY$:IF I$="C" OR I$="c" THEN GOTO 320
118 IF I$="F" OR I$="f" THEN FE=0
120 IF FAX=2 THEN GOTO 160
125 IF C=2 THEN N=N-(2*N)
126 FOR D=1 TO R
130 X=X+V:Y=Y+N
135 IF X=>450 THEN X=450
136 IF X=<0 THEN X=0
137 IF Y=>250 THEN Y=250
138 IF Y=<0 THEN Y=0
140 PUT(X,Y),B,XOR:FOR RT=1 TO Q:NEXT
    RT:PUT(X,Y),B,XOR
150 NEXT D:GOTO 100
160 FOR D=1 TO R:X=X-V:Y=Y+N
```

```
170 IF X=>450 THEN X=450
175 IF X=<0 THEN X=0
180 IF Y=>250 THEN Y=250
185 IF Y=<0 THEN Y=0
190 PUT(X,Y),A,XOR:FOR RT=1 TO Q:NEXT
    RT:PUT(X,Y),A,XOR
195 NEXT D:GOTO 100
200 FOR AS=Y TO 1 STEP -10
220 PUT(X,AS),B,XOR:PUT(X,AS),B,XOR:NEXT AS
230 PUT(X,0),B,XOR:LOCATE 10,20:PRINT"Y O U R   F I
    S H  I S  D E A D ."
240 I$=INKEY$:IF I$="" THEN GOTO 240
250 GOTO 10
300 RE=INT(1+3*RND(1))+346:PSET(X,RE),6:DRAW"R1 D1
    L1 U1":KAR=0:DE=DE+1:IF DE=>20 THEN GOTO 200
310 GOTO 100
320 FOR TI=0 TO 645:PSET(TI,346),3:DRAW"D3":NEXT
    TI:KAR=0:GOTO 100
```

• • •

Turning FISH.BAS into a game that plays swimmingly—
replete with goals, a scorecard, and the like—presents a
significant challenge. Perhaps going the route of the once-
hyper-popular Tamagotchi digital pets makes the most
sense here.

Floating Natasha
LOAD "TATA.BAS"

Ok

RUN_

I think you'll agree that the stuffed animal Natasha is cute enough to warrant her own chapter (and program):

Run **TATA.BAS** and you'll be treated to Natasha floating to and fro on-screen.

• • •

TATA.BAS works similarly to **FISH.BAS**. For animation and other types of graphics movement, there should be no doubt by this point: **PUT** and **GET**, hand in hand with **PCOPY**, are your best options.

• • •

TATA.BAS
```
10 RANDOMIZE TIMER:KEY OFF:SCREEN 7:SCREEN
   9:SCREEN 9,,0,1:PALETTE 8,32:PALETTE
   9,55:PALETTE 5,47:PALETTE 13,56:X=120:Y=195
240 CLS
250 PSET(120,95),13:DRAW"R100 D70 L100 U70"
```

```
260 PAINT(125,99),1,13:PSET(134,165),13:
    DRAW"M131,160 M130,155 M131,150 M135,145
    M139,146 M144,147 M151,148 M160,148 M165,147
    M168,149 M172,151 M177,153 M183,155 M193,157
    M202,159 M211,160 M220,160":PAINT(169,159),9,
    13
265 DRAW"C13 BM135,145 M128,149 M129,146 M126,145
    M121,148 M121,142 M125,139 M120,136 M120,130
    M127,128 M124,127 M122,125 M125,124 M127,123
    M124,122 M122,120 M128,119 M132,118 M128,111
    M128,104 M132,109 M134,106 M137,108 M141,102
    M144,107 M151,100"
270 DRAW"M150,107 M154,107 M164,98 M159,107
    M169,103 M163,111 M174,106 M179,106 M181,108
    M178,108 M171,112 M180,114 M173,115 M180,117
    M183,124 M175,119 M181,129 M176,128 M180,137
    M173,135 M174,140 M171,142 M174,145 M167,145
    M168,149"
273 DRAW"BM134,141 M131,123 M133,120 M137,117
    M142,116 M151,115 M163,116 M171,120 M171,124
    M162,141 M156,143 M141,143 M134,141 BM132,131
    M142,127 M145,128 M146,134 M155,134 M157,130
    M160,128 M164,128 M167,131":PAINT(151,122),5,
    13
275 PAINT(152,111),10,13:PAINT(153,138),9,13:
    PSET(146,135),13:DRAW"M148,136 M153,136
    M155,134 BM151,136 M151,138 M150,138
    M150,136":PAINT(150,135),8,13
278 PSET(147,139),12:DRAW"M153,139 M153,140
    M148,140 C13 BM154,139 M158,138 M161,137
    BM146,139 M140,138 M138,137"
280 PSET(136,124),13:DRAW"M136,122 M137,120
    M139,119 M141,119 M143,121 M143,123 M136,124
    BM138,124 M141,125 M143,123":PAINT(140,121),
    2,13:PAINT(141,124),15,13
282 PSET(157,123),13:DRAW"M159,121 M162,120
    M164,121 M164,123 M164,124 M164,125
    M157,123":PAINT(162,122),2,13:PSET(158,123),13
    :DRAW"M160,126 M163,125":PAINT(161,125),15,13
285 DIM PA(1000):GET(119,95)-(221,165),PA:CLS
290 CLS:PCOPY 0,1:SCREEN 9:CLS:COLOR
    10,15:RANDOMIZE TIMER
300 T=INT(1+5*RND(1))
305 V=INT(1+5*RND(1))
```

```
306 C=INT(1+5*RND(1))
307 B=INT(1+2*RND(1))
308 N=INT(1+2*RND(1))
309 IF B=2 THEN V=-(V)
310 IF N=2 THEN C=-(C)
311 FD=INT(1+1000*RND(1))
320 FOR A=1 TO T
325 PUT(X,Y),PA,XOR
330 FOR DF=1 TO FD:NEXT DF
340 PUT(X,Y),PA,XOR
350 X=X+V:Y=Y+C
351 IF X=<1 THEN X=1
352 IF X=>535 THEN X=535
353 IF Y=>270 THEN Y=270
354 IF Y=<1 THEN Y=1
355 NEXT A
360 GOTO 300
```

● ● ●

Wrap a narrative—and a game—around Natasha (a.k.a. Tata). She's simply too adorable not to, don't you think?

Moving in Stages
LOAD "STAGE.BAS"

Ok

RUN

Shigeru Miyamoto created *Mario Bros.* in 1983. Although groundbreaking and popular, his best work was yet to come two years later.

Super Mario Bros. differs in one key respect to its predecessor: levels can scroll. Although *Super Mario Bros.* wasn't the first side-scrolling game—*Defender* (1980) has that honor—it brought side- and parallax scrolling to the masses, helping both to launch the eight-bit Nintendo Entertainment System to stratospheric sales and create a thousand side-scrolling imitators, of which very few (e.g., the *Mega Man* series) were up to par.

GW-BASIC has no built-in feature to scroll stages, but there are a couple of very limited workarounds. (The main problems are speed and flicker, so please keep your expectations in check.) Let take a look at several programs.

• • •

CAR.BAS, which places you inside a car via a dashboard view, loops the white-painted lines of a road toward the viewer to trick the eye into thinking the car's moving forward. Not "real" scrolling—just a visual trick—so the program's not exactly *Stunts*, which is probably the most innovative PC racing game of all time (heck, the program's not even *The Ford Simulator*).

STAGE1.BAS and **STAGE2.BAS** scroll a wireframe background beneath rocket ships. You control the speed of the ships by pressing the + and − keys. This is a step closer to *Super Mario Bros.*, but the ships don't interact with the scrolling backgrounds—although in **STAGE2.BAS** you can control the position of the ship as well as speed thrusts. Pay attention in the code to the use of **DRAW** relative movement versus absolute movement.

Finally, **ROADER.BAS** gives you a taste of overhead scrolling à la *Spy Hunter* (1983). You can use the + and − keys to control the speed of the vehicles, but you can't move them left or right.

• • •

CAR.BAS

```
10 KEY OFF:SCREEN 7:CLS:SCREEN 7,,0,1:COLOR
   14,7:CLS
20 CIRCLE(230,30),40,15
30 PAINT(230,30),14,15
40 PSET(0,60),8:DRAW"R10 U10 R10 D10 R10 U20 R20
   D20 R10 U10 R10 D10 R10 U30 R20 D30 R10 U10 R10
   D10 R10 U20 R30 D20 R10 U10 R10 D10 R10 U10 R20
   D10 R10 U30 R10 D30 R10 U20 R20 D20 R10 U10 R10
   D10 R10 U30 R20 D30 R10 D5 L320"
50 PAINT(140,50),8,8
60 PSET(0,130),8:DRAW"M150,65 M320,130"
70 PAINT(40,90),2,8:PAINT(270,90),2,8
80 CIRCLE(230,30),40,8
90 PAINT(20,10),1,8:PAINT(300,10),1,8
100 CIRCLE(230,30),40,8
105 PSET(0,160),8:DRAW"R320"
106 PAINT(5,165),5,8
```

```
107 CIRCLE(50,180),50,6:CIRCLE(50,180),49,6:
    CIRCLE(50,180),48,6:CIRCLE(50,180),47,6:CIRCLE
    (50,180),3,6
108 PSET(50,180),6:DRAW"NE30 ND50 NH30"
109 CIRCLE(190,190),20,6:CIRCLE(240,190),20,6:
    CIRCLE(290,190),20,6:PAINT(190,190),2,6:PAINT(
    240,190),2,6:PAINT(290,190),2,6:PSET(0,130),6:
    DRAW"M5,65 M315,65 M320,130":PSET(0,60),6:DRAW
    "R320":PAINT(10,63),6,6:PCOPY 0,1:SCREEN 7
110 FOR V=67 TO 85 STEP 5
120 PSET(150,V),15
130 DRAW"D2 BD1 D3 BD3 D5 BD5 D8 BD8 D12 BD12 D15"
135 FOR G=1 TO 400:NEXT G
140 PSET(150,V),0
145 DRAW"D2 BD1 D3 BD3 D5 BD5 D8 BD8 D12 BD12 D15"
150 NEXT V
160 GOTO 110
```

STAGE1.BAS

```
0 T=0:D=0
10 KEY OFF:SCREEN 7:COLOR 15,0:CLS
11 CIRCLE(90,60),5,14:CIRCLE(110,60),5,14:
   CIRCLE(130,60),5,14:CIRCLE(150,60),5,14
12 PAINT(90,60),12,14:PAINT(110,60),8,14:
   PAINT(130,60),8,14:PAINT(150,60),8,14
13 PSET(80,50),14:DRAW"R80 D20 L80 U20"
14 PAINT(120,60),3,14
15 LOCATE 1,12:COLOR 14:PRINT"MJL Enterprises"
16 PSET(79,49),12:DRAW"R80 D20 L80 U20"
20 T=0:A$="R320 U70 R70 D40 R90 D30 R100 U50 E10
   R100 F10 D50 R50 U10 R100 D10 R30 U60 E20 R30
   F20 D60 R100 U80 R50 D40 R50 D40 R70 U20 E10
   R100 F10 D20 R400"
21 PSET(50,20),14:DRAW"M60,20 M61,10 M90,20
   M150,20 M200,30 M150,40 M50,40 M50,20"
22 PSET(50,20),14:DRAW"M40,18 M40,30 M50,28 M50,32
   M40,30 M40,42 M50,40"
23 PSET(60,20),14:DRAW"M90,20":PSET(37,20),14:
   DRAW"M10,30 M37,40 BM37,37 C12 M20,30 M37,23"
24 PSET(150,20),14:DRAW"M147,24 M147,36 M150,40"
25 PSET(80,30),14:DRAW"M110,36 M140,30
   M80,30":PSET(90,40),14:DRAW"M60,50 M60,40"
26 PAINT(170,30),7,14:PAINT(110,33),7,14:
   PAINT(100,25),12,14:PAINT(70,16),4,14
```

```
27 PAINT(45,25),7,14
28 PAINT(45,35),7,14:PAINT(73,43),4,14
29 PSET(51,21),4:DRAW"R97":PSET(51,39),4:DRAW"R97"
30 C$=INKEY$:T=T-D:PSET(T,180),15:DRAW
   A$:PSET(T,180),0:DRAW A$
35 IF T=<-1348 THEN T=0
40 IF C$="+" THEN D=D+1
45 IF C$="-" THEN D=D-1
50 IF D=<0 THEN D=0
55 IF D=0 THEN PAINT(90,60),12,14
60 IF D=1 THEN PAINT(90,60),9,14:
   PAINT(110,60),8,14
65 IF D=100 THEN PAINT(110,60),10,14:
   PAINT(130,60),8,14
70 IF D=299 THEN PAINT(150,60),10,14:
   PAINT(130,60),8,14
75 IF D=200 THEN GOTO 100
76 LOCATE 10,11:COLOR 12:PRINT"Mph-";D
90 GOTO 30
100 PAINT(130,60),10,14:PAINT(110,60),8,14:
    PAINT(150,60),8,14
110 GOTO 30
```

STAGE2.BAS

```
10 D=0:T=0:X=160:Y=85:KEY OFF:SCREEN 7:COLOR
   15,0:CLS
15 B$="S4 R320 U10 R60 D10 R50 E40 R10 F40 R10 U70
   E10 R90 F10 D50 R80 D10 F10 R50 U70 R50 D70 R90
   U10 R10 D10 R320"
20 I$=INKEY$
30 T=T-D
40 IF I$="6" THEN X=X+10
50 IF I$="4" THEN X=X-10
60 IF I$="8" THEN Y=Y-10
70 IF I$="2" THEN Y=Y+10
71 IF I$="9" THEN X=X+5:Y=Y-5
72 IF I$="3" THEN X=X+5:Y=Y+5
73 IF I$="1" THEN X=X-5:Y=Y+5
74 IF I$="7" THEN X=X-5:Y=Y-5
75 IF I$="-" THEN D=D-10
76 IF I$="+" THEN D=D+10
77 IF D=<0 THEN D=0
78 LOCATE 3,1:PRINT"Speed:";D
```

```
80 PSET(X,Y):DRAW"S4 M-5,-4 M-8,-1 M-8,+1 M-2,+5
   M+2,+2 M+5,+1 M+7,+0 M+8,+0 M+5,-2 M-4,-2"
85 PSET(X,Y),0:DRAW"S4 M-5,-4 M-8,-1 M-8,+1 M-2,+5
   M+2,+2 M+5,+1 M+7,+0 M+8,+0 M+5,-2 M-4,-2"
90 PSET(T,180),12:DRAW B$
95 PSET(T,180),0:DRAW B$
96 IF T=<-936 THEN T=0
100 GOTO 20
```

ROADER.BAS

```
0 KEY OFF:SCREEN 7:COLOR 15,2:CLS:LOCATE
  1,15:PRINT"Roader v1.0"
1 PSET(110,40),8:DRAW"R90 D90 L90
  U90":PAINT(140,50),8,8:PSET(105,45),15:DRAW"R90
  D90 L90 U90":PAINT(120,60),2,15
2 COLOR 12:LOCATE 7,15:PRINT"Select Car":COLOR
  4:LOCATE 9,15:PRINT"Car 1":LOCATE
  10,15:PRINT"Car 2":LOCATE
  11,15:PRINT"View":LOCATE 12,15:PRINT"Exit"
3 T$=INKEY$
4 IF T$="1" THEN B$="C8 U10 E5 F5 D10 L10":GOTO
  700
5 IF T$="2" THEN B$="C8 U14 E1 R8 F1 D14 G1 F1 L10
  E1 H1":GOTO 700
6 IF T$="V" THEN GOTO 500
7 IF T$="E" THEN CLS:END
8 GOTO 3
10 D=0:T=-100:KEY OFF:SCREEN 7:COLOR
   15,7:CLS:PSET(140,100):DRAW
   B$:PAINT(145,90),COL,8
20 PSET(100,0),8:DRAW"D200":PSET(170,0),8:
   DRAW"D200":PAINT(10,10),2,8:PAINT(290,10),2,8
30 I$=INKEY$:T=T+D:PSET(137,T):DRAW"D10 BD10 D10
   BD10 D10 BD10 D10 BD10 D10 BD10 D10 BD10 D10
   BD10 D10 BD10 D10 BD10 D10 BD10 D10 BD10 D10
   BD10 D10 BD10 D10 BD10 D10 BD10 D10 BD10 D10
   BD10 D10 BD10 D10 BD10 D10 BD10 D10 BD10 D10
   BD10 D10 BD10 D10 BD10 D10
36 LOCATE 1,1:PRINT"Speed:";U
37 U=INT(D*10)
40 PSET(137,T),0:DRAW"D10 BD10 D10 BD10 D10 BD10
   D10 BD10 D10 BD10 D10 BD10 D10 BD10 D10 BD10 D10
   BD10 D10 BD10 D10 BD10 D10 BD10 D10 BD10 D10
   BD10 D10 BD10 D10 BD10 D10 BD10 D10 BD10 D10
```

313

```
    BD10 D10 BD10 D10 BD10 D10 BD10 D10 BD10 D10
    BD10 D10 BD10 D10 BD10
41  IF I$="+" THEN D=D+SPD
42  IF I$="-" THEN D=D-SPD
43  IF D=<0 THEN D=0
44  IF D=>100 THEN D=100
45  IF T=>-80 THEN T=-100
50  GOTO 30
500 CLS:PSET(0,128),8:DRAW"R320":PAINT(10,10),1,
    8:CIRCLE(260,20),30,14:PAINT(260,20),14,14
510 PSET(100,10),12:DRAW"L10 D10 R10 BR10 U10 R10
    D5 L10 R10 D5 BR10 U10 R10 D5 L10 R5 F5 BR20
    U10"
520 PSET(60,120),8:DRAW"M77,107 M90,100 M104,95
    M120,91 M140,91 M160,93 M175,97 M173,107
    M170,120"
530 PSET(150,120),8:DRAW"L50":PSET(80,120),8:
    DRAW"L20"
540 CIRCLE(90,120),10,8:CIRCLE(160,120),10,8
550 PAINT(120,100),5,8:PAINT(90,120),15,8:
    PAINT(160,120),15,8
560 PSET(0,128),8:DRAW"R320"
580 LOCATE 20,12:COLOR 15:PRINT"Top Speed:?
    m.p.h.":LOCATE 21,12:PRINT"0-60 0.7 seconds"
595 FOR GH=1 TO 15000:NEXT GH
600 CLS:PSET(0,128),8:DRAW"R320":PAINT(10,10),1,8
    :CIRCLE(260,20),30,14:PAINT(260,20),14,14
605 PSET(80,120),8:DRAW"M110,90 M119,88 M180,88
    M190,90 M199,103 M207,97 M208,105 M200,120
    M190,120"
610 PSET(100,10),12:DRAW"L10 D10 R10 BR10 U10 R10
    D5 L10 R10 D5 BR10 U10 R10 D5 L10 R5 F5 BR20
    R10 L10 U5 R10 U5 L10"
620 PSET(170,120),8:DRAW"L50":PSET(100,120),8:
    DRAW"L20":CIRCLE(110,120),10,8:CIRCLE(180,120)
    ,10,8
630 PAINT(120,100),14,8:PAINT(110,120),7,8:
    PAINT(180,120),7,8
640 LOCATE 20,12:COLOR 15:PRINT"Top Speed:?
    m.p.h.":LOCATE 21,12:PRINT"0-60 6.2 seconds"
650 FOR GH=1 TO 15000:NEXT GH
660 GOTO 0
700 IF T$="1" THEN COL=5:SPD=1
710 IF T$="1" THEN GOTO 10
```

314

```
720 IF T$="2" THEN COL=14:SPD=.1
730 IF T$="2" THEN GOTO 10
```

● ● ●

All four programs in this chapter suffer from the same problem: crippling flicker due to limited speed-processing capabilities. The challenge: Using a variety of speed-optimization algorithms, can you make a true, interactive side-scrolling game in GW-BASIC? Would flipping between invisible SCREENs or using the PCOPY statement be enough to deal with the issues?

Only up to a point. Consider, for example, the following program.

SQURE.BAS
```
10 SCREEN 7:CLS:KEY OFF:COLOR 15,0:CLS
15 SCREEN 7:CLS:SCREEN 7,,0,1
20 PSET(100,20):DRAW"M260,20 M260,170 M100,170
   M100,20":PAINT(170,70),12,15
25 PSET(30,60),6:DRAW"M160,60 M160,140 M30,140
   M30,60":PAINT(100,80),14,6
30 PCOPY 0,1:FOR GH=1 TO 6000:NEXT GH:SCREEN 7:CLS
40 SCREEN 7,,2,3
50 PSET(100,20),15:DRAW"M260,20 M260,170 M100,170
   M100,20":PAINT(170,70),12,15
60 PSET(40,60),6:DRAW"M180,60 M180,140 M30,160
   M40,60":PAINT(120,80),14,6
70 PCOPY 2,3:FOR GH=1 TO 6000:NEXT GH:GOTO 15
```

SQURE.BAS alternates between two images of convex polygons. Even though flicker is nonexistent once the images toggle back and forth, both flicker and slowdown make their presence felt at run time—right when the images are drawn initially on-screen—so GW-BASIC programs necessitating rapid movement, like car racing games, will always have a lot of trouble firing on all cylinders.

Put and Get Drawing
LOAD "PUTGET.BAS"

Ok

RUN_

POSITION.BAS introduced savable images into the fray, but suffered from two key drawbacks: the images were saved as coded BASIC programs, and there was no way to undo drawing commands.

PUTGET.BAS tackles both of those problems head-on. Although the method of drawing on-screen is similar, the images are saved as *.dat* files (data files), and can be loaded as-is—they do not appear as coded DRAW statements.

● ● ●

Lines 469 and 510 introduce two GW-BASIC statements we haven't utilized before: BSAVE, which saves an image file, and BLOAD, which loads an image file.

● ● ●

PUTGET.BAS
```
5 CLEAR:C=1:C2=1:X=180:Y=62
10 KEY OFF:SCREEN 7:SCREEN 9:COLOR 8,55:PALETTE
   8,32:PALETTE 6,20:CLS:LOCATE 10,20:PRINT"Put and
   Get Graphics v1.0":FOR TY=1 TO 5000:NEXT
   TY:SOUND 1000,.35:CLS
11 LOCATE 10,14:INPUT"Memory usage for picture
   (max = 14500):";DI
12 LOCATE 11,14:INPUT"Load picture onto
   screen(Y/N)";AD$:CLS
13 IF AD$="Y" OR AD$="y" THEN GOTO 500
```

```
15 PSET(1,1),8:DIM H(2):GET(1,1)-(1,1),H:
   PSET(1,1),0
30 I$=INKEY$
35 PUT(X,Y),H,XOR:FOR FG=1 TO 100:NEXT
   FG:PUT(X,Y),H,XOR
40 IF I$="6" THEN X=X+1
41 IF I$="+" THEN C=C+1
42 IF I$="-" THEN C=C-1
43 IF C=<0 THEN C=15
44 IF C=>16 THEN C=1
45 IF I$="4" THEN X=X-1
50 IF I$="2" THEN Y=Y+1
55 IF I$="8" THEN Y=Y-1
60 IF I$="W" THEN Y=Y-10
65 IF I$="Z" THEN Y=Y+10
70 IF I$="A" THEN X=X-10
75 IF I$="S" THEN X=X+10
76 IF I$="L" OR I$="l" THEN GOTO 600
80 IF I$="9" THEN X=X+1:Y=Y-1
81 IF I$="D" OR I$="d" THEN GOTO 610
85 IF I$="1" THEN X=X-1:Y=Y+1
86 IF I$="P" OR I$="p" THEN GOTO 200
87 IF I$="B" OR I$="b" THEN B=B+1:GOTO 191
90 IF I$="3" THEN X=X+1:Y=Y+1
91 IF I$="M" OR I$="m" THEN C2=C2+1
92 IF C2>15 THEN C2=1
95 IF I$="7" THEN X=X-1:Y=Y-1
96 IF X<0 THEN X=0
97 IF X>639 THEN X=639
98 IF Y<0 THEN Y=0
99 IF Y>349 THEN Y=349
100 IF I$=" " THEN GOTO 160
110 IF I$="N" OR I$="n" THEN GOTO 180
120 IF I$="E" OR I$="e" THEN GOTO 220
130 LOCATE 23,1:PRINT"C=";C:LOCATE
    23,7:PRINT"P=";C2:LOCATE 23,12:PRINT X;",";Y
150 GOTO 30
160 LINE(R,S)-(X,Y),C:R=X:S=Y
170 GOTO 150
180 PSET(X,Y),C:R=X:S=Y
190 GOTO 150
191 IF B=>62 THEN B=0
192 COLOR ,B:GOTO 30
200 PAINT(X,Y),C2,C
```

```
210 GOTO 30
220 I$=INKEY$
230 PUT(X,Y),H,XOR:PUT(X,Y),H,XOR
240 IF I$="6" THEN X=X+1
250 IF I$="4" THEN X=X-1
260 IF I$="8" THEN Y=Y-1
265 IF I$="2" THEN Y=Y+1
270 IF I$="9" THEN X=X+1:Y=Y-1
280 IF I$="7" THEN Y=Y-1:X=X-1
285 IF I$="3" THEN Y=Y+1:X=X+1
290 IF I$="1" THEN X=X-1:Y=Y+1
300 IF I$="S" THEN X=X+10
310 IF I$="A" THEN X=X-10
315 IF I$="W" THEN Y=Y-10
320 IF I$="Z" THEN Y=Y+10
325 IF I$=" " THEN GOTO 340
330 GOTO 220
340 PSET(X-1,Y-1),8:A=X:B=Y
350 I$=INKEY$
360 PUT(A,B),H,XOR:PUT(A,B),H,XOR
370 IF I$="6" THEN A=A+1
375 IF I$="4" THEN A=A-1
380 IF I$="8" THEN B=B-1
385 IF I$="2" THEN B=B+1
390 IF I$="9" THEN A=A+1:B=B-1
395 IF I$="7" THEN B=B-1:A=A-1
400 IF I$="3" THEN B=B+1:A=A+1
405 IF I$="1" THEN A=A-1:B=B+1
410 IF I$="S" THEN A=A+10
420 IF I$="A" THEN A=A-10
425 IF I$="W" THEN B=B-10
430 IF I$="Z" THEN B=B+10
435 IF I$=" " THEN GOTO 440
436 GOTO 350
440 DIM L(DI):GET(X,Y)-(A,B),L
450 FOR GH=1 TO 5000:NEXT GH
455 CLS:LOCATE 10,13:INPUT"Save under (include
    drive, name, and .DAT extension)";F$
460 DEF SEG:BSAVE F$,VARPTR(L(0)),DI:END
500 CLS:LOCATE 10,13:INPUT"Drive for
    files:";DA$:FILES DA$:INPUT"Saved under (in
    clude drive, name, and .DAT extension)";F$
510 DEF SEG:BLOAD F$,VARPTR(M(0))
520 CLS:PUT(10,10),M,XOR:GOTO 15
```

```
600 COLOR C:LINE INPUT O$:COLOR 8:GOTO 30
610 I$=INKEY$
620 PUT(X,Y),H,XOR:PUT(X,Y),H,XOR
630 IF I$="6" THEN X=X+1
640 IF I$="4" THEN X=X-1
650 IF I$="8" THEN Y=Y-1
660 IF I$="2" THEN Y=Y+1
665 IF I$="9" THEN X=X+1:Y=Y-1
670 IF I$="7" THEN Y=Y-1:X=X-1
675 IF I$="3" THEN Y=Y+1:X=X+1
680 IF I$="1" THEN X=X-1:Y=Y+1
685 IF I$="S" THEN X=X+10
690 IF I$="A" THEN X=X-10
695 IF I$="W" THEN Y=Y-10
700 IF I$="Z" THEN Y=Y+10
705 IF I$="E" OR I$="e" THEN GOTO 30
706 IF I$="N" OR I$="n" THEN PSET(X,Y),0
710 GOTO 610
```

● ● ●

PUTGET.BAS gives you a blank canvas. The upshot: you have the freedom to draw up to the limits of GW-BASIC—and your own patience. For example, take a look at this image that I sketched using PUTGET.BAS:

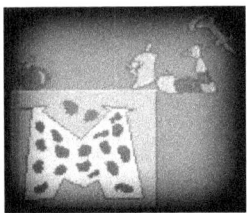

But, on the downside, there are quite a few keyboard commands to remember while working with PUTGET.BAS. Displaying all the commands on-screen in a heads-up-like display would clutter things up, but, as it stands now, the program is terribly un-user-friendly.

Better Drawing
LOAD "FUN.BAS"

Ok

RUN_

PUTGET.BAS is tough to work with, largely because it's so open-ended: lots of commands with virtually no prompting.

FUN.BAS solves some of these problems, but at a cost: you're restricted to drawing in a small rectangular area of the screen. But the image-manipulation options are much more clearly stated.

• • •

Like with PUTGET.BAS, BSAVE, which saves *.dat* files, and BLOAD, which loads *.dat* files, are used here.

• • •

```
FUN.BAS
5 CLEAR:C=1:C2=1:X=180:Y=62
10 KEY OFF:SCREEN 7:SCREEN 9:COLOR 15,0:CLS:LOCATE
   1,15:PRINT"*F*U*N* Version 1.0 Standard Drawing
   Block"
11 LOCATE 14,7:PRINT"Press + or - to find your
   color":LOCATE 15,7:PRINT"Press M to select your
   Paint color":LOCATE 16,7:PRINT"Press B to find
   your background color":LOCATE 17,7:PRINT"Press E
   to take image in box and transpose to clear
   screen"
13 LOCATE 18,7:PRINT"Press L to load a saved im
   age":LOCATE 19,7:PRINT"Press F to save an image"
```

```
15 PSET(1,1),15:DIM H(2):GET(1,1)-(1,1),H:
   PSET(1,1),0
20 PSET(175,42),15:DRAW"R170 D120 L170 U120"
30 I$=INKEY$
35 PUT(X,Y),H,XOR:FOR FG=1 TO 100:NEXT
   FG:PUT(X,Y),H,XOR
40 IF I$="6" THEN X=X+1
41 IF I$="+" THEN C=C+1
42 IF I$="-" THEN C=C-1
43 IF C=<0 THEN C=15
44 IF C=>16 THEN C=1
45 IF I$="4" THEN X=X-1
50 IF I$="2" THEN Y=Y+1
55 IF I$="8" THEN Y=Y-1
60 IF I$="W" THEN Y=Y-10
65 IF I$="Z" THEN Y=Y+10
66 IF I$="L" OR I$="l" THEN GOTO 285
70 IF I$="A" THEN X=X-10
75 IF I$="S" THEN X=X+10
80 IF I$="9" THEN X=X+1:Y=Y-1
85 IF I$="1" THEN X=X-1:Y=Y+1
86 IF I$="P" OR I$="p" THEN GOTO 200
87 IF I$="B" OR I$="b" THEN B=B+1:GOTO 191
88 IF I$="F" OR I$="f" THEN GOTO 310
90 IF I$="3" THEN X=X+1:Y=Y+1
91 IF I$="M" OR I$="m" THEN C2=C2+1
92 IF C2>15 THEN C2=1
95 IF I$="7" THEN X=X-1:Y=Y-1
96 IF X<175 THEN X=175
97 IF X>175+170 THEN X=175+170
98 IF Y<42 THEN Y=42
99 IF Y>42+120 THEN Y=42+120
100 IF I$=" " THEN GOTO 160
110 IF I$="N" OR I$="n" THEN GOTO 180
120 IF I$="E" OR I$="e" THEN GOTO 220
130 LOCATE 21,1:PRINT"Color";C:LOCATE 21,15:PRINT
    "Paint";C2:LOCATE 21,29:PRINT"Background";B
150 GOTO 30
160 LINE(R,S)-(X,Y),C:R=X:S=Y
170 GOTO 150
180 PSET(X,Y),C:R=X:S=Y
190 GOTO 150
191 IF B=>62 THEN B=0
192 COLOR ,B:GOTO 30
```

```
200 PAINT(X,Y),C2,C
210 GOTO 30
220 DIM M(9999):GET(176,43)-(176+168,43+118),M
230 COLOR ,0:CLS
240 RANDOMIZE TIMER
250 Z=INT(1+460*RND(1)):E=INT(1+195*RND(1))
260 PUT(Z,E),M,XOR
270 FOR VA=1 TO 3000:NEXT VA:PUT(Z,E),M,XOR:CLS
276 IF B=>62 THEN B=0
280 GOTO 250
285 CLS:FILES"C:":INPUT"What is file name (with
    extension)";F$
290 DEF SEG:BLOAD F$,VARPTR(M(0))
291 CLS:PUT(180,62),M,XOR:CLEAR:GOTO 11
300 GOTO 230
310 DIM M(9999):GET(176,43)-(176+168,43+118),M
320 CLS:INPUT"What is the file name (please use
    extension .DAT after inputting name)";F$
330 DEF SEG:BSAVE F$,VARPTR(M(0)),9999
340 GOTO 230
360 GOTO 300
```

• • •

Although a step in the right direction, **FUN.BAS** still suffers from many of the same issues as **PUTGET.BAS**. Refining the code even more by finding the best compromise between user-friendliness and flexibility is paramount.

Star Fields and Spaceships
LOAD "TE.BAS"

Ok

RUN_

Let's put aside the usual chapter formatting rules, and use PUTGET.BAS (or FUN.BAS) to construct a user-controlled spaceship flying through a star field.

• • •

First, let's see if we can make a program that displays a star field scrolling from right to left—giving the illusion that your ship is floating from left to right. Each star's coordinates need to be saved in an array, so that all of the stars can be moved as a group easily; in addition, when a star reaches the left side of the screen, it should be immediately transported to the right side of the screen.

STARFIELD.BAS
```
10 KEY OFF:SCREEN 9:COLOR 15,0:CLS
20 DIM X(30):DIM Y(30)
30 FOR T=1 TO 30:X(T)=INT(1+640*RND(1)):Y(T)=
   INT(1+320*RND(1)):NEXT T
40 FOR B=1 TO 30
45 PSET(X(B),Y(B)),15
50 NEXT B
60 FOR PAUSE=1 TO 400:NEXT PAUSE
65 FOR B=1 TO 30
70 PRESET(X(B),Y(B))
75 X(B)=X(B)-1
80 IF X(B)<0 THEN X(B)=640
85 NEXT B
90 GOTO 40
```

• • •

Next, let's draw a spaceship. The ship should have fire-like thrust emerging from the rear. How about something like this?

But the thrust wouldn't be static in real life—it would be rapidly growing and shrinking in volume. Therefore, after saving the image above as **SHIP1.DAT**, I reloaded it, made a couple of additions, and saved my new picture as **SHIP2.DAT**:

Notice the bigger thrust column out the back of the spaceship. Alternating these two ship images should give us a nice illusion of forward momentum.

• • •

The program **TE.BAS** puts together all the pieces—the star field, the ship animation, and the user-movement commands. (Note: if you don't draw and save the two ship *.dat* files, **TE.BAS** will not run.)

TE.BAS
```
10 KEY OFF:RANDOMIZE TIMER:SCREEN 7:SCREEN 9:
   CLEAR:COLOR 15,0:CLS:DEF SEG:BLOAD
   "SHIP1.DAT",VARPTR(KL(0))
20 PUT(10,10),KL,XOR:CLEAR:BLOAD"SHIP2.DAT",VARPTR
   (LK(0)):PUT(50,50),LK,XOR:CLEAR
30 DIM K1(1000):GET(4,10)-(75,25),K1:DIM K2(1000):
   GET(47,53)-(119,69),K2:CLS
31 X=100:Y=100
32 DIM XX(30):DIM YY(30)
```

```
33 FOR T=1 TO 30:XX(T)=INT(1+640*RND(1)):YY(T)=INT
   (1+320*RND(1)):NEXT T
35 I$=INKEY$
40 PUT(X,Y),K1:FOR TY=1 TO 800:NEXT TY:PUT(X,Y),K1
45 IF I$="6" THEN X=X+10
50 IF I$="4" THEN X=X-8
55 IF I$="8" THEN Y=Y-10
60 IF I$="2" THEN Y=Y+10
61 FOR B=1 TO 30
62 PSET(XX(B),YY(B)),15
63 NEXT B
70 I$=INKEY$
75 PUT(X,Y-1),K2:FOR TY=1 TO 800:NEXT TY:PUT(X,Y-
   1),K2
80 IF I$="6" THEN X=X+10
85 IF I$="4" THEN X=X-8
90 IF I$="8" THEN Y=Y-10
95 IF I$="2" THEN Y=Y+10
96 FOR B=1 TO 30
97 PRESET(XX(B),YY(B))
98 XX(B)=XX(B)-5
99 IF XX(B)<2 THEN XX(B)=640
100 NEXT B
110 GOTO 35
```

• • •

Once run, it's immediately apparent how sluggish the ship's movements are; even though flicker isn't *that bad*— although it's noticeably worse in **TE.BAS** than **STARFIELD.BAS**—the more items that GW-BASIC has to move on-screen or simply account for, the slower the program's going to run.

Teeing Off
LOAD "GOLF.BAS"
Ok
RUN_

Ah, golf. A tough game to play, an even tougher game to watch on television.

But golf can sometimes be fun to play interactively on a computer screen. When you run **GOLF.BAS**, you'll first be given instructions on how to construct your course. Then, after creating the course, you will be able to play a couple of rounds. Your facility with tapping the spacebar determines your success on the green.

• • •

Like **TE.BAS**, several *.dat* images must be loaded before running the program. One, a logo-image file called **GOLFTI.DAT**, is optional; the other, a flag-in-the-hole drawing file called **FLAG.DAT**, is not.

Both images, shown below, can be constructed with either **PUTGET.BAS** or **FUN.BAS**. The flag's color is supposed to be red, but the "hole" it's planted in *must* be gray, which is **COLOR 7**, otherwise the **POINT** command won't register a win.

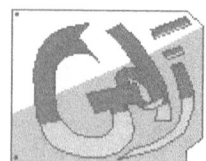

The golf ball travels from one location to another using simple algebra: the movement subroutine finds the slope between the old and new locations of the ball and runs a FOR/NEXT loop between the two coordinate pairs (see lines 4000 to 4060 for the details).

• • •

GOLF.BAS

```
10 CLEAR:VIEW PRINT:RANDOMIZE TIMER:KEY OFF:SCREEN
   9:CLS:COLOR 15,0:FOR TY=1 TO 5000:NEXT TY:COLOR
   15,42:CLS:FOR TY=1 TO 3000:NEXT TY
20 BLOAD"GOLFTI.DAT",VARPTR(A(0)):PUT(250,100),A,
   XOR:CLEAR:DIM A(5000):GET(252,102)-(365,186),A
25 LOCATE 16,32:PRINT"COURSE DESIGNER":LOCATE
   19,31:PRINT"- press any key -"
30 I$=INKEY$:IF I$="" THEN 30
31 GOTO 2000
35 COLOR ,21:CLS
40 PUT(510,240),A,XOR
50 PSET(100,62),8:DRAW"M500,62 M500,233 M100,233
   M100,62"
60 COLOR 8:CIRCLE(120,280),25:CIRCLE(200,280),25:
   CIRCLE(280,280),25:CIRCLE(360,280),25:CIRCLE(440
   ,280),25
70 PAINT(120,280),10,8:PAINT(200,280),2,8:
   PAINT(280,280),1,8:PAINT(440,280),15,8
75 BLOAD"FLAG.DAT",VARPTR(F(0)):PUT(355,270),F,
   XOR:CLEAR:DIM F(500):GET(356,270)-(369,289),F:
   PUT(356,270),F,XOR:PUT(356,270),F,XOR:PAINT(365,
   280),10,8
80 PALETTE 14,55:PAINT(440,280),14,8
85 LOCATE 18,15:PRINT"G":LOCATE
   18,25:PRINT"R":LOCATE 18,35:PRINT"O":LOCATE
   18,45:PRINT"F":LOCATE 18,55:PRINT"T":COLOR
   10:LOCATE 1,26:PRINT"GOLF Course Designer"
90 COLOR 8:LOCATE 2,24:PRINT"E-  Exits screen to
   play"
100 CIRCLE(10,10),3,15:PAINT(10,10),15,15:DIM
    AA(10):GET(8,8)-(12,12),AA:PSET(10,10),0
    :X=300:Y=120
110 I$=INKEY$
```

```
120 PUT(X,Y),AA:PUT(X,Y),AA
125 IF I$="" THEN 110
130 IF I$="6" THEN X=X+1
135 IF I$="4" THEN X=X-1
140 IF I$="8" THEN Y=Y-1
145 IF I$="2" THEN Y=Y+1
150 IF I$="3" THEN X=X+1:Y=Y+1
160 IF I$="7" THEN X=X-1:Y=Y-1
165 IF I$="9" THEN X=X+1:Y=Y-1
170 IF I$="1" THEN X=X-1:Y=Y+1
175 IF I$="A" THEN X=X-10
180 IF I$="W" THEN Y=Y-10
185 IF I$="Z" THEN Y=Y+10
190 IF I$="S" THEN X=X+10
200 IF X<100 THEN X=100
205 IF X>500 THEN X=500
210 IF Y<62 THEN Y=62
215 IF Y>233 THEN Y=233
220 IF I$=" " THEN GOTO 810
225 IF I$="N" OR I$="n" THEN GOTO 820
230 IF I$="G" OR I$="g" THEN PAINT(X,Y),10,8
240 IF I$="r" OR I$="R" THEN PAINT(X,Y),2,8
250 IF I$="O" OR I$="o" THEN PAINT(X,Y),1,8
260 IF I$="F" OR I$="f" THEN GOTO 830
265 IF I$="T" OR I$="t" THEN PAINT(X,Y),14,8
280 IF I$="E" OR I$="e" THEN GOTO 920
800 GOTO 110
810 LINE(R,S)-(X,Y),8:R=X:S=Y:GOTO 110
820 PSET(X,Y),8:R=X:S=Y:GOTO 110
830 B$=INKEY$
840 PUT(X,Y),F,XOR:PUT(X,Y),F,XOR
850 IF B$="6" THEN X=X+1
860 IF B$="4" THEN X=X-1
870 IF B$="8" THEN Y=Y-1
880 IF B$="2" THEN Y=Y+1
890 IF B$=" " THEN GOTO 900
895 GOTO 830
900 PUT(X,Y),F
905 FLAGX=X:FLAGY=Y
910 GOTO 110
920 COLOR 8:FOR GH=14 TO 38:PSET(262,GH),0:DRAW
    "R115":NEXT GH:FOR TY=237 TO 300:PSET(80,TY),
    0:DRAW"R390":NEXT TY:LOCATE 2,34:PRINT"game"
```

```
930 COLOR 8:LOCATE 19,22:PRINT"PLEASE LOCATE
    TEEING-OFF POINT"
940 I$=INKEY$
945 PUT(X,Y),AA,XOR:PUT(X,Y),AA,XOR
950 IF I$="6" THEN X=X+1
960 IF I$="4" THEN X=X-1
970 IF I$="8" THEN Y=Y-1
980 IF I$="2" THEN Y=Y+1
990 IF I$="S" THEN X=X+10
991 IF I$="A" THEN X=X-10
992 IF I$="W" THEN Y=Y-10
993 IF I$="Z" THEN Y=Y+10
994 IF I$=" " THEN GOTO 1005
1004 GOTO 940
1005 E=1:GF=X:FG=Y:FOR IU=251 TO 264:PSET(165,IU),
     0:DRAW"R244":NEXT IU:PSET(X,Y),12
1010 LOCATE 19,22:INPUT"What is PAR";PAR
1015 FOR IU=251 TO
     264:PSET(165,IU),0:DRAW"R244":NEXT IU
1020 LOCATE 3,24:PRINT"Par on course is:";PAR
1025 STR=1:LOCATE 4,23:PRINT"Current stroke
     is:";STR
1026 IF POINT(X+1,Y+1)=2 THEN E=2
1027 IF POINT(X+1,Y+1)=10 THEN E=1
1028 IF POINT(X+1,Y+1)=14 THEN E=5
1030 PSET(100,62),3:DRAW"M500,62 M500,233 M100,233
     M100,62"
1040 LOCATE 19,22:INPUT"Wind strength(1-5)";WS
1045 FOR IU=251 TO
     264:PSET(165,IU),0:DRAW"R244":NEXT IU
1050 RANDOMIZE
     TIMER:H=INT(1+4*RND(1)):G=INT(1+WS*RND(1))
1051 IF H=1 THEN LOCATE 22,29:PRINT"E at ";G;"
     MPH"
1052 IF H=2 THEN LOCATE 22,29:PRINT"W at ";G;"
     MPH"
1053 IF H=3 THEN LOCATE 22,29:PRINT"N at ";G;"
     MPH"
1054 IF H=4 THEN LOCATE 22,29:PRINT"S at ";G;"
     MPH"
1056 I$=INKEY$
1057 IF I$="E" OR I$="e" THEN END
1058 TU=INT(1+15*RND(1)):PSET(GF,FG),TU
1059 IF I$="" THEN GOTO 1056
```

```
1060 PUT(GF,FG),AA,XOR:X1=GF:Y1=FG:PUT(GF,FG),
     AA,XOR
1065 FOR FG=243 TO 52 STEP -E:PSET(90,FG),15:
     DRAW"L10":FOR NB=1 TO 100:NEXT
     NB:PSET(90,FG),0: DRAW"L10":I$=INKEY$:IF I$="
     " THEN GOTO 1075
1070 NEXT FG
1075 FOR GF=90 TO 510 STEP E:PSET(GF,243),15:DRAW
     "D10":FOR NB=1 TO 100:NEXT NB:PSET(GF,243),0:
     DRAW"D10":I$=INKEY$:IF I$=" " THEN GOTO 1081
1080 NEXT GF
1081 IF POINT(GF,FG)=2 THEN E=2
1082 IF POINT(GF,FG)=10 THEN E=1
1083 IF POINT(GF,FG)=14 THEN E=5
1085 IF H=1 THEN GF=GF+G
1090 IF H=2 THEN GF=GF-G
1095 IF H=3 THEN FG=FG-G
1100 IF H=4 THEN FG=FG+G
1120 STR=STR+1
1150 IF POINT(GF,FG)=7 THEN GOTO 1175
1155 IF POINT(GF,FG)=1 THEN STR=STR+1
1160 IF POINT(GF,FG)=3 THEN STR=STR+1
1165 IF POINT(GF,FG)=0 THEN STR=STR+1
1167 GOSUB 4000 'MOVE THE BALL
1168 PSET(GF,FG),15:LOCATE 4,23:PRINT"Current
     stroke is:";STR
1170 GOTO 1050
1175 LOCATE 21,29:COLOR 11:PRINT"INTO THE
     HOLE!!!":COLOR 8
1180 I$=INKEY$:IF I$="" THEN GOTO 1180
1190 GOTO 920
2000 CLS:PRINT"Instructions:----------------------
     ----------------------------------------------
     "
2010 PRINT:PRINT"First, the course must be drawn.
     Do this with the numeric keypad (NUMLOCK on),
     and other keys such as the spacebar. Press-
     ing:"
2020 PRINT"N -  Starts a new pixel, and you draw
     relative to that point."
2025 PRINT"SPACE -  Draws a line from the point of
     the last position to the current cursor posi
     tion."
```

```
2030 PRINT:PRINT"You make the enclosed object
     painted to a rough, green, etc. by moving
     cursor inside of it and pressing appropriate
     letter (above icons at bottom of screen."
2040 PRINT:PRINT"Hitting the Ball -- when stroke
     begins, press space at when the line is
     traveling downward, and again when it is
     traveling horizontally to achieve an X,Y po-
     sitioning for the ball on the course."
2050 PRINT:PRINT:PRINT"      - press any key to
     begin game -"
2060 I$=INKEY$:IF I$="" THEN 2060
2070 GOTO 35
4000 'SUBROUTINE FOR MOVING BALL
4005 X2=GF:Y2=FG
4010 SLOPE=(Y2-Y1)/(X2-X1)
4020 IF X1<X2 THEN ST=1 ELSE ST=-1
4025 YA=Y1    'Set initial y-value
4030 FOR LOOP=X1 TO X2 STEP ST
4040 PUT(LOOP,YA),AA,XOR:FOR PAUSE=1 TO 100:NEXT
     PAUSE:PUT(LOOP,YA),AA,XOR
4045 IF X1<X2 THEN YA=YA+SLOPE ELSE YA=YA-SLOPE
4047 IF (INT(LOOP)=FLAGX AND INT(YA)=FLAGY) THEN
     GOTO 1175   'CHECK TO SEE IF YOU WON
4048 IF POINT(LOOP,YA)=7 THEN GOTO 1175   'CHECK
     IN ANOTHER WAY TO SEE IF YOU'VE WON
4050 NEXT LOOP
4060 RETURN
```

• • •

Although it *sort of* looks like golf, **GOLF.BAS** doesn't really *feel* like golf in terms of player control. Although you can design pretty courses, the terrain doesn't make much of a difference when you're "hitting" the ball, though there are consequences to landing in the rough and in the sand; plus, worst of all, you can't even save the courses you've constructed. It's enough to leave you all teed off.

On-Screen Graph Paper
LOAD "GP.BAS"

Ok

RUN_

When drawing, you might require more precision—
perhaps even to the level of a pixel at a time, like in the
following sketch:

GP.BAS gives you that, along with a bonus feature: the
ability to save a mirror image of the picture you've just
created. If you're making a platform game, this feature is
really handy: not having to redraw (let's say) a VW Bug
from the reverse direction will save you quite a bit of time
and frustration.

• • •

The reflected image is created on-the-fly, while you're laying down the pixels; otherwise, **GP.BAS** works similarly to
PUTGET.BAS.

• • •

GP.BAS

```
10 VIEW PRINT:RANDOMIZE TIMER:KEY OFF:SCREEN
   9:COLOR 8,56:CLS:PALETTE 8,32:PALETTE
   6,20:X=1:Y=1:M=505:N=50
11 A=629:B=180
15 PSET(10,10),8:DRAW"R3 D2 L3 U2 R1 D1 R1":DIM
   U(10):GET(10,10)-(14,14),U
16 CLS
20 FOR T=0 TO 300 STEP 4:PSET(0,T),8:DRAW"R500":
   NEXT T
30 FOR T=0 TO 500 STEP
   4:PSET(T,0),8:DRAW"D300":NEXT T
40 I$=INKEY$
50 PUT(X,Y),U,XOR:PUT(X,Y),U,XOR:PUT(X,Y),U,XOR:
   PUT(X,Y),U,XOR
60 IF I$="6" THEN GOTO 350
70 IF I$="4" THEN GOTO 360
80 IF I$="8" THEN GOTO 370
90 IF I$="2" THEN GOTO 380
95 IF I$="B" OR I$="b" THEN COLOR ,56
96 IF I$="R" OR I$="r" THEN COLOR ,55
97 IF I$="K" THEN GOTO 400
100 IF X<0 THEN X=1
110 IF X>497 THEN X=497
115 IF Y<0 THEN Y=1
120 IF Y>297 THEN Y=297
125 IF I$="+" THEN C=C+1
126 IF I$="-" THEN C=C-1
127 IF C>15 THEN C=0
128 IF C<0 THEN C=15
129 LOCATE 23,5:PRINT"C=";C
130 IF I$=" " THEN PAINT(X+1,Y+1),C,8:GOTO 310
300 GOTO 40
310 PSET(M,N),C:PSET(A,B),C:GOTO 40
350 X=X+4:M=M+1:A=A-1
351 IF M>629 THEN M=629
352 IF M<505 THEN M=505
353 IF N>124 THEN N=124
354 IF N<50 THEN N=50
355 IF A>629 THEN A=629
356 IF A<505 THEN A=505
357 IF B>254 THEN B=254
358 IF B<180 THEN B=180
359 GOTO 100
```

```
360 X=X-4:M=M-1:A=A+1
361 IF M>629 THEN M=629
362 IF M<505 THEN M=505
363 IF N>124 THEN N=124
364 IF N<50 THEN N=50
365 IF A>629 THEN A=629
366 IF A<505 THEN A=505
367 IF B>254 THEN B=254
368 IF B<180 THEN B=180
369 GOTO 100
370 Y=Y-4:N=N-1:B=B-1
371 IF M>629 THEN M=629
372 IF M<505 THEN M=505
373 IF N>124 THEN N=124
374 IF N<50 THEN N=50
375 IF A>629 THEN A=629
376 IF A<505 THEN A=505
377 IF B>254 THEN B=254
378 IF B<180 THEN B=180
379 GOTO 100
380 Y=Y+4:N=N+1:B=B+1
381 IF M>629 THEN M=629
382 IF M<505 THEN M=505
383 IF N>124 THEN N=124
384 IF N<50 THEN N=50
385 IF A>629 THEN A=629
386 IF A<505 THEN A=505
387 IF B>254 THEN B=254
388 IF B<180 THEN B=180
389 GOTO 100
400 DIM Q(1500):GET(503,48)-(632,126),Q:DIM
    Y(1500):GET(503,177)-(632,257),Y
410 CLS:PRINT:PRINT:INPUT"Save as (Drv., name,
    .DAT)";D$
420 DEF SEG:BSAVE D$,VARPTR(Q(0)),5000
430 INPUT"Save mirror image as well (Y/N)";V$
440 IF V$="N" THEN CLEAR:END
450 CLS:PRINT:PRINT:INPUT"Save as (Drv.,name,
    .DAT)";A$
460 DEF SEG:BSAVE A$,VARPTR(Y(0)),5000
470 CLEAR:END
```

• • •

Although useful, **GP.BAS** also suffers from a lack of user-friendliness, in addition to not being able to load image files. You have your work cut out for you.

Stamps

LOAD "STAMP.BAS"

Ok

RUN_

Though similar to **GP.BAS**, **STAMP.BAS** actually takes as its inspiration *Mario Paint* (1992), the first Super Nintendo game to use a mouse. A "stamp" in *Mario Paint* was a 16-pixel by 16-pixel image. **STAMP.BAS** gives you that same canvas: 16 by 16, where you can draw, save, and load stamps. In fact, you can even turn any ASCII code into a stamp to edit and save.

• • •

Lots of **PSET** and **PAINT** statements are needed to set up the drawing easel, but it's well worth it—**STAMP.BAS** has one of the cleanest, clearest user interfaces of any program in the book.

• • •

STAMP.BAS

```
10 VIEW PRINT:RANDOMIZE TIMER:KEY OFF:SCREEN
   9:COLOR 8,56:CLS:PALETTE 8,32:PALETTE
   6,20:PSET(20,20),8:DRAW"R1 D1 L1 U1":DIM
   Q(6):GET(19,19)-(22,22),Q:CLS:B=30:X=114:Y=59:
   P=1:A=370:B=80:L=20
11 PALETTE 13,55
12 INPUT"Load Image (Y/N/CC)";RE$:IF RE$="Y" OR
   RE$="y" THEN GOTO 570
13 IF RE$="CC" OR RE$="cc" THEN GOTO 600
14 CLS
```

```
15 PSET(0,35),8:DRAW"R650"
20 FOR K=1 TO 15:L=L+35:CIRCLE(L,17),15:NEXT
   K:PAINT(586,17),15,8
21 PAINT(63,17),1,8
22 PAINT(100,17),2,8
23 PAINT(135,17),3,8
24 PAINT(170,17),4,8
25 PAINT(206,17),5,8
26 PAINT(239,17),6,8
27 PAINT(274,17),7,8
28 PAINT(308,17),8,8
29 PAINT(345,17),9,8
30 PAINT(381,17),10,8
31 PAINT(414,17),11,8
32 PAINT(450,17),12,8
33 PAINT(486,17),13,8
34 PAINT(521,17),14,8
35 PAINT(556,17),15,8
40 PSET(110,55),8:DRAW"M270,55 M270,215 M110,215
   M110,55"
50 PSET(110,65),8:DRAW"R160"
51 PSET(110,75),8:DRAW"R160"
52 PSET(110,85),8:DRAW"R160"
53 PSET(110,95),8:DRAW"R160"
54 PSET(110,105),8:DRAW"R160"
55 PSET(110,115),8:DRAW"R160"
56 PSET(110,125),8:DRAW"R160"
57 PSET(110,135),8:DRAW"R160"
58 PSET(110,145),8:DRAW"R160"
59 PSET(110,155),8:DRAW"R160"
60 PSET(110,165),8:DRAW"R160"
61 PSET(110,175),8:DRAW"R160"
62 PSET(110,185),8:DRAW"R160"
63 PSET(110,195),8:DRAW"R160"
64 PSET(110,205),8:DRAW"R160"
70 PSET(120,55),8:DRAW"D160"
71 PSET(130,55),8:DRAW"D160"
72 PSET(140,55),8:DRAW"D160"
73 PSET(150,55),8:DRAW"D160"
74 PSET(160,55),8:DRAW"D160"
75 PSET(170,55),8:DRAW"D160"
76 PSET(180,55),8:DRAW"D160"
77 PSET(190,55),8:DRAW"D160"
78 PSET(200,55),8:DRAW"D160"
```

```
79 PSET(210,55),8:DRAW"D160"
80 PSET(220,55),8:DRAW"D160"
81 PSET(230,55),8:DRAW"D160"
82 PSET(240,55),8:DRAW"D160"
83 PSET(250,55),8:DRAW"D160"
84 PSET(260,55),8:DRAW"D160"
85 PSET(109,54),8:DRAW"M271,54 M271,216 M109,216
   M109,54"
100 IF RE$="Y" OR RE$="y" THEN 110
105 IF RE$="CC" OR RE$="cc" THEN 160 ELSE GOTO 300
110 FOR QE=80 TO 110 STEP 2
120 FOR QW=370 TO 416 STEP 3
130 PAINT(X,Y),POINT(QW,QE),8:X=X+10
140 NEXT QW
150 X=114:Y=Y+10:NEXT QE:GOTO 300
160 P=1:X=114:Y=59:A=370:B=80
170 FOR QE=85 TO 100 STEP 1
180 FOR QW=390 TO 405 STEP 1
190 PAINT(X,Y),POINT(QW,QE),8:X=X+10
200 NEXT QW
210 X=114:Y=Y+10:NEXT QE
220 P=1:X=114:Y=59:A=370:B=80
230 FOR QE=84 TO 101:FOR QW=390 TO 405:
    PSET(QW,QE),0:NEXT QW,QE
235 P=1:X=114:Y=59:A=370:B=80
240 FOR QE=59 TO 219 STEP 10
245 FOR QW=114 TO 274 STEP 10
250 PSET(A,B),POINT(QW,QE):DRAW"R2 D1 L2 U1":A=A+3
255 NEXT QW
260 A=370:B=B+2:NEXT QE
270 P=1:X=114:Y=59:A=370:B=80
300 I$=INKEY$
310 PUT(X,Y),Q,XOR:PUT(X,Y),Q,XOR
320 IF I$="6" THEN X=X+10:A=A+3
330 IF I$="4" THEN X=X-10:A=A-3
340 IF I$="8" THEN Y=Y-10:B=B-2
350 IF I$="2" THEN Y=Y+10:B=B+2
360 REM IF I$="7" THEN X=X-10:Y=Y-10
400 IF X<114 THEN X=114:A=370
410 IF X>264 THEN X=264:A=415
420 IF Y<59 THEN Y=59:B=80
430 IF Y>209 THEN Y=209:B=110
440 IF I$=" " THEN GOTO 510
450 IF I$="+" THEN P=P+1
```

```
460 IF I$="-" THEN P=P-1
470 IF P<0 THEN P=15
480 IF P>15 THEN P=0
490 IF I$="E" OR I$="e" THEN GOTO 520
495 LOCATE 18,15:PRINT" PAINT COLOR IS ";P
500 GOTO 300
510 PAINT(X,Y),P,8:PSET(A,B),P:DRAW"R2 D1 L2
    U1":GOTO 300
520 DIM R(900):GET(367,78)-(420,113),R
530 CLS:PUT(150,50),R,XOR
540 LOCATE 15,3:INPUT"Save under (drive, file
    name, and .DAT)";D$
550 DEF SEG:BSAVE D$,VARPTR(R(0)),1000
560 END
570 INPUT"Drive for Files:";DA$:FILES
    DA$:INPUT"Saved under (including drive, name,
    and .DAT extension)";F$
580 DEF SEG:BLOAD F$,VARPTR(M(0))
590 CLS:PUT(367,78),M,XOR:
    PSET(364,113),0:DRAW"R100":GOTO 15
600 CLS:PRINT:PRINT"Press + and - to locate the
    CHR$ character you want...."
601 PRINT"Press C to rotate colors and press <ESC>
    to exit with character choice."
605 WA=33:CC=1
610 TR$=INKEY$
615 IF TR$="" THEN GOTO 610
620 IF TR$=CHR$(27) THEN GOTO 650
625 IF TR$="+" THEN WA=WA+1
630 IF TR$="-" THEN WA=WA-1
631 IF TR$="C" THEN CC=CC+1
632 IF CC>15 THEN CC=1
633 IF WA>255 THEN WA=33
634 IF WA<33 THEN WA=255
635 COLOR CC:LOCATE 7,50:PRINT CHR$(WA):LOCATE 6,
    50:PRINT"#";WA
640 GOTO 610
650 CLS:COLOR CC:LOCATE 7,50:PRINT CHR$(WA):COLOR
    8:GOTO 15
```

• • •

Refreshingly, there's little in **STAMP.BAS** to complain about, although the program's far from perfect (of course). Tweaks to the interface—perhaps even adding mouse input, just as *Mario Paint* had nearly a quarter of a century ago—are worth exploring.

Drawing in Three Dimensions
LOAD "3DPLOT.BAS"

Ok

RUN

We've pored over a lot of different drawing programs thus far, but they've all had one thing in common: all of the images have been in two dimensions. Let's add a dimension to the mix.

Handling three dimensions on a computer screen is a bit tricky, since the screen itself projects images in only two dimensions.

Recall that, in an earlier chapter, we examined rotating images by using trigonometric functions: any rotation at angle θ about the origin is given by

$$(x \cdot \cos\theta - y \cdot \sin\theta, x \cdot \sin\theta + y \cos\theta)$$

But in three dimensions, we have to account for a third axis—the z-axis—which is orthogonal (perpendicular) in space to the other two axes, x and y. In order to visualize the three axes, you may want to point your right thumb upward and have your index finger pointing outward along with your middle finger facing toward your palm; this is the so-called right-hand rule, a quick way of orientating the three axes.

The trick to rotating objects in three dimensions is to rotate around one axis at a time. For instance, if we wish to rotate around the x-axis in three dimensions, we only need to get new y and z coordinates (since x remains constant):

$$\left(x, z \cdot \sin\theta + y \cdot \cos\theta, z \cdot \cos\theta - y \cdot \sin\theta\right)$$

And if it's y-axis rotation we're after, the formula for the ordered triple looks like this:

$$\left(x \cdot \cos\theta - z \cdot \sin\theta, y, x \cdot \sin\theta + z \cdot \cos\theta\right)$$

Likewise, for rotation about the z-axis, we obtain

$$\left(y \cdot \sin\theta + x \cdot \cos\theta, y \cdot \cos\theta - x \cdot \sin\theta, z\right)$$

That covers the mathematics of rotation. But there's one more outstanding issue: projecting a three-dimensional world onto a two-dimensional monitor; this is termed "translation."

$$\left(x \cdot scalefact \div z, y \cdot scalefact \div z\right)$$

The *scalefact* (scale factor) above should be around 256 to avoid as much distortion as possible.

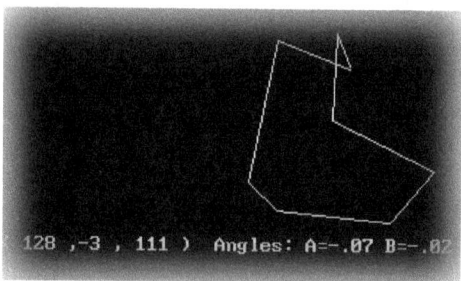

Run **3DPLOT.BAS** to put all of this mathematical theory to the test. Move the drawing cursor with the numeric keypad, and use the spacebar to set vertices for a three-dimensional wireframe image. You can adjust the image (along with the cursor) using *J*, *K*, *I*, or *M*, and change the color of the lines by pressing *P*. Rotating about any of the three axes requires you to simply press *x*, *y*, or *z* (uppercase letters increase the angle measure; lowercase letters decrease the angle measure). Typing *R* immediately resets the image to the default values. Finally, when your drawing is complete, pressing the ESCAPE key produces, on-screen, a program listing of the coordinates of your wireframe image.

• • •

At the start you are presented with a number of options: the **SCREEN** display, the starting coordinates, and the scaling factor. It takes a bit of trial and error to see which starting coordinates make the most sense—let alone which scaling factor.

Afterward, in lines **15** to **50**, a number of arrays are created and variables initialized. Read through the coded comments carefully.

As usual, an **INKEY$** handles the user input, sending the program to subroutines for rotation and movement. Hitting ESCAPE prompts **3DPLOT.BAS** to type up a program on-screen of the coordinates of the wireframe image you've just drawn, whilst clearing the interpreter's queue of **3DPLOT.BAS** (examine lines **5000** to **5050**).

• • •

3DPLOT.BAS
```
10 KEY OFF:SCREEN 9:COLOR 15,0:CLS
11 PRINT:PRINT"3D PLOT":PRINT"You are permitted to
   make a wire-frame shape of at most 30 ordered
   triples.":PRINT"Press the SPACEBAR to set a
   point; press ESCAPE to create the program out
   put.":PRINT
12 INPUT"Screen 7, or Screen 9 (enter number)";SCR
13 INPUT"Start at
   X=";XTEMP:INPUT"Y=";YTEMP:INPUT"Z=";ZTEMP:INPUT"
```

```
    Scaling constant (ENTER = 256 = stand-
    ard)";SCA:IF SCA=0 THEN SCA=256
14 SCREEN SCR:COLOR 15,0:CLS
15 DIM SHAPEX(30):DIM SHAPEY(30):DIM
   SHAPEZ(30):DIM SHAPECOL(30):E=1    'Set arrays
   and elements for wireframe shape--maximum of 30
   coordinate triples
17 DIM TEMPX(30):DIM TEMPY(30):DIM TEMPZ(30)
   'Set up arrays for the temporary display of the
   ordered triples of the constructed shape
20 X=XTEMP:Y=YTEMP:Z=ZTEMP    'Initial coordinates
   for x, y, z
25 IF Z=0 THEN Z=.5    'Making sure there's no di
   vision by zero error here
30 A=0:B=0:C=0     'Angles for x, y, z respectively
35 XX=0:YY=0     'Set to zero; use the I, J, K, and
   N letters to move the image quickly
40 COL=15    'Initial cursor color = white
50 SCALE=SCA    'Scaling constant
100 I$=INKEY$
102 IF E=1 THEN 105
103 PSET(TEMPX(1)*SCALE/TEMPZ(1)+XX,TEMPY(1)*
    SCALE/TEMPZ(1)+YY),SHAPECOL(1):FOR LOOP=2 TO
    (E-1):LINE -(TEMPX(LOOP)*SCALE/TEMPZ(LOOP)+XX,
    TEMPY(LOOP)*SCALE/TEMPZ(LOOP)+YY),SHAPECOL(LOO
    P):NEXT LOOP    'Draws wireframe shape so far
105 PSET(X*SCALE/Z+XX,Y*SCALE/Z+YY),COL    'Cursor
    location, projected onto 2-d screen
107 LOCATE 22,1:PRINT"(";INT(X);",";INT(Y);",";
    INT(Z)")";"  Angles:
    A=";A;"B=";B;"C=";C;"_P_en _R_eset"
108 IF I$="" THEN 100
109 CLS
110 IF I$="8" THEN Y=Y-1
120 IF I$="2" THEN Y=Y+1
130 IF I$="4" THEN X=X-1
140 IF I$="6" THEN X=X+1
145 IF I$="J" OR I$="j" THEN XX=XX-10
146 IF I$="K" OR I$="k" THEN XX=XX+10
147 IF I$="I" OR I$="i" THEN YY=YY-10
148 IF I$="M" OR I$="m" THEN YY=YY+10
150 IF I$="+" THEN Z=Z+1
160 IF I$="-" THEN Z=Z-1
```

```
165 IF Z=0 THEN Z=.5    'Avoids division by zero
    error; so z isn't allowed to be zero
170 IF I$="X" THEN A=A+.01:GOSUB 2000
180 IF I$="x" THEN A=A-.01:GOSUB 2000
190 IF I$="Y" THEN B=B+.01:GOSUB 2000
200 IF I$="y" THEN B=B-.01:GOSUB 2000
210 IF I$="Z" THEN C=C+.01:GOSUB 2000
220 IF I$="z" THEN C=C-.01:GOSUB 2000
230 IF I$="R" OR I$="r" THEN GOSUB 3000
240 IF I$="P" OR I$="p" THEN COL=COL+1
250 IF COL>15 THEN COL=1
260 IF I$=CHR$(32) THEN GOSUB 4000    'Hitting
    SPACE sends program to make a new point in the
    shape
270 IF I$=CHR$(27) THEN GOSUB 5000    'Pressing
    ESCAPE ends program, prints out DAT for the
    shape's coordinates
500 GOTO 100
2000 'ROTATION SUBROUTINE
2001 'ROTATE AROUND X-AXIS (ANGLE A)
2005 'First, rotate cursor ordered triple
2010 NEWZ=COS(A)*Z-SIN(A)*Y
2020 NEWY=SIN(A)*Z+COS(A)*Y
2030 Z=NEWZ:Y=NEWY
2031 'Next, rotate each point of the so-far-
     constructed wireframe object's ordered tri
     ples (if anything exists)
2032 IF E=1 THEN 2050    'If there's no object
     yet, jump forward
2033 FOR LOOP=1 TO E-1
2035 TEMPZ(LOOP)=COS(A)*SHAPEZ(LOOP)-
     SIN(A)*SHAPEY(LOOP)    'Change to z
2036 TEMPY(LOOP)=SIN(A)*SHAPEZ(LOOP)+COS(A)
     *SHAPEY(LOOP)    'Change to y
2037 NEXT LOOP
2050 'ROTATE AROUND Y-AXIS (ANGLE B)
2060 NEWX=COS(B)*X-SIN(B)*Z
2070 NEWZ=SIN(B)*X+COS(B)*Z
2080 X=NEWX:Z=NEWZ
2081 'Next, rotate each point of the so-far-
     constructed wireframe object's ordered tri
     ples (if anything exists)
2082 IF E=1 THEN 2100  'If there's no object yet,
     jump ahead
```

```
2083 FOR LOOP=1 TO E-1
2085 TEMPX(LOOP)=COS(B)*SHAPEX(LOOP)-
     SIN(B)*SHAPEZ(LOOP)    'Change to x
2086 TEMPZ(LOOP)=SIN(B)*SHAPEX(LOOP)+COS(B)
     *SHAPEZ(LOOP)    'Change to z
2087 NEXT LOOP
2100 'ROTATE AROUND Z-AXIS (ANGLE C)
2110 NEWY=COS(C)*Y-SIN(C)*X
2120 NEWX=SIN(C)*Y+COS(C)*X
2130 Y=NEWY:X=NEWX
2131 'Next, rotate each point of the so-far-
     constructed wireframe object's ordered tri
     ples (if anything exists)
2132 IF E=1 THEN 2140   'If there's no object yet,
     jump ahead
2133 FOR LOOP=1 TO E-1
2135 TEMPY(LOOP)=COS(C)*SHAPEY(LOOP)-
     SIN(C)*SHAPEX(LOOP)    'Change to y
2136 TEMPX(LOOP)=SIN(C)*SHAPEY(LOOP)+COS(C)*
     SHAPEX(LOOP)    'Change to x
2137 NEXT LOOP
2140 RETURN
3000 'Reset to starting coordinates and angles
3010 X=XTEMP:Y=YTEMP:Z=ZTEMP:A=0:B=0:C=0:COL=15
3011 IF Z=0 THEN Z=.5    'Making sure there's no
     division by zero
3015 IF E=1 THEN RETURN    'If there's no drawing,
     no need to reset position of that too
3016 FOR LOOP=1 TO E-1
3017 TEMPX(LOOP)=SHAPEX(LOOP):TEMPY(LOOP)=
     SHAPEY(LOOP):TEMPZ(LOOP)=SHAPEZ(LOOP)
3018 NEXT LOOP
3020 RETURN
4000 'Create new line of wireframe drawing
4010 SHAPEX(E)=X:TEMPX(E)=X
4020 SHAPEY(E)=Y:TEMPY(E)=Y
4030 SHAPEZ(E)=Z:TEMPZ(E)=Z
4040 SHAPECOL(E)=COL
4050 E=E+1
4060 IF E>30 THEN GOSUB 5000    'Must end program
     if there are more than 30 ordered triples to
     the shape
4070 RETURN
5000 SCREEN 9:CLS:LNUM=10:COUNT=0
```

```
5005 'PRINT OUT PROGRAM WITH SHAPE'S DATA
5010 FOR DUMMY=1 TO E-1
5015 IF COUNT=>2 THEN COUNT=0:LNUM=LNUM+10
5017 IF COUNT=0 THEN PRINT
5020 IF COUNT=0 THEN PRINT LNUM;" DATA
     ";INT(SHAPEX(DUMMY));",";INT(SHAPEY(DUMMY));"
     ,";INT(SHAPEZ(DUMMY));",";SHAPECOL(DUMMY);","
     ;
5030 IF (COUNT<>0 AND COUNT<2) THEN PRINT
     ;INT(SHAPEX(DUMMY));",";INT(SHAPEY(DUMMY));",
     ";INT(SHAPEZ(DUMMY));",";SHAPECOL(DUMMY);",";
     :COUNT=COUNT+1
5035 IF COUNT=0 THEN COUNT=COUNT+1
5040 NEXT DUMMY
5050 LOCATE 1,1:NEW
```

● ● ●

3DPLOT.BAS is hardly ready for primetime—it has a number of display quirks besides just a limiting thirty co-ordinates per wireframe image.

To improve the program, you might want to get ahold of a good book on three-dimensional graphics programming, such as *High-Performance CAD Graphics in C* (1986) by Lee Adams, which not only presents the mathematical theory behind the practice, but also relays relevant sample code. Adams's book (and he has others, if you can manage to find them), especially, is wonderful; the C programs can, with a little thought and care, be converted to GW-BASIC.

Let's end this chapter with a personal anecdote. When I was in high school, I searched far and wide for any resources on programming true 3D graphics specifically for GW-BASIC and repeatedly came up empty-handed. At around this time, because of frustrations with this 3D-graphical Gordian Knot and other logistical issues, my interest for BASIC was waning; I was instead consumed with learning Fortran, PASCAL, and especially C++, when I stumbled onto the Adams's text at a local book wholesaler. Reading through chapter 10—called "The Cube," which presents a rotating wireframe cube on-screen—it suddenly occurred to me: Why not simply take these C image-manipulation algorithms and translate them into GW-BASIC code? My key insight—and looking back, it's not so impressive, but cut me some slack, I was still in high school—was that the mathematics rooting the graphics were largely (though hardly completely) programming-language independent.*

Adams's book, along with a comprehensive text like *Introduction to Computer Graphics* (1993) by James D. Foley et al., will not only help you turn **3DPLOT.BAS** into a more useful program, but will also provide you with the coding foundation to create more powerful GW-BASIC three-dimensional software.

---

* Quick, but important and necessary, clarification: The code for **3DPLOT.BAS** (and all other programs in this book) is wholly my creation, for better or for worse, taking nothing from other programmers' code.

Mousetrap

LOAD "MOUSE.BAS"

Ok

RUN

If you're intent on using a mouse in GW-BASIC, you'll have to overcome a number of hurdles. Luckily, there's some sample code on the web, but it's a complicated patchwork of assembly language calls. See the following websites for the details:

- http://content.gpwiki.org/GW-Basic/Mouse
- http://www.gw-basic.com/blog/mouse-functionality-by-daryl-dubbs
- http://computer-programming-forum.com/12-visual-basic/82a8e868d5c52243.htm

Thomas C. McIntire, in the online article "GW-BASIC and Windows Marriages," explains concisely why interfacing with "Mickey" is so difficult.

> There is one fundamental reason why GW-BASIC contains no mouse commands or functions: They would have made the interpreter too big for the box…. Mouse programming in GW-BASIC is certainly possible, nonetheless. Making such programs work well on a Windows machine requires a little patience, and a rudimentary understanding of the underlying software architecture.

You can read the rest of McIntire's expansive article at http://www.o-bizz.de/qbtuts/blastoff/gwbaswin.html.

Alternatively, the GW-BASIC emulator PC-BASIC offers mouse support through the **PEN** statement (**PEN**, when used in GW-BASIC, looks for light pen input, not mouse input). The following PC-BASIC-exclusive program, **MOUSE.BAS**, demonstrates how to leverage **PEN** to interface with a mouse. Clicking the left mouse button registers a "-1" on-screen, and the coordinates of the cursor's position are continually updated.

● ● ●

MOUSE.BAS
```
10 CLS:KEY OFF:SCREEN 9:SCREEN 0
20 PEN ON
30 X=PEN(1):Y=PEN(2):Z=PEN(3):C=PEN(4):D=PEN(5)
35 LOCATE 13,1:PRINT"Shows '-1' if left button
   clicked:";Z
40 LOCATE 15,1:PRINT "LEFT CLICK TO SEE MOUSE-
   POINTER COORDINATES: (";X;",";Y;")"
45 LOCATE 17,1:PRINT"Shows mouse coordinates in
   real-time: (";C;",";D;")"
50 IF INKEY$<>CHR$(27) THEN 30
60 CLS:PEN OFF
70 END
```

● ● ●

Most any drawing program could be improved through a mouse interface; games and other utilities would also benefit from "Mickey." **MOUSE.BAS** gives you a template, albeit one that only works for PC-BASIC.

But purists should rightly complain: PC-BASIC isn't *really* GW-BASIC. The reality is that no matter how you spin it, interfacing with a mouse in GW-BASIC requires parsing assembly code. And if that's what it takes, then the most devoted GW-BASIC enthusiasts wouldn't have it any other way.

Epilogue

Ok

RUN_

I never wanted GW-BASIC to go gentle into that good night, even though it's so clearly fraught with limitations—and without special software supports it won't even run on a modern Windows PC anymore!—but it might be best to let it go. If you agree, then, like a depressed former pet owner shopping for a new puppy most resembling the dog just put out to pasture, maybe we should wise up and shop for some successors to fill the void.

And GW-BASIC has its share of successors. Briefly: First came Microsoft QBasic, which was based on Microsoft's QuickBASIC, in the mid-1990s. Although it's not a direct successor, Microsoft Visual Basic, a drag-and-drop programming language, arrived on the scene in the early '90s. And Microsoft Small Basic, intended as a training ground for Visual Basic, is newest on the scene, having only arrived less than a decade ago.

If we expand our scope to products outside of the Microsoft family, BASIC has widely proliferated, with new variants still being created today.

But let's explore just the Microsoft successors. First, though, a little mathematics is in order.

● ● ●

A *hailstone number*, also referred to as a $3n+1$ sequence, can be defined as

$$f(n) = \begin{cases} \dfrac{n}{2} \text{ if } n \text{ is even} \\ 3n+1 \text{ if } n \text{ is odd} \end{cases}$$

It's interesting to see how many iterations a starting seed takes to reach 1 (if ever—Lothar Collatz hypothesized that any natural number eventually converges to one; formally, his hypothesis is called the Collatz conjecture).

For example, consider the number 6. Plugged into the formula, 6 is even, so we divide it by 2 to obtain 3. But 3 is odd, so we take 3x3+1 = 10. And 10 is even, so we divide by 2: our result is 5. If we keep this up, we find that 6 takes eight iterations to land at 1.

A GW-BASIC hailstone program might look like this:

```
HAILSTON.BAS
10 KEY OFF:SCREEN 9:COLOR 15,0:CLS
20 PRINT"Hailstone Numbers!"
30 STEPS=0
40 LINE INPUT"Enter an initial number: ";NUM$
45 NUM=VAL(NUM$)   'Converts string to number
50 WHILE NUM<>1
60 STEPS=STEPS+1
70 REMAINDER=NUM MOD 2
80 IF REMAINDER=0 THEN NUM=NUM/2 ELSE
   NUM=NUM*3+1
90 PRINT NUM;"  ";
100 WEND
110 PRINT
120 PRINT"Steps to 1: ";STEPS
130 PRINT"Press any key to exit..."
140 IF INKEY$="" THEN 140 ELSE CLS:END
```

The program's pretty self-explanatory; after taking the input of an initial seed, HAILSTON.BAS uses modular arithmetic to juggle the number back down to 1. (Although be sure not to miss the VAL function in line 45: it converts a string variable to a numerical one. STR$ is the complementary function, which converts a numerical variable into a string variable.)

Here's a screenshot of sample output for an initial seed of **67**:

QBasic, most similar to GW-BASIC, can handle most of the program as it stands now, except the line numbers aren't necessary and line **10**'s screen-display statements need to be tweaked.

Small Basic is another matter entirely, however. Below is the code for the analogous hailstone program:

```
hailstone.sb
1  TextWindow.WriteLine("Hailstone Numbers!")
2  steps = 0
3  TextWindow.Write("Enter an initial number:
   ")
4  num = TextWindow.ReadNumber()
5  While num <> 1
6  steps=steps+1
7  remainder = Math.Remainder(num, 2)
8  If (remainder = 0) Then
```

```
9    num=num/2
10 Else
11    num=num*3+1
12 EndIf
13 TextWindow.Write(num + "  ")
14 EndWhile
15
16 Textwindow.WriteLine("")
17 Textwindow.WriteLine("Steps to 1: " +
   steps)
18 TextWindow.Pause()
19 Program.End()
```

Glancing through the Small Basic code, the GW-BASIC family resemblance shines through. The line numbers, which show for aesthetic reasons only, appear on-screen as you're typing the code. But there are stylistic differences that go beyond the merely aesthetic. For instance, the If/Then statements are grouped in blocks, terminated by an EndIf. This is much more convenient that GW-BASIC's approach, which can group at most two commands for each conditional statement.

Here's the output of **hailstone.sb**, again with an initial seed of **67**.

The `Textwindow` serves as your input/output venue for text, although other types of windows are possible for graphical displays.

Small Basic also encourages you to publish your programs straight to the web with a single button—I did that with **hailstone.sb**. What follows is one more SB program, which you won't find on the web, called `hailstones of hailstones.sb`.

```
hailstones of hailstones.sb
1   TextWindow.WriteLine("Hailstone Numbers -
    to the next level!")
2   steps = 0
3   TextWindow.Write("Enter an initial number:
    ")
4   num = TextWindow.ReadNumber()
5   While num <> 1
6    While num <> 1
7   steps=steps+1
8   remainder = Math.Remainder(num, 2)
9   If (remainder = 0) Then
10    num=num/2
11  Else
12    num=num*3+1
13  EndIf
14  TextWindow.WriteLine(num)
15  EndWhile
16
17  Textwindow.WriteLine("Steps to 1 in this
    iteration: " + steps)
18  num=steps
19  steps=0
20  itersteps = itersteps + 1
21  EndWhile
```

`hailstones of hailstones.sb` finds the number of steps an initial seed requires to iterate to 1 and treats *that number* as a new initial seed—and so on—until settling down to 1 (if ever).

The screenshot below shows output for an initial seed of **7**.

```
Hailstone Numbers - to the next level!
Enter an initial number: 7
22
11
34
17
52
26
13
40
20
10
5
16
8
4
2
1
Steps to 1 in this iteration: 16
4
2
1
Steps to 1 in this iteration: 4
2
1
Steps to 1 in this iteration: 2
1
Steps to 1 in this iteration: 1
Steps to 1 after all iterations: 3
Press any key to continue...
```

Small Basic, a free software package, sells you hard on "upgrading" to Visual Basic, by, for example, automatically converting with the click of a button the SB code you've written to VB code straightaway. Temping, but Visual Basic is a whole different animal—at a whole different level of complexity—that BASIC creators John Kemeny and Thomas Kurtz would be hard-pressed to recognize.

• • •

Irv Gordon, a retired New York school teacher, landed in the *Guinness Book of World Records* not for some incredble feat of strength, nor for some unusual genetically expressed deformity, nor even for some amazing trick of mental dexterity.

Rather, Gordon holds the world record for highest vehicle mileage, at over three million miles, all travelled in his plucky little red 1966 Volvo P1800S coupe. How did he do it? A little luck, coupled with a lot of repairs and even more regular maintance.

Maybe the remaining handful of hard-core GW-BASIC programmers aren't akin to depressed pet owners, mouring what they've lost. Maybe they're more like classic car lovers, perfectionists looking for that ever-elusive replacement part, tinkering endlessly, working with (virtual) tools to solve and resolve the most unpredictable of problems that repeatedly crop up, though those classic cars (or a classic computer language) may be stand-ins for idealized versions of the past, like the symbolic green light on Daisy's dock in *The Great Gatsby*.

From a practical standpoint, classic cars might not have GPS navigation, or automatic parking assist, or any of the many other latest technological frills, but they're wonderfully compatible with gasoline and with roads—and thus can still get you from point A to point B. Similarly, GW-BASIC might not permit the latest in programming semantics, but an amazingly wide variety of algorithms can still, with a bit of jury-rigging, run on it just fine.

Matthew Crawford, in his book *Shop Class As Soulcraft* (which was inspired by *Zen and the Art of Motorcycle Maintenance*), laments a world in which we put down our tools and dispose of our things at the first sign of trouble.

> A decline in tool use would seem to betoken a shift in our relationship to our own stuff: more passive and more dependent. And indeed, there are fewer occasions for the kind of spiritedness that is called forth when we take things in hand for ourselves, whether to fix them or to make them. What ordinary people once made, they buy; and what they once fixed for themselves, they replace entirely or hire an expert to repair, whose expert fix often involves replacing an entire system because some minute component has failed.

Irv Gordon kept his Volvo running for all these years and for all those millions of miles because he didn't throw out his baby car with the proverbial bath water (and antifreeze). He ignored the siren song of planned obsolescence and fixed the car instead.

Likewise, us few GW-BASIC faithful keep the spirit of line-numbered, unstructured old-school BASIC programming just barely alive, like a flickering flame withstanding gusts of wind, in the face of the temptations of modern, more sophisticated languages, as we heed the *Ok* prompt and beat on, boats against the current, borne back ceaselessly into the past.

Statements, Functions, and Commands

Ok

RUN

Some, but not all, of the following comprehensive list of statements (which direct a program to do something), functions (which return a value to the user), and commands (which are usually reserved for direct mode instruction) are used in this book's programs. There are also several reserved variables for user input and debugging.

• • •

The Statements.

BEEP	DEFDBL	GET	LOCATE
CALL	DEFSNG	GOSUB-RETURN	LOCK
CHAIN	DEFSTR	GOTO	LPRINT
CIRCLE	DEF SEG	IF	LPRINT USING
CLOSE	DEF USR	INPUT	LSET
CLS	DIM	INPUT#	MID$
COLOR	DRAW	IOCTL	NEXT
COM(n)	END	KEY	ON COM(n)
COMMON	ENVIRON	KEY(n)	ON KEY(n)
DATA	ERASE	LET	ON PEN
DATE$	ERROR	LINE	ON PLAY(n)
DEF FN	FIELD	LINE INPUT	ON STRIG(n)
DEFINT	FOR	LINE INPUT#	ON TIMER(n)

The Statements. (continued)

ON ERROR GOTO	PSET	SCREEN	WIDTH
ON-GOSUB	PRINT	SHELL	WINDOW
ON-GOTO	PRINT USING	SOUND	WRITE
OPEN	PRINT#	STOP	WRITE#
OPEN COM(n)	PRINT# USING	STRIG	
OPTION BASE	PUT	STRIG(n)	
OUT	RANDOMIZE	SWAP	
PAINT	READ	TIME$	
PALETTE	REM	UNLOCK	
PALETTE USING	RESTORE	VIEW	
PLAY	RESUME	VIEW PRINT	
POKE	RETURN	WAIT	
PRESET	RSET	WHILE-WEND	

The Functions.

ABS	EOF	LEN	PLAY(n)	STICK
ASC	EXP	LOC	PMAP	STR$
ATN	EXTERR	LOF	POINT	STRING$
CDBL	FIX	LOG	POS	TAB
CHR$	FRE	LPOS	RIGHT$	TAN
CINT	HEX$	MID$	RND	TIMER
COS	INP	MKD$	SCREEN	USR
CSNG	INPUT$	MKI$	SGN	VAL
CVD	INSTR	MKS$	SIN	VARPTR
CVI	INT	OCT$	SPACE$	VARPTR$
CVS	IOCTL$	PEEK	SPC	
ENVIRON$	LEFT$	PEN	SQR	

The Commands.

AUTO	FILES	NEW	TROFF
BLOAD	KILL	PCOPY	TRON
BSAVE	LIST	RENUM	
CHDIR	LLIST	RESET	
CLEAR	LOAD	RMDIR	
CONT	MERGE	RUN	
DELETE	MKDIR	SAVE	
EDIT	NAME	SYSTEM	

The Variables.

CSRLIN

ERL

ERR

INKEY$

ERDEV($)

• • •

For more detailed information on syntax and semantics, the very best online GW-BASIC manual is available at http://www.antonis.de/qbebooks/gwbasman/. And by far the most thorough book reference, unfortunately out of print, is called *The GW-BASIC Reference* (1990) by Don Inman and Bob Albrecht.

Index of Programs

Ok

RUN_

A short description of every program in the book follows. Note: a *t* means the program is text-based, a *gt* means graphics-based, a *PC* refers to PC-BASIC emulator code, and an *SB* denotes Small Basic code.

● ● ●

3DPLOT.BAS—(gt, *p.* 343). Allows the drawing and saving of 3D images.

ADD.BAS—(t, *p.* 134). Adds two very large numbers.

AGEBMI.BAS—(t, *p.* 30). Calculates a user's BMI and hours, minutes, and seconds of life lived.

AIRPLANE.BAS—(gt, *p.* 249). Shows a third-person view of an airplane.

ALARM.BAS—(t, *p.* 32). Sets a timed alarm.

ART1.BAS—(gt, *p.* 252). Shows connected lines shooting all over the screen.

ARTIF.BAS—(gt, *p.* 302). Displays a small fish bobbing around the screen.

AVGCALC.BAS—(t, *p.* 57). Calculates weighted averages.

BACKWRIT.BAS—(t, *p.* 20). Writes backwards on-screen.

BJACK.BAS—(t, *p.* 138). Plays a game of blackjack.

BOUNCE.BAS—(gt, *p.* 185). Shows a bouncing circle.

BOUNCEB.BAS—(gt, *p.* 201). Demonstrates a bouncing ball simulation.

BOXGAME.BAS—(gt, *p.* 258). Runs the "Box Game."

CAR.BAS—(gt, *p.* 310). Shows a first-person shot of a car dashboard.

CHAOS.BAS—(gt, *p.* 222). Experiments with mathematical chaos.

CHRGC.BAS—(t, *p*. 70). Scrolls through all ASCII character codes.

CIRCLE1.BAS—(gt, *p*. 183). Expands and collapses a circle.

CIRCLE2.BAS—(gt, *p*. 183). Presents pie slices of circles.

CIRCLE3.BAS—(gt, *p*. 184). Expands and shrinks circles, ad infinitum.

CIRCOL.BAS—(gt, *p*. 184). Ever-expanding circles of random colors fly out of the screen.

CIROV.BAS—(gt, *p*. 185). Displays different circle designs.

CIRMAKER.BAS—(gt, *p*. 184). Allows for a number of circle-customization options.

COIN.BAS—(gt, *p*. 186). Shows a rotating coin.

COIN2.BAS—(gt, *p*. 186). Presents a face's opening and closing mouth.

COLMAK.BAS—(gt, *p*. 256). Places colored patterns throughout the screen.

COLORS.BAS—(gt, *p*. 300). Shows all sixty-four available colors.

COMSPORT.BAS—(gt, *p*. 235). Runs the "Com-Sport" game.

CONE.BAS—(t, *p*. 90). Approximates the volume of cones using thinly sliced cylinders.

COPER.BAS—(t, *p*. 38). Calculates lower and upper bounds in time for a prediction.

CRYSTAL.BAS—(gt, *p*. 193). Shows images of colored crystals.

DERBY.BAS—(gt, *p*. 298). Runs the "Kentucky Derby" game.

DERIVE.BAS—(t, *p*. 51). Outputs mathematical derivatives of monomials.

DICE.BAS—(t, *p*. 60). Rolls two fair dice repeatedly.

DICE2.BAS—(t, *p*. 62). Rolls two dice of *n* number of sides.

DIFF.BAS—(gt, *p*. 212). Graphs slope fields of differential equations.

DISEASE.BAS—(t, *p*. 27). Calculates the probability you have a disease.

DM.BAS—(t, *p*. 65). Suggests decisions, like a Magic 8-Ball.

DMOLTION.BAS—(gt, *p*. 256). Allows the user to destroy whatever's on-screen.

DOTS.BAS—(gt, *p*. 193). Creates line patterns.

DOTTER.BAS—(gt, *p.* 194). Moves lots of dots around the screen.

DRWRND.BAS—(gt, *p.* 253). Moves colored boxes rapidly around the screen.

EFFECTS.BAS—(gt, *p.* 227). Displays a variety of visual effects.

EQUATION.BAS—(t, *p.* 55). Solves one-variable equations by utilizing approximation methods.

ETCH.BAS—(gt, *p.* 254). Draws patterns of varying sizes.

FACTY.BAS—(t, *p.* 112). Finds factorial numbers.

FBSCORES.BAS—(t, *p.* 40). Determines permutations of a football team's final points total.

FEATHER.BAS—(gt, *p.* 269). Displays a falling feather.

FIBO.BAS—(t, *p.* 35). Prints the Fibonacci sequence.

FICTION.BAS—(t, *p.* 126). Presents a work of interactive fiction.

FISH.BAS—(gt, *p.* 303). Displays a big swimming fish.

FLASH.BAS—(t, *p.* 122). Creates electronic flashcards.

FLIP.BAS—(t, *p.* 101). Runs the "Flip Game."

FRACTAL1.BAS—(gt, *p.* 195). Multiple self-similar patterns are drawn on the screen.

FUN.BAS—(gt, *p.* 320). Allows the user to load and save small images.

FUNC.BAS—(t, *p.* 47). Defines and evaluates mathematical functions at given values.

GOLF.BAS—(gt, *p.* 327). Runs the "Golf" game.

GP.BAS—(gt, *p.* 333). Permits the user to draw images using on-screen graph paper.

HAILSTON.BAS—(gt, *p.* 352). Calculates hailstone numbers.

hailstone.sb—(SB, *p.* 353). Calculates hailstone numbers.

hailstones of hailstones.BAS—(gt, *p.* 355). Finds the hailstone numbers of hailstone numbers.

HEART.BAS—(gt, *p.* 195). Presents a heart monitor-like display.

INTROGR.BAS—(gt, *p.* 177). Introduces rudimentary GW-BASIC graphics options.

LCD.BAS—(t, *p.* 77). Finds the lowest common denominator of two numbers.

LINER.BAS—(gt, *p.* 195). Draws random Tinker Toy-like designs.

LINES.BAS—(gt, *p.* 193). Stretches randomly colored lines across the screen horizontally.

LINES2.BAS—(gt, *p.* 193). Stretches randomly colored lines across the screen vertically.

LOTTERY.BAS—(t, *p.* 98). Generates lottery numbers according to various specifications.

MATRIX.BAS—(t, *p.* 43). Performs matrix operations.

MONEY.BAS—(t, *p.* 22). Repeatedly doubles your starting money.

MORSE.BAS—(t, *p.* 73). Converts letters of the alphabet to Morse code.

MOUSE.BAS—(PC, *p.* 350). Allows for a mouse interface.

MOVE.BAS—(gt, *p.* 214). Moves a trapezoid.

MUSIC.BAS—(t, *p.* 72). Randomly plays musical notes.

OK.BAS—(gt, *p.* 226). Displays a blinking "Ok" button.

OPENING.BAS—(gt, *p.* 268). Places you inside a movie theater at the start of a picture.

PAINT.BAS—(gt, *p.* 217). Runs a very simple painting program.

PALM.BAS—(gt, *p.* 265). Displays a drawing of a palm tree, using code generated from **POSITION.BAS**.

PASCAL.BAS—(t, *p.* 84). Generates rows of Pascal's triangle.

PERCOMB.BAS—(t, *p.* 114). Outputs the results of permutations and combinations.

PI.BAS—(gt, *p.* 189). Approximates pi using measurements from an on-screen circle.

PIER.BAS—(t, *p.* 87). Approximates pi using an infinite series.

POKER.BAS—(t, *p.* 144). Plays a game of poker.

POSITION.BAS—(gt, *p.* 261). Allows the user to draw and save images.

PRIMES.BAS—(t, *p.* 81). Determines if inputted numbers are prime.

PSEUDO.BAS—(t, *p.* 67). Generates pseudorandom numbers without using the **RND** function.

PUTGET.BAS—(gt, *p.* 316). Permits the user to draw, load, and save images of any size.

QPP.BAS—(gt, *p*. 219). Runs the "Quiz-Per-Play" game.

RNDCHR$.BAS—(t, *p*. 70). Shows random ASCII codes all over the screen.

ROADER.BAS—(gt, *p*. 313). Presents an overhead view of a car riding on a road.

ROTATION.BAS—(gt, *p*. 244). Utilizes a rotation matrix to create colorful patterns.

SAVER.BAS—(gt, *p*. 196). Runs a screensaver.

SE1.BAS—(gt, *p*. 247). Demonstrates image rotation.

SE2.BAS—(gt, *p*. 248). Demonstrates both image rotation and scaling.

SIGMA.BAS—(t, *p*. 54). Prints out the sum of finite summations.

SINCOS.BAS—(gt, *p*. 243). Shows multiple circle demos using trigonometric functions.

SLANTEXT.BAS—(gt, *p*. 200). Shows text large and slanted.

SLOPE.BAS—(gt, *p*. 204). Experiments with different slopes of linear equations.

SNOW.BAS—(gt, *p*. 193). Displays many (identical) snow-flakes on-screen.

SORT.BAS—(t, *p*. 95). Sorts items in a list using a bubble sort procedure.

SPIN.BAS—(gt, *p*. 246). Spins a yellow line around the screen using the **TA** command.

SPIRAL.BAS—(t, *p*. 92). Categorizes spirolaterals.

SPREAD.BAS—(t, *p*. 118). Calculates several measures of dispersion, such as standard deviation.

SROB.BAS—(gt, *p*. 249). Displays a rotating, growing box.

SQRT.BAS—(t, *p*. 76). Uses a recursive algorithm to find the square root of a number.

SQURE.BAS—(gt, *p*. 315). Displays a flicker-free animation.

STAGE1.BAS—(gt, *p*. 311). Scrolls a wireframe background beneath an immobile rocket ship.

STAGE2.BAS—(gt, *p*. 312). Scrolls a wireframe background beneath a mobile rocket ship.

STAMP.BAS—(gt, *p*. 336). Allows the user to construct small stamp-like images.

STARFIELD.BAS—(gt, *p*. 323). Displays a star field scrolling from left to right.

STARS.BAS—(gt, *p.* 192). Sprinkles stars randomly on the screen.

STARS2.BAS—(gt, *p.* 192). Scrolls random stars upward.

STARS3.BAS—(gt, *p.* 192). Presents static images of stars.

STROOP.BAS—(t, *p.* 108). Presents the Stroop test.

SW.BAS—(gt, *p.* 291). Runs the "Space Wars" game.

TARGET.BAS—(gt, *p.* 229). Runs the "Target Game."

TATA.BAS—(gt, *p.* 306). Shows a floating Natasha.

TAXES.BAS—(t, *p.* 25). Calculates sales tax.

TE.BAS—(gt, *p.* 324). Shows a spaceship flying through a star field.

TEST.BAS—(gt, *p.* 257). Tests image scaling and rotation.

TOWEL.BAS—(gt, *p.* 272). Runs an interactive presentation about towels.

TUNNEL.BAS—(gt, *p.* 184). Creates different types of circles on-screen.

TYPEPRAC.BAS—(t, *p.* 105). Runs a timed typing practice game.

UNITCIR.BAS—(gt, *p.* 243). Uses trigonometric functions to rotate images.

WORDS.BAS—(gt, *p.* 199). Displays words with a larger font (lighter/thinner).

WORDS2.BAS—(gt, *p.* 199). Displays words with a larger font (darker/thicker).

WPB.BAS—(t, *p.* 130). Loads a GW-BASIC word processor.

XYGRAPH.BAS—(gt, *p.* 208). Graphs mathematical functions.

Acknowledgments

Ok

RUN_

Books don't write themselves. It takes a lot of hard work. Without the ongoing support of my parents and friends, and the mathematical instruction and inspiration I have received over the years from a handful of teachers (especially Louis, Ned, Carlos, Tom, and Lisa, but Fred and Jo-anne laid the foundation) and friends (especially recreational mathematics talks with Yan, Bob, Rich, Gavin, and Scott), not only would my life be much emptier, but my bookshelves would be at least several books barer. But any mistakes in the text, mathematical or otherwise, are solely my own.

About the Author

MARK JONES LORENZO, a teacher, is the author of *Affront to Meritocracy: Stories of Overlooked Talents, Ignored Abilities, and Hidden Truths*. He lives in Pennsylvania with his dogs.

www.ingramcontent.com/pod-product-compliance
Lightning Source LLC
Chambersburg PA
CBHW070849180526
45168CB00005B/1751